A LAWYER'S CASE
FOR HIS
FAITH

AUTHOR OF
A Lawyer's Case for God & A Lawyer's Case for the Resurrection

JIM JACOB, ESQ.

TABLE OF CONTENTS

INTRODUCTION

THE REASON FOR THIS BOOK

MY BIG BLUNDER AT THE VATICAN

By the age of 22, I was already a staunch atheist. I had come to the conclusion that, despite being raised Jewish, religion was nothing more than a false way for individuals to feel that life had a greater meaning. I agreed with Karl Marx that religion was nothing more than an "opiate of the masses."[1] I thought that being a part of a religion was simply a waste of time and money; not to mention, it meant that I had to sit through extremely boring services. Despite my atheism and dislike for religion, I nonetheless became very concerned one day that I had greatly upset a priest at the Vatican in Rome, of all places. That did not seem like a wise thing to do! Let me explain this most memorable experience.

Between college and law school, I was fortunate enough to have three months to backpack across Western Europe. Despite my atheism at the time, I knew that one tourist attraction I did not want to miss was the Vatican. Upon my arrival at the Vatican, I noticed that it seemed like an incredibly holy and tranquil place. I was intrigued by its beauty, and decided to purchase an audio tour to learn more about one of the cathedral's history, artwork, stained glass, and statuary.[2] I opened the door to a booth with a sign on it that said "English," believing it was the place where I could hear the tour in my native language. To my surprise, I had walked into a confessional booth for people who spoke English! As you probably know, in a confessional booth people *privately* confess their sins to a priest. I had startled both parties, and quickly closed the door. I thought, "Oy vey, what a place to do such a thing!" I knew that I had to linger for a while and apologize profusely to the priest. I waited for what seemed like an eternity. When the confession was finally over, I apologized, and the priest was extremely forgiving and understanding. I remember he lovingly said, "No harm done, son." Whew!

I was always struck by the graciousness that the priest had shown me in my moment of embarrassment, as I had interrupted a very memorable and personal experience for someone else. To this day, decades later, the love that I felt from the priest has stuck in my mind. This was one experience among many that would begin to whittle away at my negative perceptions of those who were involved in religion.

GROWING UP JEWISH

Let's rewind a bit. There was really no reason for me to place any added spiritual significance to the Vatican or the reaction of the priest, because I was raised Jewish. I had a Bar Mitzvah at the age of 13 and graduated from religious school. However, due to my lack of attention, I came away with virtually no knowledge about Jewish religious beliefs. I lived a secluded life in a suburb of St. Louis affectionately referred to as "Jew City" due to its large Jewish population. To help paint the picture, on the Jewish holidays when the Jewish kids stayed home from school, there were only *three* students in attendance in my grade school classes. On Sundays, I would occasionally see families all dressed up and going to church. It all looked so surreal to me—like they were from another world.

MY LIFE AS AN ATHEIST

I had become an atheist during my late teens and stopped attending any religious services in my early 20s. I knew that I did not believe what was being taught, and I felt that it was hypocritical to go. In fact, I felt religious institutions were filled with hypocrites whose "holy" behavior usually vanished as soon as they returned home after services, if not sooner.

My atheism was basically by default, as my decision was certainly not an informed one. I had never spent must time reading the Bible or any other religious materials, and had never talked about spirituality with my friends. I did not know much about the significance or background of the various Jewish holidays we celebrated. About all I knew was that we ate matzah on Passover, fasted on Yom Kippur, and we got off of school for some holidays—of course, I took part in that tradition! I remember trying to fast one Yom Kippur when I was about eight years old. The aroma of cooked bacon (of all things) did me in, and I broke my fast early in the morning.

MY LEGAL CAREER IN KANSAS CITY

I graduated from law school in Kansas City in 1978. Thankfully, during law school I snagged much more than a diploma: somehow I also convinced the most beautiful woman in town to marry me. My wife, Cathy, is the second of eight children from a close-knit Italian Catholic family. They all got along so well and seemed to deeply love and care for one another. This touched

3

me. I desired to feel that joy and inner-peace that they all seemed to have. I sensed that it was due to their faith in Jesus. But I believed that because I was Jewish, that "Catholic stuff" would never work for me. Despite being intrigued by their faith, I remained apathetic in my religious beliefs and pursuits.

BEGINNING TO BELIEVE IN SOMETHING

At the age of 31, my atheism was seriously challenged with the birth of our first child. I vividly recall my astonishment when I observed a fully-formed, fully-functioning human being enter the world from another human being. Although I had obviously always known this fact, actually witnessing it was something else entirely. I was taken aback by how miraculous the creation of life seemed. As the memory began to fade and late night feedings and smelly diapers took its place, I pushed aside my astonishment and continued to put spirituality on the back burner.

Since religion was not important to me, I allowed Cathy to raise our children as she deemed fit. She expressed a desire to expose them to Jewish customs, but began taking them to Catholic Church. Although initially I did not care what religion my children were affiliated with (as I believed they were all a waste of time anyway), I was unsettled when I saw my children identifying with Catholicism, which was still quite foreign to me.

I was reminded of something my older brother had told me when I was pondering whether I could marry Cathy since she was Catholic. I shared with him my concern that one day my kids might "cross" themselves, which I felt would be hard to watch. He shared with me that my kids could do a lot worse things in this world than cross themselves. That piece of wisdom alleviated my concern at the time. But now when I saw my kids crossing themselves, my brother's sage advice did not totally relieve my discomfort. Cathy would have allowed the family to attend synagogue as well, but that did not seem right since I had not attended synagogue for several years. However, I always had in the back of my mind that *one day* I needed to read the Bible to learn what this religious stuff was all about.

About this time, a friend urged me to read C.S. Lewis' popular book *Mere Christianity*. I took this advice, which turned out to be one of the best decisions I have ever made. Lewis meticulously lays out the logical case for God and His Son, Jesus. Although I was reading Lewis' book as a skeptic, his detailed analysis still made incredible sense to me. The barriers I had constructed against God and Jesus were beginning to erode, and I wanted to learn more.

Shortly after I finished *Mere Christianity*, Cathy learned that a Messianic congregation was starting in Kansas City. Neither of us had any idea what that was. We soon discovered that a Messianic congregation consists of Jews and non-Jews worshipping Yeshua (Jesus' Hebrew name, which means "salvation") in a Jewish style— lighting candles on Friday night, honoring the Sabbath on Saturday, reading the weekly Torah portion (parsha) in Hebrew, and so on. It sounded like an interesting solution for our family, so I agreed to check it out.

From the moment I walked in to my first Messianic gathering, I was drawn to the love and unity of the people in attendance. It was similar to the love I had seen in Cathy's family and experienced from my interaction with the priest at the Vatican. I enjoyed these services so much that we started attending fairly regularly. I had never experienced anything exactly like this, yet it seemed so natural to me. I felt like I was being restored to my Jewish roots; it just seemed right in my *kishkes* (Yiddish for guts).

One night, my heart was touched deeply after hearing the story of Rose Price, a Holocaust survivor. She had been raised as an observant orthodox Jew, which is among the strictest sects of Judaism. After enduring the horrors of the Holocaust, Rose eventually married and had children. She was extremely angry, and had abandoned her faith in God. To add to her grief, her daughter and husband had become followers of Yeshua. Despite Roses' anger, she was intrigued as she witnessed wonderful changes in them. She began to meet more and more followers of Yeshua, and was drawn to learn more. She decided to start reading the Old Covenant (Old Testament/Hebrew Scriptures/Tanakh). Little by little, she began to understand and feel the love of the God. She was especially moved by the Book of Isaiah in the Old Covenant which spoke of the Messiah who would come and be "(w)ounded because of our transgressions...and with his stripes we were healed... as a lamb that is led to the slaughter...yet he bore the sin of many," (Isaiah 53:5,7,12).[3]

After studying the Old Covenant in depth, Rose began to read the New Covenant (New Testament/Messianic Scriptures/ Brit Chadasha). She began to see that Yeshua was a kind man who clearly appeared to be the Messiah of Israel who had been prophesied for centuries to the Jewish people. She asked Yeshua to reveal Himself to her if He was real, and He did! Her intense anger against God was transformed into a love for God and His Son, Yeshua, and her life was forever radically changed.

A few years later, Rose felt that God was telling her to visit Germany and to forgive the Nazis. She obeyed, and was able to speak to thousands of Germans about forgiveness, and publically profess her forgiveness of the Nazis. One of those in attendance had been in charge of punishment at a camp in which she had been imprisoned! After forgiving those who had inflicted so much pain and agony on her and her family within the concentration camps, Rose's anger, bitterness, and unrest subsided, and she had more peace in her heart. Even her health, previously very poor, improved dramatically.[4]

After hearing Rose's incredible story and sincerely desiring to know the truth, I bowed my head, closed my eyes, and asked God to let me know if He was real. I opened my eyes, and nothing had changed. There was no parting of the Red Sea or booming voice from the sky. Oh well, at least I tried! However, God soon let me know in a subtle way that He was indeed very real.

Previously, I would often use profanity when I was around men. Starting the very next day, curse words would come to my lips but I no longer wanted to utter them. I had not even made a decision to stop cursing. It just did not feel right to swear. I was not quite sure what had taken place. I now know that this was God beginning to change me: a habit of mine had been broken, and I was beginning to be transformed.

Although I still had not accepted Yeshua as my Messiah and the Son of God, my family and I began attending the Messianic congregation weekly. Even though I continued to be drawn by the love I felt, it was difficult for me, being raised Jewish, to accept Yeshua as the Messiah. I did not know much about what Jews believed, but I knew that Jews *did not* believe in Yeshua. Nonetheless, the teachings at our Messianic congregation were still revelatory to me. I read where hundreds of years in advance, the Jewish prophets in of the Old Covenant predicted specific details about Yeshua's coming in Jerusalem.[5] I learned that Jewish people wrote all 66 of the books of the Old *and* New Covenants (with the possible exception of the Gospel of Luke and the Book of Acts). I learned that Mary, the mother of Yeshua, was not Catholic but was actually Jewish! I was discovering that many of the things I had previously rejected as being "Christian" and "un-Jewish" were actually *extremely* Jewish.

BECOMING A BELIEVER IN YESHUA

A few months after hearing Rose's testimony, our rabbi scheduled a t'vilah, (water immersion/ mikvah/ baptism) service. I have since learned that water immersion is actually a very Jewish ritual![6] At the time, I thought this would be just another enjoyable event to attend, so I signed up. I did not realize that it held any sort of deeper spiritual meaning. On the way to the immersion,

Cathy pointed out to me that before being immersed I would be asked to publicly declare my belief in Yeshua as the Son of God. I was shocked! Oh no! I didn't realize I would have to do that!

When I arrived, I vividly recall getting out of our car and nervously pacing back and forth in the gravel parking lot beside the lake as I pondered what to do. I thought of backing out, but recalled that our rabbi had printed a flyer with the names of those participating in the water immersion, and mine was listed! I believed that if I backed out, I would offend everyone who thought this was a significant event. But I also reasoned that I could not lie and say that I believed if I did not. I searched my soul, and eventually decided that I could acknowledge Yeshua as the Messiah. He had been changing my life. It was true! So, I proceeded with the t'vilah.

Accompanied by the rabbi and many observers, I stood waist deep in a lake, proclaimed my faith in Yeshua, and immersed my entire body in the water. When I came out of the water, it felt as if I jumped five feet in the air. It was absolutely exhilarating! Cathy was re-immersed that day as well, and we embraced soaking wet. That glorious day was the day that I became a follower of Yeshua! Since then my life has been forever changed.

Shortly after professing my belief in Yeshua as the Messiah, I began to personally experience the inexplicable peace I had witnessed among Cathy's family and other believers in Yeshua. Before becoming a follower of Yeshua, I believed I could solve all of my problems with my own strength and intellect. This was truly exhausting and frustrating at times. After choosing to follow Yeshua, the challenges of life did not disappear, but they were nowhere near as unnerving. I was no longer relying solely on my own strength, but on God's. What a relief! It was immediately evident to me that God's ways far surpassed mine.

As you have briefly read, the walls I had constructed against Yeshua took *years* to be dismantled. This was mostly because I erroneously thought that believing in Yeshua meant I had to become a Christian. I have since learned that is not true! In fact, the initial followers of Yeshua were almost exclusively Jewish.[7] When Yeshua became a part of my life, I started becoming much more involved in Judaism than I had ever been in my entire life! I learned that His last name was not Christ. Christ is simply the Greek word for Messiah, or anointed one. The Hebrew word for Messiah is Mashiach, and the Mashiach is spoken of extensively in Judaism. Not only had my heart been changed, but my eyes had also been opened to who Yeshua was—a Jew! I have discovered that it is actually very Jewish to worship Yeshua as the Jewish Messiah.

I realize what I have just shared may tempt some of my Jewish readers to want to immediately throw down this book. For most of my life, I would have almost certainly had the same urge. I would have viewed someone claiming Yeshua is the Jewish Messiah to be a traitor, and someone who was attempting to destroy my Jewish identity. However, if you are like I was, you may have made decisions about God, the Bible, and Yeshua without ever actually studying or analyzing these important topics.

We make choices every day. For the bigger decisions, such as buying a new car, accepting a job offer, or choosing a spouse, we often dedicate significant amounts of time, energy, and research into determining our best options. If we investigate other matters so extensively, why would we not research what we believe about the spiritual realm? Is there an issue that is more worthy of our attention? If you become dissatisfied with your new car, you can sell it. If you make the wrong job choice, you can quit. If you pick the wrong spouse, your absolute worst-case scenario is about 75 years of unhappiness. But if you make the wrong choice about the spiritual realm, the repercussions could be eternal.

BEFORE WE BEGIN

I do not intend to attempt to *im*pose my beliefs on you. Instead my purpose is to *ex*pose you to information of which I was unaware when I had rejected belief in Yeshua. My desire is to share what has greatly impacted my life, and I believe can do the same for yours.

I think it would be helpful if I provide an analogy that puts into perspective why I, and others, wish to share our beliefs. Imagine that you fell into a roaring river during a storm, and were drowning. A man named Joseph dove into the pond and rescued you. Joseph stayed with you as you recovered from this ordeal and has become your best friend. Joseph has clearly impacted your life significantly. Any opportunity you could, you would tell people about Joseph—how he has saved your life, and the powerful impact he has had on you. You would want people to meet Joseph and get to know what an amazing person he is. That is what it is like as a follower of Yeshua. Yeshua has mercifully changed the direction of my life (and countless others) and I simply want to share Him with people I meet so they can get to know Him too *if* they choose to do so. The decision ultimately belongs to each of us.

I wrote this book to address some of the foundational topics regarding the spiritual realm that I did not research for decades.[8] I have attempted to condense the material into an "easy-to-read" style. There are already countless brilliant theological books on every topic addressed in this book; however, we often do not have the time or dedication to pick up a book several hundred pages in length.[9] Further, you will notice that I use Hebrew terminology periodically. For example, Jesus will be referred to by His Hebrew name, Yeshua. I used to be extremely distracted by stereotypical Christian terms, so I hope to alleviate any potential negative pre-conceived thoughts some may have about those terms while presenting the evidence.

I have one final request. Before a judge will allow a person to serve as a juror on a case, the potential juror will be asked if he or she can set aside any biases to serve fairly and impartially on the jury, thereby giving both sides a fair trial. I would ask the same of you, as you most likely have certain beliefs about God, the Bible, and Yeshua. Each juror is further instructed by the judge to not make up his or her mind or draw any conclusions until *all* of the evidence has been presented and examined. I simply ask you to do the same. I believe when analyzed in its entirety, the evidence presented will firmly establish that God exists, the Bible is historically accurate, and Yeshua is the Messiah of Israel spoken of in the Old Covenant.

CHAPTER 1

ARE WE ABSOLUTELY SURE THAT THERE ARE NO ABSOLUTES?

CAN WE ALL BE CORRECT?

Is there such a thing as absolute truth? Some feel there is not. The belief that there is no absolute truth is known as relativism. It advocates that everything is... relative. That is, the idea of "truth" is subjective and dependent upon factors relative to one's upbringing and culture. Many relativists contend that since we all come with our own unique perspectives, it is narrow-minded to claim that there is such a thing as absolute truth.

Relativism works when we are dealing with tastes and preferences. I enjoy peanut butter ice cream; my wife prefers vanilla. There is not an absolute truth of which ice cream is better; there is simply a distinction that is based on our personal tastes. But obviously *preferences* or *opinions* are different than *facts*. Contradictory facts cannot be equally valid. To claim that every viewpoint regarding certain undeniable facts has the same merit is clearly demonstrated to be illogical.

To analyze whether absolute truth exists, let's first examine basic facts about our physical world. We can all agree that there are absolute truths in the physical realm. For example, we all need oxygen to live. We cannot claim that breathing oxygen may work for some, but breathing helium will work for others if they choose the "helium path." Breathing helium instead of oxygen may certainly produce some hilarious short-term results, but will ultimately end poorly if relied upon exclusively. Clearly, it is an absolute truth that oxygen is necessary for our survival. Similarly, gravity absolutely exists regardless of one's belief. Even if someone does not believe gravity exists, if he or she walks off a 10-story building, the hard truth will soon be discovered.

While absolute truth is clearly evident in the physical world, are there also uncompromising truths in the spiritual realm, or the dimension that exists beyond our five senses? The word "spiritual" may immediately bring negative connotations for some. However, if you are like the approximately 90% of Americans who believe God (or a higher power) exists, then you do believe in some sort of spiritual, or supernatural, realm.[10] Although individuals have many different beliefs about the specifics of the spiritual realm, it is undeniable that there are certain foundational spiritual truths surpassing subjectivity. For example, either God exists, or does not exist. Whether something or someone exists is an absolute truth: I cannot exist to some people and not to others. Clearly, both sides of these dichotomous realities cannot be true.[11] Similar to learning whether gravity exists before we venture off a rooftop, it seems wise to learn if God exists, and whether He has put into place rules that will impact us during this life and beyond.

WE ALL BELIEVE IN ABSOLUTE TRUTHS

Relativism is also paradoxical. Everyone believes in absolute truth, even if his or her opinion is that there is no such thing as absolute truth. Those who claim relativism applies in the spiritual realm accept their belief as an absolute truth. Or put another way, some are absolutely certain that there is no such thing as absolute spiritual truth. Although relativism is often praised in our culture, it is actually a concept that contradicts itself. It proposes its own absolute—that there are no absolutes.

Our culture commonly defines "tolerance" as being synonymous with recognizing that all ideas are equally valid. Although admirable, the definition of tolerance is often misunderstood. Clinging to the notion of relativity does not allow us to escape the inevitability of the exclusive nature of certain spiritual truths. That is, spiritual truth by its very nature is exclusive and rejects that with which it is incompatible.

Having a high level of tolerance does not come from accepting all beliefs as truth. Rather, tolerance is apparent by how we treat others who may hold contrasting beliefs from our own. We must learn to understand tolerance in a manner that is logically consistent with the undeniable reality of certain absolute truths. In other words, we should love those with whom we disagree, but not simply accept their views as another "truth" that works for them. Doing so can actually be unloving as their misunderstanding of truth could be harmful to them.[12]

If someone believes that two contradictory spiritual beliefs can work for different people, then they are essentially espousing that both spiritual beliefs are nothing more than placebos (i.e., any benefit is psychological and comes from our minds rather than a real source). For instance, if someone advocates that some can believe Yeshua was just a prophet *and* others can believe that Yeshua was God in the flesh, they are ultimately saying that it does not matter—it is all relative. Both of these beliefs cannot simultaneously be true. Yeshua cannot *just* be a prophet and *also* God. To say He can be both is to ultimately advocate that He is neither. A more in-depth analysis of the contradictory nature of different spiritual beliefs can be found in Appendix A.

There are clearly absolute truths regarding the spiritual realm. Either God exists, or He does not. As will be thoroughly discussed in Chapter 7, either the Messiah has already come as a suffering servant, or He has not.[13] I did not explore these topics for the first 39 years of my life. I deeply regret that I missed out on having a relationship with God all those years because I chose to ignore and not investigate spiritual matters. These are issues that warrant our attention. They lie at the heart of the common inquiries: why we are here, and what is our purpose in life. We will spend the remainder of this book exploring the evidence for varying viewpoints and other absolute spiritual truths. I find the evidence for the beliefs presented to be extremely compelling. It is my hope that you will, too.

CHAPTER 2

DOES GOD EXIST?

DOES SCIENCE OPPOSE GOD?

Sir Isaac Newton concluded that, "The thumb alone would convince me of God's existence."[14] Despite this famous scientist's declaration, nowadays it takes more than a thumb to convince some people to believe in the existence of God. In some circles, God is deemed an illusion initially created by ancient people. Some argue that when primitive people did not understand why something happened, they attributed it to the work of a higher power. They claim since we now have greater scientific understanding, we no longer have the need to attribute anything to God. Contrary to what some skeptics suggest, believing in God does not stand in opposition to rationality and science.

Some contend that our existence is a result of a series of uncalculated events: the universe came into existence and despite the tremendous odds against it, had the precise properties required to sustain life. They believe that there is nothing supernatural about the process. Others believe everything ultimately began because of a creator.

This issue has often manifested itself in two camps: those who believe in evolution, and those who believe in intelligent design. However, these two camps do not need to stand in staunch opposition. Those who believe in evolution, and those who believe in intelligent design both must address the same issues (which will be discussed in this chapter). Simply put, evolution is not the issue of this chapter—the existence of God is the issue.[15]

Before beginning our exploration of whether there is evidence that God exists, it is important to remember the tremendous limitations of our finite minds in comprehending an eternal, infinite God. In paraphrasing renowned author C.S. Lewis, Timothy Keller writes:

> If there were a God, he wouldn't be another object in the universe that could be put in a lab and analyzed with empirical methods. He would relate to us in the way a playwright relates to the characters in a play. We [characters] might be able to know quite a lot about the playwright, but only to the degree the author chooses to put information about himself in the play. Therefore, in no case could we "prove" God's existence as if he were an object wholly within our universe like oxygen and hydrogen or an island in the Pacific.[16]

In other words, if there truly is a creator whose powers go significantly beyond the limits of our world, we will never fully understand, know, or be able to study Him as we would the elements of this world. Please do not misunderstand me; I am not advocating for blind faith. Those who believe in God also need credible and persuasive evidence to support their position. However, coming to terms with our limitations will account for a better exploration of the evidence. Although we will be unable to conceptualize the entirety of an infinite God with our finite minds, the evidence for a creator is still extraordinary.

In the following pages, our focus will be on three compelling pieces of evidence for God. We will delve into the question of how it all began, examine how incredibly fine-tuned the conditions are for our existence, and determine whether our morality and emotions could have developed naturally. These pieces of evidence will be labeled:

Exhibit 1: The Big Bang
Exhibit 2: The Fine-Tuning of the Universe
Exhibit 3: Our Morality and Emotions

Exhibit 1: The Big Bang—How Did It All Begin?

Do space and time go on forever? Until quite recently, most scientists assumed that our universe had no beginning. This all changed after the discovery of radiation that was emitted during the beginning of the universe—today referred to as the "big bang." This discovery scientifically proved that there was a beginning of our universe. Dr. Francis Collins, one of the leaders of the Human Genome Project and the current director of the National Institutes of Health, has concluded that the big bang is compelling evidence for a creator. Collins writes:

> The big bang cries for a divine explanation. It forces the conclusion that nature had a defined beginning. I cannot see how nature could have created itself. Only a supernatural force that is outside of space and time could have done that.[17]

Collins' beliefs were echoed by Max Planck, founder of the quantum theory and one of the most acclaimed physicists of the 20th century. Planck's exhaustive research left him totally convinced that there was a "conscious and intelligent mind" that has created all matter.[18]

Robert Jastrow, who is an astronomer, physicist, and founder of NASA's Goddard Institute of Space Studies, also believes the existence of a creator is "a scientifically proven fact:"

> Astronomers now find they have painted themselves into a corner because they have proven, by their own methods, that the world began abruptly in an act of creation to which you can trace the seeds of every star, every planet, every living thing in this cosmos and on the earth. And they have found that all this happened as a product of forces they cannot hope to discover… That there are what I or anyone would call supernatural forces at work is now, I think, a scientifically proven fact.[19]

Additionally, prominent cosmologist Dr. Stephen Hawking concedes the improbability of the beginning of our universe without a divine creator. In his book *A Brief History in Time*, Hawking marvels at how precise the initial properties would have to be for the creation of our universe. He writes:

> It would be very difficult to explain why the universe should have begun in just this way, except as the act of a God who intended to create beings like us.[20]

This remarkable precision observable in our universe will be discussed in further depth in the next section. Although Hawking has since acknowledged that he does not believe in a god, he seemed to be at a loss for explaining the beginning of the universe without attributing it to a higher power.[21]

Now we must ask ourselves: what caused the big bang, or what caused the beginning? Is Collins' conclusion correct—does "the big bang [cry] for a divine explanation?"[22] Well-known international debater and analytic philosopher Dr. William Lane Craig solves this conundrum using the Kalam Cosmological Argument, which proposes that nothing can begin to exist without a cause. Since the universe began to exist, there must be a cause. Further, the initial cause would have to be more powerful than the thing it is creating. Thus, the force causing our universe to come into existence has to be beyond the realities of our world. In other words, the force that created our vast universe would have to be uncaused, timeless, and extremely powerful.[23] More simply, something had to come first; there has to be a constant cause or origin from which everything is created. Although the Kalam Cosmological Argument alone cannot justify belief in a higher power, it forces one to consider—what is this uncaused, timeless, powerful force?

This leads to an objection sometimes raised by those who do not believe in God. They may pose the question, "Well, who created God?" The short answer to that question is—no one. However, if someone were to hypothetically discover who created God, then we would undoubtedly wonder who created that hypothetical creator. We will always wonder who created the creator of the creator, and so on. Clearly, the idea of an eternal being or force is something that is difficult for us to wrap our brains around. However, our difficulty to conceptualize the concept does not invalidate its truthfulness.

Further, similar questions can be posed to those who are skeptical of a creator. What created the initial matter that led to the big bang? What created the initial matter that created the initial matter?

Some have attempted to resolve this objection by claiming that the universe created itself. Hawking's famous conclusion is at the forefront of such beliefs. He claims that, "Because there is a law such as gravity, the universe can and will create itself from nothing."[24] This belief is fundamentally flawed, as it does not actually address the original issue. Even if it were theoretically possible for the universe to create itself, it would only be possible if the requisite law of gravity existed before the universe was created. Where did the law of gravity come from? How was it initially put into place?[25] Again, we are led to the same never-ending series of questions. Clearly, something has always had to exist; matter cannot erupt out of nothing without some extraordinary force causing its creation.

Or posed another way, even if you believe that the beginning of the universe can be explained by some unknown substance or force we have yet to discover, we are still left with the unanswerable question of what would have caused that hypothetical substance or force. We will never truly have an answer of what was the *initial* cause (with every new discovery will be the realization that we do not know what caused the new thing we have discovered). Either believing in God as that beginning and constant force, or believing we will eventually discover the cause of the beginning of the universe will require a degree of faith. Which alternative sounds more plausible? Perhaps you are still unsure at this time. Please read on and weigh the additional evidence presented. The cumulative evidence heavily tips the scales in favor of a creator.

Exhibit 2: The Fine-Tuning of the Universe—What are the Odds?

In recent years, the scientific community has been stunned to discover how incredibly complex, sensitive, and precise the conditions are for the universe to permit the origin and development of life. The universe appears, in fact, to have been intricately fine-tuned from the precise moment of its inception to our eventual existence. Some readers may see the buzzword "fine-tuned" and immediately scoff. This is an argument that some feel has been overused to prove the existence of God. However, this argument stands as *additional* evidence that significantly increases the probability that there was a creator involved rather than simply chance.

The properties of our universe and Earth would have to be extremely delicate, balanced, and precise to create an inhabitable world. Collins notes that in order for life to both emerge and survive, 15 constant scientific forces had to be fine-tuned within remarkably limited ranges:

> When you look from the perspective of a scientist at the universe, it looks as if it knew we were coming. There are 15 constants—the gravitational constant, various constants about the strong and weak nuclear force, etc.—that have precise values. *If any one of those constants was off by even one part in a million, or in some cases, by one part in a million million, the universe could not have actually come to the point where we see it.* Matter would not have been able to coalesce, *there would have been no galaxy, stars, planets or people.* That's a phenomenally surprising observation. It seems almost impossible that we're here. And that does make you wonder—gosh, *who was setting those constants anyway?* Scientists have not been able to figure that out, (emphasis added).[26]

Thus, Collins recognizes the virtual impossibility of these 15 foundational forces of our world simply occurring by chance.

On the following page are some of the many examples of the properties and forces that, if even slightly altered, would have made life on Earth unsustainable.[27]

- If dark energy were even slightly denser, our universe would have expanded too quickly and would have immediately collapsed.

- If the force of gravity were marginally stronger, every star would be a blue giant (extremely hot, large star). If the force of gravity were slightly weaker, every star would be a red dwarf (smaller, relatively cooler stars). If our sun were either a blue giant or red dwarf, life would have never been able to begin on Earth. If the strength of gravity were simply infinitesimally changed by 1 part in 10 to the 100th power, life could not exist.

- If Jupiter or another large planet had not formed in our solar system, meteorites and asteroids would constantly bombard Earth.

- If Earth were either slightly closer or further away from the sun, life-sustaining water would remain in solid form (as ice), or as a gas. Earth is in the perfect position for water to be able to take three forms: liquid, solid, and gas. Similarly, if the distance between the sun and Earth were altered by .01%, life as we know it would have been unsustainable. It would have either been too hot, or too cold for our eventual existence.

- Earth's plate tectonics constantly recycle the air, ensuring the potentially poisonous carbon dioxide levels do not get either too high or too low. Without this recycling, our atmosphere would be unsustainable for life.

Leading scientists acknowledge how extraordinarily improbable the odds are for our existence. Dr. Freeman Dyson has received worldwide recognition for his work in physics, quantum electrodynamics, and nuclear engineering. He has scientifically observed the incredible design in our universe and concludes:

> The more I study the universe and study the details of its architecture, the more evidence I find that the universe in some sense knew we were coming.[28]

Even Hawking concedes the immense improbability of our existence. He writes:

> The universe and the laws of physics seem to have been *specifically designed for us.* If any one of about 40 physical qualities had more than slightly different values, life as we know it could not exist: either atoms would not be stable, or they wouldn't combine into molecules, or the stars wouldn't form the heavier elements, or the universe would collapse before life could develop, and so on, (emphasis added).[29]

Dr. Paul Davies, an astrophysicist and Templeton Prize laureate, likewise concludes, "It seems as though somebody has fine-tuned nature's numbers to make the Universe... The impression of design is overwhelming."[30]

If she were inclined to study science, it seems Goldilocks would have deemed the universe "just right" for our existence. After reviewing just a few of the examples of the specific parameters required for life to be sustained, it seems illogical to conclude that our universe could have begun by mere chance. As Davies has noted, the fingerprints of a Designer are everywhere.

However, some do not believe the incredibly fine-tuned universe is evidence for a creator. They may refer to several theories to support their position. In a court of law, in addition to offering compelling evidence to support your position (as has been set forth previously), it is important to critique the opposition's theories of the case as well. Thus, in the following section, I will critique the two most popular rebuttal theories to the fine-tuning argument.

Rebuttal A: The Anthropic Argument
Rebuttal B: The Multiverse Hypothesis

Analysis of Rebuttal A: The Anthropic Argument

One of the most common rebuttals in response to the position that a fine-tuned universe points to a creator is the anthropic argument. This argument essentially reasons, of course it seems as if the universe was engineered precisely for our existence. If the conditions were anything but what they are now, we would not exist or be able to marvel at the statistical improbabilities of our existence. Anthropic proponents contend that no matter how sophisticated and precise conditions in our universe seem to be, they are not evidence for the existence of a creator. They are only evidence of *our* existence.[31]

The anthropic argument maintains that if a creator designed the universe to fall within the specific and necessary parameters, we would eventually be able to discuss their significant improbability. If the improbabilities just happened by chance, then we would still be able to discuss their improbability. Much like the "who created God" question, the anthropic argument is a cyclical rebuttal because it does not truly refute the existence of a creator. Rather, the anthropic argument simply points to the fact that although it seems impossible for life to erupt, it did. So they argue that the improbability is irrelevant. Similarly, the anthropic argument fails to offer *any* explanations for how matter and the necessary forces in the universe originated.

I am not implying that the evidence for a higher power lies *solely* in how perfectly our universe appears to have been hard-wired for our existence. However, the incredible improbability of our existence significantly adds to the probability that there is a creator behind it all, rather than our existence being just a chance statistical phenomenon.

The often-used analogy by philosopher John Leslie helps illuminate the weakness of the anthropic argument.[32] In his analogy, Leslie surmises that there is a man sentenced to death by a firing squad of 50 expert marksmen, each firing from six feet away. Now imagine that each of these 50 marksmen misses the condemned man. The man would reflect on how improbable the event was, but its improbability is irrelevant as his ability to reflect is obviously proof that the improbable occurred. The anthropic argument essentially stops there, marveling at this improbability. However, with such an incredible improbability, it seems far-fetched to assume each shooter just happened to miss by chance. Logic would reason that they were bribed, or there was some sort of explanation for their incredibly bad shots. In other words, the remarkable improbability makes chance extremely unlikely and points to an underlying cause.

Although it is possible that our world just happened to have every necessary requirement for our existence by chance, is this truly the most plausible explanation? As with the poor marksmen, is it truly more rational to attribute the finely tuned universe to *chance*, or does it perhaps make more sense to draw the conclusion there is something, or *someone* greater intervening?

Analysis of Rebuttal B: Multiverse Hypothesis

Another rebuttal to the position that the fine-tuned universe points to a creator is the multiverse hypothesis. This hypothesis speculates that there are an infinite number of universes, rendering the immense improbability of the existence of our universe to be at least somewhat plausible. It essentially reasons that if you have an infinite number of chances for something nearly impossible to happen, you are bound to defy the odds at least once. However, it seems that the possible existence of an infinite number of universes does nothing to increase the significant improbability of *our* universe being the universe where life erupts.

Further, the multiverse hypothesis is just that: a hypothesis. Although scientists are currently attempting to discover whether an infinite number of universes are even a possibility, they have found *no* evidence to prove that it is true. Although it is possible that there are an infinite number of universes (as this theory is nothing more than an unconfirmed unproven possibility), is this idea truly so much more plausible to accept than the existence of a creator?

More importantly, the multiverse hypothesis does not rule out the existence of a creator. If scientists were to eventually discover that there were an infinite number of universes, then we would return to the same question: what caused the infinite universes to begin in the first place? Davies reiterates this point in stating:

> The general multiverse explanation is simply naïve deism (belief in a higher power) dressed up in scientific language. Both appear to be an infinite unknown, invisible and unknowable system… It is basically just a religious conviction rather than a scientific argument, (parenthetical added).[33]

As was the case with the anthropic argument, the multiverse theory fails to offer any answers as to how the universes and the necessary forces (i.e., gravity) came into existence.

Also, if there were a machine or mechanism creating universes, or a universe generator of sorts, this generator would have to be extraordinarily powerful and capable of creating with incomprehensible precision. As was noted with the Kalam Cosmological Argument, the initial creator has to be greater than the thing it is creating. This generator would have to be far more powerful than our unfathomably vast universe. It would have to possess the immensely powerful capabilities to create a universe so precisely fine-tuned to eventually permit and sustain conditions for life. Again, is random chance truly more logical to believe in than God? The multiverse hypothesis brings us right back to the issues we face with a single universe, and it too offers no evidence to refute the existence of a creator. It seems to take more faith to believe in the multiverse hypothesis than it does to believe in a creator. Biologist Dr. Richard Dawkins disagrees with this assertion as he contends:

> The multiverse, for all that it is extravagant, is simple. God, or any intelligent, decision-taking, calculating agent, would have to be highly improbable in the very same statistical sense as the entities he is supposed to explain.[34]

Essentially, Dawkins proposes that because a hypothetical creator would have to be initially extremely complex, it is illogical to believe in a higher power. His argument comes from a reductionist mindset, or the idea that everything starts simply and becomes more complex (much like evolution—from speck to life).

Notably, in the documentary *Expelled,* Dawkins concedes that, "No one knows how it got started." He goes on to speculate that molecular biologists might eventually discover the "signature of some sort of designer."[35] He validates this reasoning by claiming that there may be another civilization somewhere that has evolved to higher levels of intellect than us. He conjectures that somehow, this alien civilization was able to bring life to

Earth (thus, making this hypothesized civilization the creator or "designer" of life on Earth).

The first and most obvious issue with this belief (as I imagine you have already picked up on) is the question of how those non-discovered, higher-intelligence, extra-terrestrial beings were created. Even if these hypothetical beings ultimately evolved from a speck of matter, where did that initial matter come from? Dawkins' theory, again, leaves us with no explanation of how it all began.

Those who cling to these obscure and hypothetical beliefs are often doing so because such beliefs are different and no longer rooted in what they consider to be "primitive" religious ideals. But is it truly more rational to disregard any belief in a higher power through the claim that life did not begin on this planet but in another galaxy, and somehow that life was transported to Earth? This reasoning does nothing more than reassign to a planet in another galaxy the problems naturalists face when they reject the existence of a creator. By conceding, "we do not know how life began, but it probably did not begin here," skeptics are still left with the same issue of origin—*how did it begin*? We should not cling to traditional beliefs merely for the sake of traditionalism, but we should be cautious of the allure of logically incoherent beliefs simply because they are new.

Dawkins continues to hold to his reductionist beliefs, even while discussing hypothetical aliens. He ascertains that these evolved beings (who somehow brought life to Earth) would have had to begin simply and then evolve to higher levels of intellect. As noted, the reality is that the force that created our universe would have to be incredibly powerful and sophisticated in order to create the complex, intricate world in which we live. As I believe has been demonstrated, belief in the existence of a creator seems far more rational and supported by the evidence than the alternatives offered.

Exhibit 3: Our Morality and Emotions—Where Did They Come From?

We Seem to Have an Innate Sense of Morality and Justice

"He cut in line! That's not fair! It wasn't his turn!" These words often cried out by an impatient young child (or adult) speaks to something greater—the belief that there is a distinction between what is "right" and what is "wrong." The debate regarding the origin of this embedded distinction between moral and immoral behavior is one that has occupied the stage in nearly every realm of ethics and theology for as long as these branches of thought have existed. In the following section, we will join the conversation. More specifically, we will examine two of the leading trains of thought today regarding the origin of morality: that our morality is a result of millions of years of random adaptations, or that our morality is actually evidence for a creator.

Initially, it should be acknowledged that some do not believe there is an underlying moral code ingrained in us. They reason morality is simply a social construct that has been developed over the course of time. There are simply behaviors that are either accepted or rejected in any given community depending upon the culture. This is often referred to as cultural moral relativism. Despite this neutral attitude towards morality, few actually accept it in practice.

If individuals witnessed a community committing cannibalism towards its disabled children, few would claim, "It is simply a result of my social constructs that I view this behavior as wrong." Nearly everyone would label that as awful and immoral behavior and want to intervene. Some in that community would most likely also be troubled by the grotesque conduct.

For a less extreme example, most individuals living in western communities believe women should be allowed the equal opportunity to pursue an education (and more people are standing up for this right in all cultures around the globe).[36] Clearly, people across many cultures become upset when other cultures refuse to offer women this equal opportunity for education. Most cultures view the opportunity to receive an education as an inherent right of all human beings. But where did this "right" come from? If there is no ingrained moral law establishing that human beings should be treated equally, is this right to equal educational opportunities simply a result of our culture? If that is the case, perhaps societies that do not honor this right have simply evolved differently (neither better nor worse). If it is just a result of our own culture to view this behavior as correct, do we have a right to impose our beliefs on other cultures? How do we know that their culture didn't get it right and we are simply the unenlightened ones?

Despite this proposal for cultural moral relativism, in practice, virtually everyone holds innate principles and laws in their minds when categorizing moral and immoral behaviors. Often, we are unaware that we have created these categories until an event or situation arises (i.e., the prohibition of the education of women). Within our consciences are certain beliefs of fairness and equality that should not be crossed. We hold to the fundamental tenet that all people are created equal and should be treated accordingly. This principle is far more acceptable in our society than the idea of "survival of the fittest." Is it more reasonable to conclude these moral underpinnings evolved? Or is it more reasonable to perhaps conclude that a just and fair God embedded them in us?

Distinction Between Moral Values and Moral Duties

It should be noted that every act does not need to be deemed "moral" and "immoral." William Lane Craig makes the distinction between moral *values* and moral *duties*.[37] Moral values deem something to be good or bad, but are *subjective*. For example, some may say it is good to go to a four-year university. Depending on the individual involved, this may be a true statement. But someone who has skills in carpentry and chooses to go to a trade school is not behaving inherently *bad*. The individual may actually be making the better choice for his or her career path. Thus, higher education paths are subjective.

On the other hand, moral duties determine something to be right or wrong and are *objective*. For example, most would concede that the murder of an *innocent* individual is wrong. This is an objective assessment and is not dependent upon personal choices.

Some may argue that the claim that there is a universal morality of sorts is fallacious because our distinction of moral acts has changed over time. As C.S. Lewis illuminates in *Mere Christianity* (a book I highly recommend), although the distinction of what is "moral" has changed, the general underlying principles have remained the same. He writes:

> Men have differed as regards what people you ought to be unselfish to—whether it was only your own family, or your fellow countrymen, or everyone. But they have always agreed that you ought not to put yourself first. Selfishness has never been admired.[38]

The true question lies in determining whether these consistent underlying principles (such as unselfishness) have been ingrained in us by a creator, or have arisen out of purely natural processes. Recently, evolutionary psychology has gained notoriety in attempting to explain human values and emotions purely through natural biological processes. However, if the point of evolution is to preserve our own life ("survival of the fittest") then why does society deem it wrong to steal from the elderly lady walking down the street? Clearly, it would give someone an advantage to steal, as it would help their survival and well being because they would then have access to more resources. When we attempt to explain morality without the existence of God, it often becomes convoluted and difficult. As I believe will be clearly demonstrated, the existence of morality is simply unexplainable without the existence of a creator.

Humanity Has Different Moral Standards than the Animal Kingdom

Are we truly just a random mass culmination of cells, tissue, and brain matter? Is there anything *beyond* our biology? Some have conjectured that we are nothing more than the sum of our parts. They believe we are machines that are wired to survive through the random process of natural selection. This wholly-encompassing belief, simplistically defined previously as evolutionary psychology, postulates that the theory of evolution not only explains the biological progression of life from the initial cell, but also our actions, emotions, and even our morality.

At first glance this belief may make us feel a bit uneasy because it strips away our traditional sense of humanity. It ultimately reasons that we are nothing more than "robotic" beings, or "machines" that can be fully explained through a biological progression. The entirety of humanity is essentially nothing more than a snowball rolling down the hill, accumulating the snow and other materials in its path that will prove to be the most adaptive. There is no true morality, no conscience—everything we may think and feel is just a result of what proved to be the most adaptive during the process of natural selection.

Despite the fact that human beings are considered to be just animals, we continue to hold humans to a higher standard than the rest of the animal kingdom. For instance, a cold-blooded murder is deemed evil in our society. We have enacted laws to punish those who have murdered other human beings. Would anyone seriously consider creating a criminal justice system for animals to be put on trial after murdering another animal? Would we hold investigations to determine whether their murder was an act of self-defense, or whether the animal should be incarcerated? Obviously, this sounds like a ridiculous proposition. But, if human beings are truly just biological beings, why would we not either hold animals to a higher standard, or lower the moral bar for ourselves?

Clearly, there is something that distinguishes humanity from the animal kingdom. Some may propose it is simply that human beings have developed greater capacities for empathy and morality.[39] But *how* and *why* did that development occur? Why do we not see other animals with developed abilities to empathize and determine morality that are on par with humanity?

More importantly, if we are truly only beings that have developed by natural selection over time, do "empathy" and "morality" even warrant any meaning? As Dawkins conveys, "Nature is not cruel, only pitilessly indifferent."[40] In the animal kingdom, the strong survive and the weak perish. Where did we determine that human beings should be any different? In his New York Times best-selling book *Reason for God*, Timothy Keller recognizes this hurdle for the naturalists. He describes the "unnatural-ness" of human morality.

> If violence is totally natural why would it be wrong
> for strong humans to trample weak ones? There is no
> basis for moral obligation unless we argue that nature
> is in some part unnatural. We can't know that nature
> is broken in some way unless there is some supernatu-
> ral standard of normalcy apart from nature by which
> we can judge right and wrong.[41]

Evolution Does Not Promote Absolute Truth

Further, is it reasonable to speculate that a trait such as altruism, or having a greater concern for others than for yourself, evolved? It has been suggested that even an altruistic act can be explained evolutionarily. Imagine a drastic scenario in which you have the opportunity to save one of your family members from being hit by a bus. This kind of a self-sacrificial act seems to go against the "survival of the fittest" process of evolution, and yet most would do it without hesitation (or feel guilty for not doing so). Some have suggested that we would make this instantaneous decision because we want our genes to be passed on to the next generation; that is, it is an adaptive survival trait to be sacrificial towards your own kin, because then your genes will still be passed on.[42]

But what about an altruistic act towards a complete stranger? Imagine the same scenario, but you have the opportunity to save a stranger. The stranger does not have familial genes, and yet many would perform a self-sacrificial act with very little hesitation (or again, feel forever guilty for not doing so). Dawkins describes two other reasons for altruism aside from the preservation of family genetics. He explains that a self-sacrificial act could be done to gain a good reputation, or the act could be done with the anticipation that a repayment of favors will be given in the future (providing the person survives this heroic act).

Dawkins goes on to suggest that if an instance of altruism is not explained by the above listed reasons, it is simply a result of a default in our biological programming. He describes:

> Natural selection does not favor the evolution of a cognitive awareness of what is good for your genes… What natural selection favors is rules of thumb, which work in practice to promote the genes that built them.[43]

Dawkins concludes natural selection does not favor *truth*, but *general rules of thumb*. Or, in other words, he proposes that there is no such thing as absolute truth; rather, there are merely behaviors that have proven to be adaptive in the progression of natural selection. This creates a serious problem. If, as some believe, our minds are molded purely by natural selection, then we are not relying on fixed standards of truth but simply upon whatever beliefs have been most adaptive in our past. Charles Darwin shared a similar concern after noting that animals did not understand truth and do not have the same rational cognitive abilities as humans. He writes:

> With me the horrid doubt always arises whether the convictions of man's mind, which has been developed from the mind of lower animals, are of any value or at all trustworthy. Would any one trust in the convictions of a monkey's mind, if there are any convictions in such a mind?[44]

Evolution does not preserve absolute truth; it simply seeks to promote the survival of an organism. Or put another way, the content or truthfulness of a belief does not matter, only whether that belief is adaptive. To presume the process of natural selection can explain all facets of human life seems not only over-simplified, but also fundamentally flawed. If we are truly only the result of natural selection, then there is no preservation of absolute truth, only of adaptive behavior.

Our Moral Compass Is Evidence of a Creator

Returning to the issue of morality, neuroscientist Dr. Sam Harris has argued that our morality can be objectively and scientifically mapped without an ingrained moral law. He argues that we can create a landscape of morality in which the peaks are moral actions, and the valleys of the landscape are immoral actions. He suggests that the actions and behaviors promoted by some cultures are objectively better than others. The distinction is merely determined by whether the actions and behaviors promote the "well-being of conscious creatures." If they do, the actions are moral. If they do not, they are immoral.[45] However, where did this objective standard come from?

Harris presumes this "moral map" does not have simply one peak of morality. Rather, there are numerous situations in which the decision made can be deemed moral, even if it differs from another peak. What are often more clear are the "valleys," or those societies, actions, and cultures which clearly squander the well-being of conscious creatures. He reasons that we can all clearly see when some societies perform heinous acts. For instance, it would be difficult to find anyone (except perhaps radical anti-Semitics) who would believe that the Holocaust was a moral event. The Holocaust led to the kidnapping, torture, and murder of millions of innocent individuals. It is clear, by any humane standard, that the Holocaust was evil.

My initial encounter with Harris' argument left me intrigued. After further reflection and research, however, I was able to see the logical fallacies in his reasoning. If we are truly only a result of our biological adaptive mechanisms, is there objective morality? Is anything objective? The belief that everything can be explained naturally proposes that there is no internal truth as everything comes from the natural or material world.

By this logic, there is no "good" or "evil"—there is only the "adaptive" and "un-adaptive." Clearly, others would reject this idea. Most (including Harris) believe that there is some standard by which acts can be measured. Harris measures these acts by the "well-being of the conscious creature." But what does this even mean? Does it require that an individual be clothed, fed, and provided with shelter, or is it deeper? Do the individuals also have to be generally satisfied with their life to be living in a moral society? Harris' argument is essentially "we can understand the well-being of conscious creatures when we see it." How? Where do we get this understanding? Is it truly plausible to say we just understand these constructs innately as a result of our biology? More importantly, if there is nothing beyond our biology, do terms like "well-being," "satisfaction," and "innately" even warrant any meaning?

If there is not some consistent standard by which morality can be measured, then again we are forced to embrace the previously critiqued idea of cultural moral relativism. This is the belief that all moral standards are flexible and dependent upon the culture. Ultimately, the theory of evolutionary psychology is also one of cultural relativism. Although it is not from one specific culture, the belief essentially says the culture that has evolved over the entire history of humanity has established moral parameters. Evolutionary psychology proposes that any distinguishing factor we may use to determine morality or well-being is based on our previous successful cultural adaptations. By this reasoning, it is wrong to propose that the Holocaust was immoral per say because there is no true distinction, or constant standard of right and wrong; it was simply an act that fell outside the parameters of the behaviors we have found adaptive over the course of history.

Following this logic, evolutionary psychologists would be forced to admit that one day, in the future, we may evolve into accepting genocide if it is presumed to be evolutionary advantageous. Comparatively, one can presume that if our ancestors would have evolved slightly differently, we could be living in a world that embraces a completely different set of moral standards. I am not suggesting that anyone who believes in evolutionary psychology is morally reprehensible. It is simply my attempt to point out the logical inconsistencies presented by this belief.

If morality cannot be logically established by evolution but we still feel there is some standard of moral truth, where does it

<del"A LAWYER'S CASE FOR HIS FAITH</del>

come from? Even if you believe morality can be objectively measured, where do the parameters for well-being or the standard by which you are objectively measuring morality come from? The reality is, without a moral lawgiver our standards cannot be objective. One could reason that prohibiting women from pursuing an education promotes a better family structure and thus, a more healthy society. Our ability to see this as fallacious by Harris' "objective" distinction may actually just be a result of our western culture.

Similar to the laws of physics governing our world, it seems that there are foundational, undeniable moral laws. It seems as if our morality is a representation of something greater—of some universal standard by which acts of humanity are measured. There is something more to us than our biology. If this were not the case, we would have no reason to conclude there were any categorizations of moral or immoral acts.

In response to those who claim they do not believe in God because there is so much evil, renowned author Ravi Zacharias points out that evil actually proves the existence of God:

> When you say there's too much evil in this world you assume there's good. When you assume there's good you assume there's such a thing as a moral law on the basis of which to differentiate between good and evil. *But if you assume a moral law, you must posit a moral Law Giver,* but that's Who you're trying to disprove and not prove. Because *if there's no moral Law Giver, there's no moral law.* If there's no moral law, there's no good. If there's no good, there's no evil, (emphasis added).[46]

Further, skeptics are forced to explain the source of good in the[4.] world if there is no God. It seems clear that there is some underlying and ultimate cause for our morality (much like the initial cause of the beginning of the existence of the universe). As Keller reasons:

> If there is no God, then there is no way to say any one action is "moral" and another "immoral" but only "I like this." If that is the case, who gets the right to put their subjective, arbitrary moral feelings into law?[47]

A purely naturalistic view of the world will leave one with the hollow feeling that there can be no distinction of morality. Unless there is a higher power or some constant force from which we base our moral distinction, our inherent sense of right and wrong acts seems unexplainable.

I am not proposing that believing in God will solve all the problems of the world. Clearly, thousands of years of hateful acts performed in the name of religion will stand as evidence against that belief. We must recognize, however, that these are acts of humans, not God. Similarly, this is not a declaration that if you are not religious, you will not be able to distinguish morality. I know many non-religious individuals who are upstanding, moral, and charitable. Just because an individual does not understand exactly how electricity works does not mean that they are unable to distinguish between what is light and what is dark. Just because someone may not personally know the moral lawgiver does not mean they cannot understand moral law.

Additionally, if we are essentially machines, how did our array of emotions develop? I know of no machine that has any emotion—although my computer seems to delight in acting up periodically. As human beings we grieve, we laugh, we rejoice, and we love. Why and how would these varied emotions have evolved? If we are truly just beings without anything more than the tangible biological exterior, these emotions do not matter. If there is no greater purpose, it does not matter whether you have lived morally or immorally; all that matters is whether you survive. Is this purposeless world one in which you wish to live? Few would claim that this kind of world sounds appealing. It seems clear there is some sort of external cause, or divine origin for our emotions and our morality. If God does not exist, then where did it come from?

CONCLUSION

As has been discussed, both believing in God and believing solely in unguided natural mechanisms require a degree of faith. But which proposition is more reasonable? We have analyzed the evidence—the big bang, our fine-tuned universe, and our qualities that separate us from the animal kingdom—and demonstrated that the existence of a creator is more strongly supported. Clearly, science and rationality do not stand in opposition to God but rather point to the existence of a creator.

As has been demonstrated, the argument is not that one must either believe in God or believe in science. Oxford professor of mathematics Dr. John Lennox refutes the claim that we must either choose to believe in science or in a creator. Lennox specifically addresses Hawking's claim that natural law can explain everything. He writes:

> What Hawking appears to have done is to confuse law with agency. His call on us to choose between God and physics is a bit like someone demanding that we choose between aeronautical engineer Sir Frank Whittle and the laws of physics to explain the jet engine.[48]

Lennox's analogy simply illustrates that although the laws of physics can explain the operation of the jet engine, there is still a creator of the jet engine (Sir Frank Whittle). It is not that there must be one or the other as both are necessary. One addresses the processes; the other addresses the creator.

Whether you believe the world is 10,000 years old or several billion, we all have to delve into the issue Lennox describes as "agency" (i.e., what was that initial cause or creative agent that forged the beginning of our universe).

The reality is that something had to come first. There is some constant agent at work in our universe. For many, many years, I believed that there was no agent and that everything came from purely natural processes. In retrospect, I realized that I never truly thought things through. My default had become atheism and the belief that everything could be explained naturally, as I assumed believing in anything else was irrational.

However, after examining the evidence for the beginning of the universe as well as the precise fine-tuned properties necessary for life to develop, I can no longer accept that everything came from nothing. There is a powerful force that created our world and enacted the physical laws by which it is governed. Without a creator, we are left wondering where those constant natural laws came from. The belief that our world developed and is governed by chance seems far more improbable than a creator.

The words and sentences on this page did not just happen by chance; they were written. Buildings do not simply appear; they are built. Similarly, our world was not formed by chance; it was created. In our culture, the idea of any spiritual or non-natural explanation is deemed to be primitive by some. But truly, what is more plausible? That our universe just happened to exist with the perfect conditions to create and sustain life, or that there was a creating force?

Similarly, it seems illogical to conclude that human beings can be completely explained as being nothing more than a result of a series of unplanned biological events. If we are no different than other animals and everything about us can be traced back to evolutionary explanations, then there is no true standard of morality or truth. We would be basing our classifications of morality and immorality solely upon things that have been the most adaptive over time, rather than on true categorizations of "good" and "evil." Our morality and emotions are simply unexplainable without the existence of a creator.

Clearly, belief in God can be explained more logically than the alternatives. Thankfully, the Creator of the universe did not put everything into place and then move on. He has far more to offer than rational arguments and logic. He extends true peace and love through the invitation to enter into a relationship with Him. This relationship can be fueled by questions; however, fuel your skepticism with the sincere desire to find truth. God is truth, and He will reveal that truth to you. Ultimately, having a relationship with the Creator is also fueled through humility in understanding that we will never have all the answers in this life. We are characters in His story, and perhaps the greatest struggle we will ever face is realizing the story is not only about us, it is also about Him.

CHAPTER 3

CAN THE OLD COVENANT BE USED
AS HISTORICAL EVIDENCE?

There are some who advocate that we should all simply focus on being good people and get rid of organized religion entirely—or at least never publicly discuss our personal religious beliefs. It is sometimes deemed intolerant to hold any religious beliefs at all, especially if you would be so bold as to presume the belief of someone else to be wrong. While at first blush this advocacy for tolerance may seem reasonable, upon further analysis, it is clearly highly illogical.

Everyone holds a spiritual belief, even if his or her belief is that there is no supernatural realm. The lack of a belief in the supernatural realm is an exclusive belief, and the belief that every spiritual belief is correct is also an exclusive belief. Ultimately, everyone holds some sort of exclusive spiritual belief. If someone believes something, they are claiming that what they believe is correct, which in turn means that everyone who does not agree with what they believe is ultimately wrong.

Often those who advocate for religious relativism (or the belief that everyone can be correct) are doing so with the underlying claim that everyone just needs to focus on being "a good person." The general desire for societal inclusion and the focus on merely being good people *sounds* like a great idea. But who determines what is good? What is good for me may not be good for you. Is abortion good or bad? Our country is split approximately 50-50 on that issue, so it seems about half of us are "not good" but think we are.[49]

Our inclination is to simply want everyone to act "good" based upon whatever subjective guidelines *we* deem most appropriate. Some advocate that we should ignore the customs of all religious practices, and instead follow this obscure standard of "being good." But, we are creating these guidelines through our own extremely limited and biased perspective based on our personal backgrounds and life experiences. Since we are creating these guidelines ourselves, there is rarely any consensus. Is this subjectivity a solid foundation upon which to base our lives and perhaps our eternal destiny?

I have lived for over 60 years and have practiced law for over 35 years. Nonetheless, I am not qualified to develop my own personal set of rules upon which to trust my physical, emotional, and spiritual well being, as well as my eternal destiny. This extremely high-risk endeavor would be a daunting task for anyone. Our life experiences are limited, and our views tend to evolve over time. When we are in our late 20s we often find our pre-teen beliefs about the world rather humorous. This same trend typically continues throughout life.

Following a road map that has proven successful for countless others over many centuries would seem to be a safer route to travel. While on vacation, would you want a tour guide who has never visited the area? I certainly would not—I would prefer a seasoned veteran. This logic certainly seems transferable to spiritual beliefs as well. If there were a supernatural realm or absolute spiritual truth, one would presume the rules governing it to have been in existence for an extremely long time.

As was discussed in the first chapter, there has to be absolute truth in the spiritual realm. There either is a God, or there is not. We cannot logically advocate for spiritual relativism. In the previous chapter, we discovered that there are rational arguments and compelling evidence for the existence of God; however, there are thousands of religions in the world. How do we choose which religion is correct? We must go where the evidence leads. For the duration of this book, we will examine the evidence supporting the beliefs of those who have faith in Yeshua, and determine whether it is a belief supported by compelling evidence. If you are interested in learning more about this topic, I have compiled a brief analysis in Appendix A demonstrating that all religions cannot be correct because they contradict one another.

FACTS ABOUT THE BIBLE

Nearly every major religion in the world has some sort of literature its followers use for instruction on how to best live their lives. Some of these religions claim their book to be a revelation from God. Many of those who believe Yeshua is the Messiah believe that the Bible was inspired by God and recorded by human beings.[50] Approximately 40 individuals wrote the Bible across three continents over the course of 1,600 years.[51] The Bible contains 66 chapters that are divided into two parts. Followers of Yeshua believe both parts depict one continuous message and were inspired by the same God.[52] The first part is called the Old Covenant (Old Testament/Hebrew Scriptures/Tanakh). The second is called the New Covenant (New Testament/Messianic Scriptures/Brit Chadasha). The distinction between the two parts occurs because the texts of the Old Covenant were written and recorded before the life of Yeshua on Earth, and the texts of the New Covenant were written after His resurrection approximately 2,000 years ago.[53]

Despite these incredibly diverse origins, the Bible is considered by many scholars to be a masterpiece of unified literature.[54] Skeptics may believe the Bible to be simply a book of ancient myths—I believed that for the first 39 years of my life. Others may think the stories are primarily fictional, but can still be looked to for wisdom. Still others, including myself now, view the Bible as a revelation from God.

If God inspired the writings of the Bible, it stands to reason that the texts and stories would be validated by other sources. In other words, we would be able to unearth evidence supporting the historical events that are recorded in the Bible. For the remainder of this chapter, we will determine whether there is evidence to validate the first 39 books of the Bible (Old Covenant). In the next chapter, we will examine the historicity of the remaining 27 books (New Covenant).

HISTORIANS SUPPORT THE ACCURACY OF THE OLD COVENANT

The deeper archaeologists dig, the more evidence they unearth which corroborates the accuracy of the Bible. Although every detail, event, and individual recorded in the Old Covenant has yet to be validated, the discoveries thus far have rendered scholars to conclude that it is a book of historical significance. Rabbi Nelson Glueck, a prominent Jewish archaeologist, concluded that archaeological discoveries have repeatedly affirmed the validity of the Bible:

> It may be stated categorically that no archaeological discovery has ever controverted a biblical reference. Scores of archaeological findings have been made which confirm in clear outline or in exact detail

historical statements in the Bible. And, by the same token, proper evaluation of biblical descriptions has often led to amazing discoveries. They form tesserae in the vast mosaic of the Bible's almost incredibly correct historical memory.[55]

Perhaps William Foxwell Albright, the American dean of biblical archaeology, sums it up best:

> Discovery after discovery has established the accuracy of innumerable details, and has brought increased recognition of the Bible as a source of history.[56]

Similarly, the highly esteemed Smithsonian Institution's Department of Anthropology, a non-religious institution, has acknowledged that:

> Much of the Bible, in particular the historical books of the old testament are as accurate historical documents as any we have from antiquity and are in fact more accurate than many of the Egyptian, Mesopotamian or Greek histories. These Biblical records can be and are used as are other ancient documents in archeological work. For the most part, the historical events described took place and the peoples cited really existed.[57]

Clearly, at the very least, portions of the Old Covenant can be viewed as historically reliable despite their religious use. In the next section, we will examine evidence that has led experts to validate the historical authenticity of the Old Covenant, including some of the archaeological evidence as well as some of the *hundreds* of accurately fulfilled predictions (prophecies).

ARCHEOLOGICAL EVIDENCE CONFIRMS THE
HISTORICAL ACCURACY OF THE OLD COVENANT

There are thousands of archeological discoveries supporting the historical accuracy of the text in the Old Covenant. Although every ancient story and character has yet to be verified by archeological discoveries, there is still an abundance of evidence to support the historical reliability of the Old Covenant—and no evidence to refute its reliability. In the following section, we will discuss a few of these discoveries and then provide the reference to where this historically confirmed individual, artifact, or event is in the Old Covenant.

Tomb of Abraham, Sarah, and their Family

Abraham, who many attribute as the patriarch (or "founding father") of Judaism, is believed to have lived around 1900 BCE.[58] Abraham bought a tomb for his family after the death of his wife, Sarah. The Old Covenant records that Abraham, his son Isaac, and his grandson Jacob, as well as their wives Sarah, Rebekah, and Leah (respectively), are all buried in this tomb. Today, the tomb can be visited in Hebron, Israel.

Old Covenant Reference: Genesis 49:31-32

There Abraham and his wife Sarah were buried, there Isaac and his wife Rebekah were buried, and there I (Jacob) buried Leah. The field and the cave in it were bought from the Hittites, (parenthetical added).[59]

House of David Inscription

King David (of David and Goliath fame) is one of the most famous individuals from the Old Covenant. Scholars have concluded that he was King of Israel from 1010-970 BCE.[60] Despite David's important role in the Old Covenant, for a long time, scholars did not find any non-biblical evidence to support his existence. Notably, this is not entirely surprising for this time in ancient Israel's history.[61]

However, in 1993, a piece of basalt (volcanic) rock was discovered containing the inscription "House of David." Archeologists confirmed this inscription was made in 841 BCE, meaning it was inscribed within the first few generations after the life of David.[62]

Notably, scholars have also unearthed a list of important places and names written by Shoshenq I of Egypt after his victory over Rehoboam and Jeroboam in 926 BCE. This list contains the inscription, "the heights of *Dwt*." Historian and Old Covenant scholar K.A. Kitchen provides an analysis of how this was most likely a reference to King David. This list was compiled within the first *50 years* of the life of David, making it very significant historical evidence![63]

Old Covenant Reference: 1 Chronicles 18:14

David reigned over all Israel, and he administered justice and equity to all his people.[64]

The Second Temple

The Western or Wailing Wall is a well-known location in Jerusalem where people often come to pray. The surrounding courtyard is the home to many joyous celebrations during the year and on Jewish holidays. This wall is actually a portion of the western retaining wall from the Second Temple. The Second Temple is discussed extensively in the Old Covenant, and stood from approximately 530 BCE until its destruction by the Romans in 70 CE.[65] The Temple was believed to be the place where God resided, and as such was regarded with extreme reverence. Since the Second Temple was such a foundational component of Judaism for over 500 years and there are many non-biblical references to it, there is virtually no debate as to whether it was a true historic location.

Old Covenant Reference: Ezra 6:3

> In the first year of King Cyrus,[66] Cyrus the king issued a decree: "Concerning the house of God at Jerusalem, let the temple, the place where sacrifices are offered, be rebuilt."[67]

Hezekiah's Tunnel

During the reign of King Hezekiah, Jerusalem was particularly vulnerable to a water shortage. This was because the water supply it had relied upon for centuries was from the spring of Gihon, which was located outside the protected city walls. The Bible records that to prevent a tragedy, King Hezekiah had a tunnel constructed in 700 BCE to transport water from the spring of Gihon to the pool of Siloam, located within Jerusalem. In the 1800s, Hezekiah's tunnel was discovered and can be waded through today on a visit to Jerusalem.

Old Covenant Reference: 2 Chronicles 32:30

> The same Hezekiah closed the upper outlet of the waters of Gihon and directed them down to the west

side of the city of David (in Jerusalem), (parenthetical added).[68]

Baruch Seals

In 1982, archaeologists unearthed 51 clay seals (bullae) of Baruch, scribe and devoted friend of the prophet Germariah (Jeremiah). One of the seals was inscribed with the name Germariah, and was discovered in the precise location in Germariah's home where it is recorded in the Old Covenant that Baruch read these parchments 2,500 years prior.[69]

Old Covenant Reference: Jeremiah 36:32

So Jeremiah took another scroll and gave it to the scribe Baruch son of Neriah, and as Jeremiah dictated, Baruch wrote on it all the words of the scroll that Jehoiakim king of Judah had burned in the fire. And many similar words were added to them.[70]

The Kings

Scholars have discovered the names of the kings recorded in the Old Covenant to be astoundingly historically accurate. After 853 BCE, 9 out of the 14 Israelite kings, and 17 out of the 20 foreign kings are also named in external sources. Similarly, while taking into consideration the context of the ancient culture, the chronology of kings recorded in the books of the Old Covenant are extremely accurate. After a thorough analysis, Kitchen confirms that, "The writers of Kings, Chronicles, and Isaiah and Jeremiah come out well here in terms of accuracy and reliability."[71]

The Dead Sea Scrolls

Perhaps the most impactful discovery to validate the Old Covenant manuscripts was the accidental discovery of the Dead Sea Scrolls in Qumran in 1949 near the Dead Sea in Israel. Before the discovery of these scrolls, the earliest manuscripts of the Old Covenant dated to around 900 CE. The Dead Sea Scrolls manuscripts were written between 100 BCE and 100 CE. These biblical manuscripts written from approximately 900 years prior were *nearly identical* to the texts from 900 CE.[72] The modern-day texts are authenticated through this very important discovery.

* *

Although every detail, individual, and event in the Bible has yet to be validated by archeological discoveries, the details we do know establish its credibility. The reality is that we will most likely never be able to completely confirm the historical accuracy of all of the ancient events and individuals of the Bible. History will never be able to be proved with 100% certainty. Dr. Michael Licona describes the process of discovering both biblical and non-biblical history:

> When historians say "x occurred" in the past, they are actually claiming the following: *given the available data, the best explanation indicates that we are warranted in having a reasonable degree of certainty that x occurred and that it appears more certain at the moment than competing hypotheses.* Accordingly we have a rational basis for believing it. However, our conclusion is subject to revision or abandonment, since new data may surface in the future showing things happened differently than presently proposed, (emphasis added).[73]

Obviously, historians cannot recreate history in a laboratory; instead, they scrutinize the available evidence to determine what occurred. Although archeological discoveries can help to validate the texts of the Old Covenant, these discoveries cannot prove beyond all doubt every detail of a historical event. With historical events and individuals who lived thousands of years ago, we simply will never have the evidence we have grown accustomed to in the 21st century. We cannot present conclusive evidence such as photographs, fingerprint analysis, or video footage to prove the life of King David. But the evidence we do have has led historians to conclude with a high degree of historical certainty that he was a man who truly lived centuries ago. A further explanation of how historical events are corroborated is discussed in Chapter 4.

Although a section listing *all* of the discoveries supporting the historicity Old Covenant would have been optimal, it was simply not plausible in this very limited section.[74] If you are interested in the topic of the historical reliability of the Old Covenant, I suggest taking the time to read K.A. Kitchen's book, *On the Reliability of the Old Testament*. As is the case with archeologists, I believe that the deeper you dig into the *scholarly* pursuit of validating the texts of the Old Covenant, the more evidence you will find that supports its historical accuracy.

FULFILLED PROPHECIES OF THE OLD COVENANT

Even if the Old Covenant can be validated historically, can it be accepted as being inspired by God? Understand, no matter what evidence historians, logicians, theologians, your pastor, your rabbi, your counselor, your parents, or whichever blogger you follow may present, no one can *prove* the Bible is a revelation from God with 100% certainty. Clearly, if you do not believe in God, you will not believe He inspired the writing of the Bible. (As was discovered in the previous chapter, however, belief in God is more strongly supported by evidence and logic than the alternative.) Similarly, no matter how truly outrageous the odds are, you can choose to explain away the fulfillment of hundreds of prophecies to mere chance. But, when does chance become a more unreasonable explanation than the intervention of God? As was previously discussed, chance is always a possibility, but we must ask ourselves, is it the most reasonable explanation?

One of the most compelling validations for the divine inspiration of the Old Covenant is the bulls-eye accuracy of its hundreds of recorded predictions (which the Bible refers to as prophecies) and their eventual fulfillment. None miss the mark! If the Old Covenant were truly inspired by God, one would assume that some of these prophecies would likewise be able to be historically validated. In this section, we will discuss some of these Old Covenant prophecies and their fulfillment.

The Scattering and Regathering of the Jewish People to the Land of Israel

After the destruction of the Second Temple in 70 CE, the Jewish people were scattered among the nations. This event, referred to as the Diaspora, was written about over 500 years prior to its occurrence!

Old Covenant Reference: Jeremiah 9:16

And the LORD[75] will scatter you among the peoples.[76]

However, it was also prophesied that the Jewish people would then be regathered to the land of Israel. In 1948, this too was fulfilled.

Old Covenant Reference: Isaiah 11:12

(God) will assemble the banished of Israel, and gather the dispersed of Judah from the four corners of the earth, (parenthetical added).[77]

No other nation has *ever* regathered after being dispersed![78] Today, Jewish people are returning to Israel from the "four corners of the earth" in record numbers.

The Kingdom of Babylon Would be Permanently Overthrown

The Jewish prophet Isaiah wrote between 701-681 BCE that Babylon would eventually be conquered and wiped out.[79] This same verse in Isaiah refers to the ancient cities of Sodom and Gomorrah. (Notably, the destruction of Sodom and Gomorrah has also been archaeologically validated.)[80] It has been confirmed that after Cyrus conquered Babylon in 539 BCE, it never again ruled as an empire, just as Isaiah foretold.[81]

Old Covenant Reference: Isaiah 13:19

Babylon, the jewel of kingdoms, the glory of the Babylonians' pride, will be overthrown by God like Sodom and Gomorrah.[82]

Further, in approximately 600 BCE, the prophet Jeremiah precisely predicted the 70-year Babylonian captivity of Judah (the Southern Kingdom of Israel), which lasted from 586 BCE to 516 BCE.[83]

Old Covenant Reference: Jeremiah 25:12

> "Then it will come to pass, when seventy years are completed, that I will punish the king of Babylon and that nation...for their iniquity," says the Lord; "and I will make it (the Babylonian Empire) a perpetual desolation," (parenthetical added).[84]

Israel's Desert Would Blossom

The ancient prophet Isaiah predicted something unthinkable—that the desert in Israel would blossom with roses and fruit.

Old Covenant Reference: Isaiah 35:1

> The wilderness and the parched land shall be glad; And the desert shall rejoice, and blossom as the rose.[85]

Old Covenant Reference: Isaiah 27:6

> In the days to come Jacob shall take root, Israel shall blossom and put forth shoots and fill the whole world with fruit.[86]

Today, Israel exports 1.5 billion roses annually, making it the third leading exporter in the world of roses to the European Union—from a country that is roughly the size of New Jersey![87] Additionally, Israel's leading export is fruit. This agricultural success has made Israel one of the leading agricultural experts in the Middle East.[88]

Rome's Rule Over Israel

Four specific aspects about the Roman rule over Israel were uncannily predicted in the Old Covenant passage in Deuteronomy quoted below. This passage was written approximately 1,400 years before the events occurred!

- Israel was under Roman rule from 63 BCE through 313 CE, (*"and they shall besiege you in all your towns throughout your land"*).

- The Roman Empire expanded "far away"—across parts of Europe, Asia, and Africa, (*"nation against you from far away, from the end of the earth"*).

- Additionally, it is recorded in ancient texts that when the Romans marched into battle, they raised the Roman Standard, which was a flag or banner that hung on a pole. An animal represented each infantry unit, and the most common was the eagle. The represented animal would be depicted on the standard as they marched into battle referring back to the biblical prophecy, (*"swooping down like the eagle"*).

- Across the expansive Roman Empire, many languages were spoken and written, but Greek was the primary language, which the Hebrew speaking Jews would not have known, (*"whose language you do not understand"*).[89]

Old Covenant Reference: Deuteronomy 28:49-52

The LORD will bring a nation against you from far away, from the end of the earth, swooping down like the eagle, a nation whose language you do not understand… And they shall besiege you in all your towns throughout your land, which the LORD your God has given you.[90]

Cyrus Would Rebuild the Walls of Jerusalem

Approximately 150 years before King Cyrus was even born, the prophet Isaiah foretold Cyrus' name and said that he would rebuild the walls of Jerusalem. What makes this prophecy even more impressive is that at the time of Isaiah's writing, the Babylonian King Nebuchadnezzar had not yet destroyed the walls of Jerusalem!

The history of King Cyrus is documented in the Cyrus Cylinder, which was discovered in 1879 and is preserved today in the British Museum.[91]

Old Covenant Reference: Isaiah 44:24-28

Thus says the LORD, your Redeemer… who says of Jerusalem, "She shall be inhabited," and of the cities of Judah, "They shall be built and I will raise up their ruins"…who says of Cyrus, "He is my shepherd and he shall fulfill all my purpose."[92]

Old Covenant Reference: Ezra 1:2

Thus says Cyrus…"The LORD, the God of heaven, has given me all the kingdoms of the earth, and he has charged me to build him a house at Jerusalem, which is in Judah."[93]

Additional fulfilled prophecies are discussed in Chapter 7, and in my first book, *A Lawyer's Case for God*.[94] The pinpoint accuracy of these predictions is unfathomable, unless God, who transcends time, language, and location, inspired the writings of the Bible. The Old Covenant confirms that the Bible is the word of the LORD:

> His (God's) way is perfect; the word of the LORD proves true, (parenthetical added), (2 Samuel 22:31).[95]

Jewish People Still in Existence

Historians and laypeople alike feel that the mere fact that the Jewish people have survived over thousands of years is powerful evidence of the existence of God who protects His people, just as He promised He would in the Bible.

Old Covenant Reference: Jeremiah 31:35-36

> Thus says the LORD, who gives the sun for light by day and the fixed order of the moon and the stars for light by night, who stirs up the sea so that its waves roar; the LORD of hosts is his name: "If this fixed order departs from before me," declares the LORD, "then shall the offspring of Israel cease from being a nation before me forever."[96]

In other words, God has promised that the Jewish people will always exist.[97] The Crusades, Spanish Inquisition, Pogroms, Holocaust, and other attempts to exterminate the Jewish people have all miraculously failed. This promise has stayed true even when the Jewish people were without a homeland for 2,000 years. No other group of people has ever kept its identity for over a few hundred years during a dispersion.

Over 300 years ago, King Louis XIV of France asked the great philosopher Blaise Pascal to give him proof of God. Pascal famously answered, "Why the Jews, your majesty, the Jews."[98]

Mark Twain, an agnostic, penned this in 1899 in Harper's Magazine about the immortality of the Jewish people:

> The Egyptian, Babylonian, and the Persian rose, filled the planet with sound and splendor, then faded to dream-stuff and passed away. The Greek and Roman followed, made a vast noise and they are gone. Other peoples have sprung up, and held their torch high for a time, but it burned out and they sit in twilight now or have vanished. The Jew saw them all, beat them all, and is now what he always was, exhibiting no decadence, no infirmities of age, no weakening of his parts, no slowing of his energies, no dulling of his alert and aggressive mind. All things are mortal, but the Jew. All other forces pass, but he remains. What is the secret of his immortality?[99]

Scientific Foreknowledge

Some have critiqued the Bible as being scientifically regressive. However, the opposite has often been the case. I will illustrate how, at times, the Bible has actually predicted scientific discoveries hundreds of years before scientists!

Air Has Weight

Date Prophesied: Approximately 6th century BCE[100]

> When he (God) *gave to the wind its weight* and appointed the waters by measure, when he made a decree for the rain and a way for the lightening of the thunder, and he saw it and declared it; he established it, and searched it out, (parenthetical and emphasis added), (Job 28:25-57).[101]

Evangelista Torricelli discovered air pressure in the mid-1600s, which proved that air had weight.[102]

Paths of the Sea

Date Prophesied: Near the end of David's life in the 10th century BCE[103]

> You have given him dominion over the works of your hands; you have put all things under his feet, all sheep and oxen, and also the beasts of the field, and the birds of the heavens, and the fish of the sea, whatever passes along the paths of the seas, (Psalm 8:6-8).[104]

Dr. Matthew Fontaine Maury discovered underwater ocean currents (paths in the sea) in the mid-1800s.[105]

Earthquake Fault Line Through the Mount of Olives

Date Prophesied: 480 BCE[106]

> On that day his (the Messiah's) feet shall stand on the Mount of Olives that lies before Jerusalem on the east, and the Mount of Olives shall be *split in two* from east to west by a very wide valley, so that one half of the Mount shall move northward, and the other half southward, (parenthetical and emphasis added), (Zechariah 14:4).[107]

Today, we know that Israel sits on the Great Rift Valley, the largest fault line in the world. Fault lines are places under the earth's surface where two tectonic plates meet. When these plates collide, it can cause an earthquake. The geological institute in Tel Aviv uncovered a major earthquake fault line running through the Mount of

Olives, making it entirely geographically plausible for it to "split in two" as this verse predicted 2,500 years ago.

Without divine intervention, it seems illogical that human beings could have accurately written about any of the above scientific facts before they were discovered. Examinations of the hundreds of fulfilled prophecies of the Old Covenant make the explanation of chance highly unlikely.[108]

THE PERCEIVED WRATH OF THE OLD COVENANT GOD

Even if the Old Covenant is validated as a historical source and could ultimately have been inspired by God, some still oppose the God of the Old Covenant. They claim He is wrathful, jealous, a control-freak, an ethnic cleanser, a misogynist, and the list goes on.[109] While reading some texts of the Old Covenant, you may even find yourself reconsidering what you previously believed about the nature of God.

The first point that must be addressed is this: even if you do not *like* God, it does not mean that He does not exist. Someone claiming God does not exist because of "Old Covenant atrocities" is the equivalency of a teenager declaring he does not have parents after a big fight with his mother and father. Clearly, the *existence* of God is not addressed when a skeptic criticizes his or her perception of God's nature. As we have discovered in the previous chapter, the evidence heavily leans in favor of the existence of a God. So, you can dislike His ways, but that opinion has *no bearing on whether He exists.*

Similarly, as archeological discoveries continue to support the validity of the Bible, it seems logical to conclude that the texts are historically accurate (as many credible historians have already validated). Just because something is recorded that we may not either understand or agree with does not mean the Bible is inaccurate. We simply may not understand the historical context in which the texts were written. Whether looking at the Bible as a book of ancient history, or as a book whose writing was inspired by God, we do not get to write off the stories we are uncomfortable with as fiction, or use them as a basis to deny His existence. To do so would be akin to ironically claiming, "God does not exist, and I hate Him."

For the purposes of page space and your time, I will only discuss two issues that often come up in the "Old Covenant atrocities" debate: whether God condones slavery and whether He approved of mass genocide. The approach and strategies utilized in the following section can be used as you come across other Bible verses that may be troubling in the future. There are also a plethora of books and websites that can help to bring historical perspective and understanding of the perceived indictments against God contained in the Bible.[110] As you will discover, I believe it is clear that the accusations against the morality of God are unsubstantiated.

Did God Approve of Slavery?

Slavery is discussed in the Old Covenant. However, it is important to understand that slavery in these biblical passages was not synonymous with the barbaric, racist Atlantic Slave Trade that existed in the United States in the 19th century. Most slavery in ancient Israel was more akin to debt servanthood where individuals had chosen to sell themselves as an employee or hired hand to another during times of financial duress. *Leviticus 25* describes this process:

> If any of your fellow Israelites become poor and sell themselves to you, do not make them work as slaves. They are to be treated as hired workers or temporary residents among you...Do not rule over them ruthlessly, but fear your God.[111]

This is an example of God providing an instruction. Slavery was not in the ideal picture of humanity.[112] But this instruction describes what

to do when individuals are in such a state of poverty that they have
to sell themselves as servants. This was not God's approval of slavery.
We need to remember that God provided instructions to individuals
operating in a world with free will. We will discuss Deuteronomy
15 below, which clearly demonstrates that God's ultimate plan is
for a world ridden of poverty. In this context, Leviticus 25 specifically instructs, "do not make them work as slaves." You might think,
"True but even if the servanthood was voluntary, there are still some
verses that seem barbaric." One such verse will be analyzed next.

Exodus 21:20-21

> And if a man beats his male or female servant with a
> rod, so that he dies under his hand, he shall surely be
> punished. Notwithstanding, if he remains alive a day or
> two, he shall not be punished; for he is his property.[113]

At first blush, this verse seems to deem the individual the *property*
of the master (implying that they are not considered a full human
being). The original Hebrew word in this verse translated into
English as "punished" in the phrase, "he shall surely be punished," is
naqam. Paul Copan, the author and editor of over 25 books including *Is God a Moral Monster*, addresses this issue. Copan writes how:

> This verb *naqam* always involves the death penalty in
> the Old Testament…This confirms that the employee/
> servant was to be treated as a human being with dig-
> nity, not as property.[114]

Unlike other ancient laws regarding servants, time and time again
the laws of the Old Covenant redeem the "personhood" of the
slave. When an individual was murdered in ancient Israel, the law
was, "an eye for an eye," (Exodus 21:24).[115] The above quoted verse

from Exodus confirms that the same punishment is required for the mistreatment of the servants. Having the same punishment gave servants the same status of "personhood" as the masters.

The second half, and more potentially problematic part of the verse is the statement that says that if the servant does not die, no further punishment is inflicted on the master who had just severely harmed another human being. However, the Old Covenant clearly describes that if the servant endures some sort of permanent ramifications for the punishment, the servant/employee is to be immediately forgiven of any debts, and is to be released from servanthood.[116] In other words, there is compensation to the servant for the harm inflicted. Copan contrasts the laws of ancient Israel with those of other ancient cultures. He writes this regarding other ancient codes: "Typically in ancient Near Eastern law codes, masters- not slaves- were merely financially compensated for injuries to their slaves."[117] These were instructions given by God to an imperfect people living in an imperfect world. Many of these "imperfections" of the world arose from the evil performed by human beings exercising their free will. During Chapter 8, we will discuss the ramifications of free will in further depth.

Perhaps the most radical and redeeming aspect of servanthood in ancient Israel was the mandatory forgiveness of all debts every seven years *and* the lavish financial blessing the employer was instructed to provide. It is written in Deuteronomy 15:

> He shall serve you six years, but in the seventh year you shall set him free. When you set him free, you shall not send him away empty-handed. You shall furnish him liberally from your flock and from your threshing floor and from your wine vat; you shall give to him as the Lord your God has blessed you.[118]

Could you imagine such a system in our world today? The ultimate goal of these instructions was to eradicate poverty and any need for servanthood. Despite the fact that some Old Covenant verses about slavery were used in the 19th century to claim that slavery was an acceptable practice, a look at these verses in-depth leads to a much different understanding.[119] The underlying heart of God is clear: ultimate and lasting freedom and forgiveness. This true freedom is a foreshadowing of what is to come through Yeshua, the Messiah.[120]

Does God Condone Mass Genocide?

Deuteronomy 20:16-17

> But in the cities of these people that the Lord your God is giving you for an inheritance, you shall save alive nothing that breathes, but you shall devote them to complete destruction, the Hittites and the Amorites, the Canaanites and the Perizzites, the Hivites and the Jebusites, as the Lord your God has commanded.[121]

Yikes! "Save alive nothing that breathes," and "devoting them to complete destruction," does not immediately paint the picture of a loving God. These commandments of total annihilation by God, and apparent success in this total destruction by the ancient Israelites, are some of the most difficult concepts for many to grasp while reading the Old Covenant. However, understanding the context behind these claims of total devastation will help us better understand the texts and the nature of God.

One of the most important points to understand about these texts is that they are using exaggerative language, which was very common in this ancient culture, especially in the context of war rhetoric.[122] It is the equivalency of sports anchors today saying something like, "That team was absolutely destroyed today." Obviously, we would understand that the team was not *literally and physically* destroyed, as this sort of exaggerative language is used in sports. This would have also been known in the ancient Near East culture with regards to war rhetoric.

The Old Covenant texts themselves actually affirm that there was *not* total destruction:

> When the Lord your God gives them over to you, and you defeat them, you must devote them to complete destruction. You shall make no covenant with them and show no mercy to them. You shall not intermarry with them, giving your daughters to their sons or taking their daughters for your sons, (Deuteronomy 7:2-3).[123]

If there were truly *complete destruction*, why would there be instructions about intermarriage? If no one were left, this would not be an issue. Clearly *all* the Hittites, Amorites, Canaanites, Perizzites, Hivites, and the Jebusites would not have been killed if there were instructions about intermarriage, despite the dramatic rhetoric.

Copan also explains the importance of the locations that the armies were attacking. He explains how Ai, Jericho, and other Canaanite cities were "mainly used for government buildings and operations, while the rest of the people (including women and children) lived in the surrounding countryside."[124] He further points out that, "There is no archaeological evidence of civilian populations at Jericho or Ai."[125] Despite the passages found regarding the conquests of Joshua and his mighty men killing everyone, "men and women, young and old, oxen, sheep, and donkeys, with the edge of the sword" the texts and the archaeological evidence suggests these were not attacks on civilian towns, (Joshua 6:21).[126] Copan sums it up well in saying:

> The biblical texts *lead us to expect* what archeology has confirmed—namely, that widespread destruction of

cities didn't take place and that gradual assimilation did. Only three cities (citadels or fortresses, as we've seen) were burned—Jericho, Ai, and Hazor... All tangible aspects of the Canaanites' culture—buildings and homes—would have remained very much intact.[127]

Again, the conquests by the Israelites have often been misinterpreted and misunderstood.

CONCLUSION

The overwhelming narrative of the Old Covenant God is one of love and grace. The Psalms declare that God is a "Father of the fatherless and protector of widows," (Psalm 68:5).[128]

Ultimately, you will run across verses that may seem contrary to a "loving" God. Before you immediately decide that the God of the Bible is inhumane and push aside any potential to gain a personal relationship with the Creator of the universe, I invite you to read them in context and to research these passages. Avoid bloggers, and learn what the scholars have to say. Discover the historical context of these texts.[129] Reading these potentially troubling texts can simply reinforce preconceived notions you may already have. But if you read the Bible as a comprehensive narrative and not just a few sound bites, I believe you will find freedom in each page and better understand the heart of God. Perhaps you will even be able to echo the sentiments of King David and continually praise God by saying:

Your steadfast love, O LORD, extends to the heavens, your faithfulness to the clouds, (Psalm 36:5).[130]

But you, O Lord, are a God merciful and gracious, slow to anger and abounding in steadfast love and faithfulness, (Psalm 86:15).[131]

The Old Covenant is a magnificent work of unified literature. The words written within these 39 books have been read and heard by hundreds of millions of people, some of who lived thousands of years ago. Think about it, your great-great-great-great-great (you get the point) grandparents could have been reading the same book you are reading. The sheer magnitude of its cultural longevity and impact alone does not prove that the Old Covenant is historically accurate. But when we examine the overwhelming historical evidence documented through archeological discoveries, we inevitably come to the same conclusion as scholars and recognize that the Old Covenant is a reliable and accurate book of history. After discovering hundreds of accurately fulfilled prophecies—with none missing the mark, it becomes apparent that the Old Covenant is not simply a book of history, but a book that has been inspired by God. As we will discover in the next chapter, it is clear that the New Covenant writings can also be looked to for history, spiritual truth, and inner-peace.

CHAPTER 4

CAN THE NEW COVENANT BE USED AS HISTORICAL EVIDENCE?

Even if the books of the Old Covenant[132] can be validated, can we accept the New Covenant[133] as historical evidence as well? Some claim there are simply too many conspiracies and too many early church power struggles to validate the books of the New Covenant. Some may read books like *The Da Vinci Code* as alternative history rather than fiction. We may hear of newly uncovered gospels hidden by power-hungry early church fathers and feel disdain towards the traditional texts of the New Covenant. (Everyone likes an underdog, right?) Despite what some skeptics may propose, the New Covenant texts *can* be used as historical evidence.[134]

The first four books of the New Covenant are the historical accounts regarding the life of Yeshua. Clearly, the accuracy of these narratives is imperative for those who believe He is the Messiah and the Son of God. These four accounts—Matthew, Mark, Luke, and John—known as the gospels, are often heavily scrutinized, and justifiably so. If the gospels and the other books of the New Covenant are historically validated, then the spiritual claims of the followers of Yeshua warrant greater attention. If they are overwhelmingly historically disproved, they can be ignored. In other words, if the claims of the followers of Yeshua are true spiritually, they should also prove to be true historically.[135]

Seeing the historical value of the New Covenant texts is paramount to understanding the next few chapters. Although there is ample extra-biblical evidence supporting the life, crucifixion, and resurrection of Yeshua, arguably some of the best evidence of these events is found in the New Covenant. Imagine if four biographies were written about the life of an individual in ancient history all within 70 years of his or her death. These works would be held in high regard for their historical value. The texts would be heavily scrutinized and their biases would be taken into account, but they would not be automatically disregarded as containing only falsities.

The focus of the remainder of this chapter will be centered on the four gospels because they contain the most *historical* information regarding the life, death, and resurrection of Yeshua. Although the other 23 books and letters of the New Covenant lend immense support and help "piece together" the life of Yeshua, it is undeniable that the gospels hold the most comprehensive, detailed information regarding His historical life. In saying this, however, it must be noted that other passages from the New Covenant can and should be used as historical evidence as well.[136]

The bias against using New Covenant texts as historical evidence runs deep, even among some followers of Yeshua. While receiving advice in the writing of this book, it was suggested that I not use any part of the Bible as evidence. Some suggested that unless an individual believed in the spiritual claims of the Bible, they would be unable to see any historical value in the texts. I am optimistic that after analyzing the obstacles individuals often have in accepting the gospels as historical evidence, you will indeed be able to see the New Covenant texts for their historical value.

This is not a plea to become a follower of Yeshua simply because some of the speculations individuals have against the Bible are sometimes misguided. I am merely appealing to your ability to think rationally and to see past some of your (potentially negative) preconceived biases in order to explore the historical validity for the life and resurrection of Yeshua.

I invite you to take a moment and think about why you may believe the Bible cannot be used as historical evidence. Is it because you have found any evidence to the contrary? Or is it because the Bible is usually associated with religious groups? As will be shown, to demand that only extra-biblical evidence be used to prove the validity of the life, death, and resurrection of Yeshua is to demand that historians ignore some of the best evidence available.

THE PROBLEM WITH HISTORY

For some, there can be a serious problem with their expectation of history. This has already been discussed in the previous chapter, but bears repeating because of how often it is overlooked. History is a puzzle which is missing many pieces. Scholars work tirelessly in an attempt to create a complete narrative of past events; however, we will *never* have all of the answers. We cannot recreate history in a laboratory; there will always be details for which we will be unable to account. As such, no event that has already happened can be re-created perfectly. This does not invalidate the process of studying history; rather, it simply means that historians have to use the best available evidence to determine what *most likely* occurred.

When individuals claim that there is no factual basis for the historical validity for the life of Yeshua or the texts of the Bible, they are often doing so from a flawed perception of how history is discovered. Although historians have yet to discover the video footage of Yeshua leaving the empty tomb, after examining historical evidence, most scholars conclude His tomb was almost certainly empty.[137] (In case you missed it, I do not actually believe we will find such video footage, and this was my attempt to illustrate some of the unrealistic expectations some may have in proving the resurrection of Yeshua.) Although we will not have such conclusive evidence, the gospels and the other books of the New Covenant provide helpful historical accounts of the resurrection.

To some, the question remains as to whether these texts can be relied upon as historical evidence. In the following section, we will review some of the more common objections against the historical validity of the New Covenant.

Claim 1: We Do Not Know What Was Originally Written
Claim 2: They Were Not Written Close Enough to the Event
Claim 3: There are too Many Contradictions
Claim 4: The Writers Were Biased
Claim 5: There is No Non-Biblical Historical Evidence

Then, in the next two chapters, we will examine the evidence for the historical validity of the life, death, and resurrection of Yeshua.

Claim 1: We Do Not Know What Was Originally Written

Individuals sometimes claim that the stories written in the New Covenant we read today are different from the narratives written in the original texts. As historians have yet to discover the original texts, this speculation is understandable. However, the sheer mass accumulation of available ancient texts should help to appease most textual uncertainty. Notably, this does nothing to validate the historical truthfulness of the texts per say (later analysis will focus on this aspect). In other words, if historians were to discover thousands of nearly identical copies of the ancient Greek drama *Oedipus the King,* it does not mean that the events in this play are historically accurate.[138] Addressing the concern of the original wording and narratives written within the texts merely validates the accuracy of the *versions* of the New Covenant we read today.

The early followers of Yeshua desired that their message be spread quickly, which means we have an incredible number of ancient copies of the New Covenant texts. Historians have discovered 5,838 fragments written in Greek (the original language of the New Covenant).[139] This is truly remarkable for ancient historical documents. By comparison, there remain only 210 copies of Plato's famous writings about the teachings of Socrates written in their original language, and no credible source doubts their accuracy.[140] The fact that there are remarkably fewer copies of Socrates teachings does not deem them to be historically inaccurate, but it does lead us to conclude that we can view the texts of the New Covenant as having a higher degree of textual certainty. Along with the Greek fragments discovered, historians have found over 25,000 New Covenant fragments in other languages, as well as 1,000,000 quotations from the New Covenant in writings of the early followers of Yeshua (i.e., letters that quote from the writings of the New Covenant).[141]

The sheer number of virtually identical "pieces" to this puzzle that have been discovered has essentially nullified any variances found within the ancient documents. In fact, although no original texts of the writings of the New Covenant have been unearthed, historians estimate we can know with 99.5% certainty what was written in the original documents by comparing these numerous manuscripts.[142]

To help illuminate this process, imagine that historians were to compare one verse in the Gospel of Matthew. They may be comparing versions of this verse written over a 1,000-year span. These versions will undoubtedly have alternative wording that may have come from a number of copying errors (i.e., misspelled and forgotten words, skipped lines). Through the mass comparison of this verse, historians would be able to see the common threads among these writings, and be able to determine what was originally written.

Notably, disregarding any of the copies of the New Covenant writings themselves, historians can nearly completely validate the accuracy of the New Covenant from the over 1,000,000 quotations from writings of the early following of Yeshua.[143] For an example of this process, think about the Gettysburg Address. If historians were to ignore any original transcripts or any writings about this speech until 100 years after it was given, they would still be able to compile the speech in its entirety by gathering quotes of it from various books, letters, and so on. A similar process can be utilized for the New Covenant. Writings of the early followers of Yeshua often contained quotations from the texts of the New Covenant, providing yet another source to further validate its historical authenticity.

Often individuals who believe we cannot gain an accurate version of what was written within the original texts of the New Covenant use the analogy of a game of telephone. In this game, an individual begins a message, whispers it to the next person in line who relays this message to the next person in line, and so on until the end. Generally, when the person at the end of the line repeats the message, it is different from the original message. Those who believe this is an accurate comparison of the writings of the New Covenant are mistaken. The copying of the New Covenant was not linear, as is the case with the game of telephone; it was geometric (one copy led to five which led to 25, and so on). This process allows historians to be able to compare a more diverse collection of copies, ultimately helping them to discern the original message with greater clarity.

As I have noted, scholars can determine the original text with 99.5% certainty. Those are great odds, but not perfect. However, these discrepancies do not have any theological or doctrinal implications. Dr. Licona reiterates this point in his lecture *The Basis of our Biblical Text Manuscripts*. He describes how one discrepancy comes from the first letter of John. The two versions of the verse are as follows:

> We are writing these things in order that *our* joy may be full, (emphasis added), (1 John 1:4), (CJB).[144]

> We are writing these things in order that *your* joy may be full, (emphasis added), (1 John 1:4), (NKJV).[145]

He explains that there is manuscript evidence for both options, so scholars are ultimately unable to determine without a doubt whether the original text said "our" or "your." However, this textual inconsistency clearly does not undermine any foundational beliefs of the followers of Yeshua.

If any non-biblical text was written over 2,000 years ago and held 99.5% textual certainty, it would be truly amazing. Dr. John Warwick Montgomery explains:

> To be skeptical of the resultant text of the New Testament books is to allow all of classical antiquity to slip into obscurity, for no documents of the ancient period are as well attested bibliographically as the New Testament.[146]

As previously acknowledged, the New Covenant texts can lead to spiritual, theological, and life changing implications. As such, its accuracy *should* be more heavily scrutinized than other works of antiquity. However, even after holding the New Covenant texts to a much higher standard, scholars are still able to verify its historical reliability as being astounding.

Claim 2: They Were Not Written Close Enough to the Event

Some presume the gospels cannot be historical because they were not written during the life of Yeshua. The majority of historians agree that the gospels were written within 35-70 years following the death of Yeshua (which occurred in approximately 32 CE).[147] New Covenant scholar F.F. Bruce dates the writing of Mark to be shortly after 60 CE (approximately 28 years after the death of Yeshua); Luke between 60-70 CE; Matthew near 70 CE; and John between 90-100 CE.[148] The gospels were completed at a time when hundreds of witnesses to the ministry, life, death, and resurrection of Yeshua were still alive to refute or attest to the accuracy of the narratives.[149]

Turning this into a more "real life" example, let's compare the dating of the gospels to present day. Starting from the year 2015, if we were to go back 28 years (the Gospel of Mark), we find ourselves in 1987. Now, I do not remember every single event that occurred in 1987, but I do remember remarkable details of an event from two years prior, the birth of my second son in 1985. I remember which hospital he was born in, details of my wife's labor, conversations I had with the doctor as the delivery approached, who was in the delivery room, and the fact that he was born on the day of the 6th game of the World Series. I even remember that the Kansas City Royals won the series 2-1 due to a blown call by first base umpire Don Denkinger. The Royals wound up winning game 7 of the World Series 11-0 the following evening.[150] Significant and out of the ordinary events in our lives (like the birth of a child) have a knack for becoming firmly etched in our memories. Undoubtedly, witnessing the miraculous ministry of Yeshua would have been extraordinary and memorable.

If we consider the latest dated gospel (the Gospel of John written approximately 70 years after Yeshua's death), and start in 2015, we find ourselves back in 1945. Any veterans of WWII can probably attest to being able to remember many, many events from that year (including the suicide of Hitler, dropping the atomic bombs on Hiroshima and Nagasaki, and the surrender of Japan). Even if those veterans have since passed away, many of their family members can still recount details of their personal experiences (as is noted from popular books/movies like *Unbroken* which is the story of a man who was held in a Japanese prison camp during WWII).[151] Human beings are able to remember the details of events that we find particularly out of the ordinary. If the claims of the followers of Yeshua are accurate, then He did live a very unusual life—one full of miraculous healings, including His eventual resurrection from the dead. If Yeshua truly did perform miraculous acts like walking on water[152] and feeding thousands with just a few fish and loaves of bread,[153] then people would have remembered these events.

Scholars believe the first letter to the Church of Corinth (1st Corinthians) was written sometime between 54 or 55 CE, a mere 23 years after the crucifixion of Yeshua.[154] In this letter, Paul discusses Yeshua's post-resurrection appearances to hundreds of people, some of whom he mentions by name.[155] Although this letter was written to a church in Greece, the resurrection occurred in Jerusalem, and the story was being told in Jerusalem. We know this because Yeshua's following was growing in Jerusalem.[156] Additionally, letters were read aloud within the communities of the followers of Yeshua, copied, and given to other communities to be read aloud.[157] Paul was making these startling claims shortly after their actual occurrence. Even without social media, if these claims had been falsified, they could have been easily disproved and any following would have dissipated.[158]

Clearly, it is not presumptuous to assume individuals would have been able to recall or refute these significant events in history. This is especially true because information at that time was primarily orally communicated. Most of the population was illiterate, so information was transmitted verbally. This leads to the question of how we are able to verify that the stories were correctly re-told. We must keep in mind that 10 of the original 12 disciples were willing to be tortured and brutally murdered for holding to their beliefs. Hundreds of eventual believers in Yeshua likewise suffered similar tragic ends.[159] If the stakes were that high—would you make up or embellish a story that would subject you to torture and death? Similarly, if you truly believed someone was the Son of God, would you ensure that His history was correctly recorded?[160]

Most importantly, if all ancient historical events required contemporaneous recordings (the recording of an event near to the time when it occurred), we would not be able to prove much of *anything* about ancient history. For instance, if we held Alexander the Great to this contemporaneous standard, we would not be able to prove his existence. The life of Alexander the Great is primarily proved using five sources. The *earliest* written evidence about his life is a work that was written around 40 CE, which is 363 *years* following Alexander the Great's death.[161] It is found in a work by Quintus Curtius Rufus entitled *The History of Alexander.* That gap from the event to the recording of the event is over 300 years longer than the gospel writings recordings about the life of Yeshua! Yet few doubt that Alexander the Great lived and was one of the most brilliant military conquerors the world has ever seen.

The expansive time span of the documentation of Alexander the Great's life does not invalidate the historical certainty that Alexander the Great truly lived. This is simply another example of how history is discovered. Despite one's theological beliefs, one must admit the life of Yeshua has far better *contemporaneous* historically documented written evidence than Alexander the Great. To deem the gospels as inaccurate on the basis that they were not recorded early enough would force us to conclude that very little can be determined about ancient history. Former director of the British Museum Sir Frederic Kenyon notes:

> In no other case is the interval between the composition of the book and the date of the earliest manuscripts so short as that in the New Testament.[162]

Claim 3: There are too Many Contradictions

Another common argument posed by individuals attempting to render the gospels as inaccurate historical documents is that they are perceived as containing contradictions. Admittedly, there *may* be some inconsistencies. In regards to the entire narrative, however, these perceived discrepancies are minor.

To begin to address this issue, we need to realize that the gospels were written as narratives from an individual perspective. Imagine that a group of college students visit the famous Louvre Art Museum in Paris, France. Each will have a slightly different perspective and story to tell of their visit. Some may describe how crowded all the rooms were. Others may say nothing about the crowds but will focus on the beauty of the artwork. Would these different accounts make every testimony inaccurate? Of course not! We would surmise the stories varied slightly because of the different perspective of the individuals sharing the narrative.

In a court of law, if testimony offered from two witnesses is the exact same, it is often argued that since different witnesses virtually never see matters exactly the same, the identical stories were rehearsed in an effort to deceive. Thus, the different perspectives of each gospel narrative actually increase their historicity because these differences indicate that there was no orchestrated effort to deceive.

An example of these seemingly contradictory accounts in the gospels is the difference in how many angels appeared to the women to proclaim the resurrection of Yeshua. The Gospel of Matthew discusses the *activity* of one angel,[163] but the Gospel of John mentions the *presence* of two angels.[164] Although they are different, these accounts are not contradictory. Matthew does not exclude the existence of another angel when he describes the activity of one angel. A radio announcer may describe the activities of a running back on the football field, but that does not exclude the other 21 players involved in the play on the field at that time. It merely means that the focus was on the running back during that particular play. Perceived discrepancies in the gospels, such as the number of angels mentioned who appeared to the women the morning of the resurrection, do not render the entire narrative inaccurate. Similarly, more often than not, these apparent contradictions are often minor details when considering the texts as a whole.

As this is one of the most often discussed reasons for not believing in the historical validity of the New Covenant, I want to highlight another example. The Gospels of Matthew,[165] Mark,[166] and Luke[167] describe a man named Simon of Cyrene who is forced to help Yeshua carry his cross when Yeshua could no longer do so Himself. The Gospel of John does not mention such an interaction.[168] Some may say this proves the accounts are falsified. Again, the omission of Simon of Cyrene in the Gospel of John is not proof that he did not help Yeshua carry His cross. John may have simply not felt it necessary to include anything about Simon of Cyrene, and instead wanted to focus on different aspects of the resurrection story.

It is also important to note that the Gospel of Mark describes Simon of Cyrene as "the father of Alexander and Rufus," (Mark 15:21).[169] Why would the writer include such an innocuous detail? Simon was already distinguished by his home of "Cyrene." There is no other mention of Alexander and Rufus in the New Covenant. It seems as if this were Mark's way of saying—don't believe me, go ask Simon's sons Alexander and Rufus for verification of what I am writing.

As with the group of college students visiting the Louvre, every gospel writer had different perspectives from which they based their narrative about Yeshua. To help illustrate this point further, I identify as a father, husband, son, brother, uncle, lawyer, and author. If someone says that I am an author, someone who only knows me as a lawyer may disagree. Although their description is an incomplete assessment, it is not inaccurate. We cannot expect every piece of historical evidence to encompass the entirety of a historical event. In the same way, we cannot expect each gospel to narrate identical details of Yeshua's life and resurrection. However, by looking at the gospels in their entirety, along with other sources, we are able to piece together a more complete description of the life, death, and resurrection of Yeshua.

Although some perceived inconsistencies within the New Covenant have yet to be reconciled by historical evidence and simply remain to be a mystery, they do not render the *entire* narrative inaccurate. Each gospel recounts miracles performed by Yeshua. They all describe how Yeshua was convicted by the Jewish Sanhedrin on charges of blasphemy, and was crucified by the Romans in Jerusalem during the Passover feast. They all record that He died within several hours of being crucified, and was buried in a sealed tomb belonging to Joseph of Arimathea. They then describe how followers of Yeshua (Mary Magdalene is mentioned in each) visited the tomb to find it empty. (The historical validity of these claims will be discussed in Chapters 5 and 6.)

To ignore the comprehensive narrative and to instead focus on apparent contradictory details as proof that Yeshua did not live is to rewrite the methods of determining history. To simply claim that we do not know exactly what happened in one small facet of the narrative does not mean we cannot utilize the writings as evidence.[170]

Claim 4: The Writers Were Biased

Some contend that since the gospels are "religious testimonies," they cannot be looked to for historical evidence. They may claim that the only evidence we can use to prove the life of Yeshua is from those who do not agree with the overall agenda of followers of Yeshua.[171] However, we all have biases. If we were to disregard every historical piece of evidence because of the bias of the original writer, we would not be able to determine *anything* about history. The bias of the original writer should be taken into account, but the historical evidence provided should not be automatically disregarded.

Similarly, every historian analyzing the evidence brings personal bias and a unique perspective. Dr. Michael Licona illustrates this point with an example in his book *The Resurrection of Jesus*. He writes how in analyzing the 9/11 attacks, American historians may presume the terrorist group al-Qaeda began as a direct response to the American invasion in the first Gulf War in 1990-91. An Israeli historian, however, may view the terrorist attacks as a response to America allying itself with Israel. Neither perspective may be necessarily wrong; each simply tells a slightly different version of the story.[172] To presume that we cannot look to the gospels and early writings of the followers of Yeshua because of their bias is to sorely underestimate the inevitability of bias in every facet of life.

Imagine if historians 2,000 years from now declared that nothing with a bias could be used to determine the accomplishments of public figures. These future historians would be unable to use Hillary Clinton's speeches, any documents she or her office drafted, and any supportive Democratic reporting to determine her accomplishments.

They would likewise be unable to look to her Republican opponents to determine what they say she accomplished. Each side would have a very specific agenda to promote. Hillary's materials would focus on how much she achieved. When specifically talking about Hillary, her Republican counterparts would assert she did not actually accomplish what she claimed, and explain why her positions/policies would be wrong for the nation (by extension, proving why theirs would be right).

In reality, the unavoidable biases within each political party would actually help future historians build a stronger understanding of Hillary's achievements. To ignore one side because they will be more positively biased is completely illogical; both sides hold biases. In the same way, the biases of the gospels and other material written regarding the life of Yeshua can actually help historians piece together a more *accurate* picture of the beliefs, movements, and ideas of the day.

It also should be noted that it appears the disciples were not in the business of putting words in the mouth of Yeshua. As is clear in the texts of the New Covenant, the early followers of Yeshua had many questions. A debate that stumped many of the early followers was whether a new believer had to adopt traditionally Jewish practices to become a true follower of Yeshua.[173] Specifically, there was a prevalent debate about whether new (gentile) followers needed to adopt the Jewish tradition of circumcision.[174]

If the disciples and writers of the New Covenant were making up stories to perpetuate their own personal agenda, why would they not simply write in a false debate in which Yeshua decided to either require or reject gentile circumcision? That would have put the matter to rest. The omission of such a debate by Yeshua is not proof, in and of itself, that the words of the New Covenant are genuine. However, it lends credibility to the idea that the writers were not deceitful, as some may have previously proposed.

The disciples seemed to believe the message they were promoting. Ten of the original 12 disciples were grotesquely tortured and murdered for their beliefs—beliefs they would have known to be either true or falsified. The disciples would have known whether the claims were true or false because many of them would have *witnessed the events recorded in the New Covenant,* including the resurrected Yeshua.[175]

The New Covenant also records the numerous shortcomings of the disciples. They did not trust Yeshua during a storm on the Sea of Galilee;[176] they bickered over who was the greatest disciple;[177] and Peter (one of the core disciples) denied that he knew Yeshua three times.[178] If you were making up a story, would you make yourself look so foolish?

Claim 5: There is No Non-Biblical Historical Evidence

Some have claimed that every story in the gospels is folklore. Although (as with the Old Covenant) every narrative, every fact, and every detail of the gospels has yet to be historically validated, claiming it is a book of folklore is inaccurate as scholars have been able to validate many details that further attest to its accuracy. (Notably, this is where the source of distinction arises as to whether it is merely a document with high *textual accuracy,* or whether it can be looked to as a document with *historical evidence.*) Some have presumed that the gospels were never meant to be recorded as facts of history. This belief is undeniably and immediately uprooted in the Gospel of Luke. The first four verses in the Gospel of Luke speak of his intention to write "an orderly account." Luke writes:

> Inasmuch as many have undertaken to compile a narrative of the things that have been accomplished among us, just as those who from the beginning were eyewitnesses and ministers of the word have delivered them to us, it seemed good to me also, having followed all things closely for some time past, to write an orderly account for you, most excellent Theophilus, that you may have certainty concerning the things you have been taught, (Luke 1:1-4).[179]

In other words, Luke is saying—what I am about to report is a carefully crafted *history from eyewitnesses* regarding the life, death, and resurrection of Yeshua. The Gospel of Luke has been heralded as a great compilation of history.[180] Luke (along with the other gospel writers) uses real people, places, and events that have been since historically validated.[181] To presume the gospels are fictional or even primarily filled with legends is to ignore what is written in the texts themselves.

Roman Official: Pontius Pilate

The writings of the New Covenant have also been validated by archeological discoveries. One historically validated character within the gospels is Pontius Pilate. The gospels record that he was the Roman Official of Judea during the life of Yeshua.[182] Along with references to Pilate in the ancient writings of historians Tacitus[183] and Josephus,[184] archeologists have discovered a stone near Jerusalem inscribed with the name of Pilate during that period.[185] This indicates that there was a Roman official with the name of Pilate during the life of Yeshua, just as the gospels record.[186]

Jewish High Priest: Caiaphas

Similarly, Caiaphas is recorded in the gospels as being the Jewish high priest during the life of Yeshua. Caiaphas' recently discovered tomb verifies that he truly lived and reigned during the crucifixion of Yeshua.[187] Although the stone of Pilate and the tomb of Caiaphas do not prove Yeshua lived a miraculous life or was resurrected from the dead, they do prove that two of the key characters in the gospel narrative truly lived during the time of His crucifixion.

Josephus: Affirms Execution of John the Baptist

Similarly, seemingly insignificant details within the Bible have been verified through other ancient writers. Flavius Josephus is one of the most well-known ancient Roman historians. He was born to a highly respected Jewish priest in Jerusalem in 37 CE, only a few years after the crucifixion of Yeshua. Jewish customs, practices, and beliefs were ingrained in Josephus throughout much of his life. He eventually joined the Romans as a historian for the Emperor Vespasian.[188] It was at the urging of the Jewish leadership that the Romans crucified Yeshua, so they clearly had no motive to perpetuate the gospel narratives if they were not true. Josephus records that John the Baptist, a first century Jewish prophet, was killed at the direction of Herod. This aligns with the gospel accounts of the death of John the Baptist. Josephus wrote in approximately 90 CE, "And so John, out of Herod's suspiciousness, was sent in chains to Machaerus, the fort previously mentioned, and there put to death."[189]

The Gospel of Mark records the same event: "Immediately the king (Herod) sent an executioner and commanded his (John the Baptist's) head to be brought. And he went and beheaded him in prison," (parentheticals added), (Mark 6:27).[190]

Josephus: Identifies James as Yeshua's Brother

Josephus also identified James as the brother of Yeshua, which the gospels described. Josephus writes, "He brought before them the brother of Jesus who was called Christ, whose name was James."[191] This is confirmed in the Gospel of Mark which also notes how those who had watched Yeshua grow up were amazed at his "wisdom" and "mighty works."

And many hearing Him were astonished, saying, "Where did this man get these things? And what

90

wisdom is that which is given to Him, that such mighty works are performed by his hands! Is this not the carpenter, the Son of Mary, and *brother of James?*" (emphasis added), (Mark 6:2-3).[192]

Remains of Crucified Body Discovered

Another significant archaeological discovery verifies the details of the crucifixion of Yeshua. Some had claimed that the gospel narrative of the crucifixion could not have been true because it was not common practice in the Roman Empire to bury their crucified victims. (The gospels record that Yeshua was buried in a tomb after His crucifixion.) However, archeologists have discovered the buried remains of a man crucified at the hands of the Romans, confirming that Yeshua could have been placed in a tomb after His crucifixion, just as the gospels record.[193]

Legacy of Yeshua

Again, comparing the historical evidence for Yeshua to the historical evidence for Alexander the Great demonstrates the unwarranted bias against historical evidence when dealing with biblical figures, especially Yeshua. Apart from the five sources of written evidence often used to prove the life of Alexander the Great (discussed previously), individuals also use the cities and legacy he left as proof of his existence. This same logic could be used for Yeshua (albeit, it is not conclusive historical logic, but helps demonstrate the reality of the prejudice nonetheless). Yeshua has a following that has been in existence for 2,000 years. The legacy of Yeshua has been in effect longer than that of Alexander the Great. So it is extremely biased to use "city" legacy of Alexander the Great as proof of his existence, and not use the lasting legacy of Yeshua.

The previously described examples are some of the *many* historically validated details of the New Covenant. The fact of the matter is that the New Covenant has an excellent track record of historical reliability. As such, it is likely that scholars will continue to discover additional evidence to further validate its historical authenticity.

CONCLUSION

Because of its theological significance and life-changing ramifications, the Bible, probably more than any other ancient historical document, has been extensively scrutinized for any statements that may be found to be historically inaccurate. History takes time to uncover, but as more discoveries are being made, the validity of the Bible is continually confirmed. As previously noted, numerous non-biblical writings and archeological discoveries confirm central points of the biblical narratives.

Prolific New Covenant scholar F.F. Bruce felt the major stumbling block for biblical skeptics came from their personal beliefs, not the historicity of the Bible. He concludes, "If the New Testament were a collection of secular writings, their authenticity would generally be regarded as beyond all doubt."[194] If historians often use ancient documents written by first and second-hand witnesses as evidence to prove a historical event, why would we ignore New Covenant texts that fulfill these credentials? Is it because of the lack of historical evidence to support the gospels, or because of one's underlying biases?

During the next two chapters, we will discover whether there is historical evidence for the life, death, and resurrection of Yeshua. Emphasis will be placed on non-biblical evidence when available; however, the texts of the New Covenant will be utilized as they too offer historical evidence. It is illogical to assume the New Covenant texts cannot be used as historical evidence simply because they are part of what some regard to be sacred writings. Although many scholars do not believe in the divine inspiration of the text, they accept the texts of the New Covenant for their historical value (having been written within 70 years following the death of Yeshua).

Perhaps you remain somewhat unconvinced. Maybe you see the New Covenant as being historically valid in some places, but unhistorical when delving into the specifics of the life of Yeshua. Some of you may think that Yeshua never lived. Others may claim that He was a great man who lived, but was never resurrected from the dead. Others may believe Yeshua lived, died, and was resurrected from the dead. As you will see in the following chapters, there is outstanding evidence validating the claims of the New Covenant: that Yeshua was a man of history who lived, died by crucifixion, and was resurrected from the dead.

CHAPTER 5

DID YESHUA TRULY LIVE AND DIE IN ISRAEL 2,000 YEARS AGO?

Can you think of a historical figure that has been the cause of more debate, more controversy, and, at times, more division in the last 2,000 years than Jesus? *Time Magazine* recently published an article listing the 100 most influential figures in history; Jesus was ranked #1.[195] Sure, the legacy Yeshua (Jesus) inspired has arguably been one of the most influential movements over the last two millennia, but this legacy alone does not prove that He is a man of history.

I am likely getting a bit ahead of myself with some readers. Some may believe, as I did for many years, that Yeshua is merely a fictional character. This belief was not based on any historical evidence, but rather on my own unwarranted biases. Still others may believe that if Yeshua lived 2,000 years ago, He was nothing like the man portrayed in the texts of the New Covenant.

Some may take a different position. They may say that Yeshua could have been a historical figure, but they have no desire to learn anything about Him. They may claim that there have been too many heinous acts done in His name to warrant any attention. However, if He is truly the most influential man of history in the last 2,000 years, it stands to reason that we should carefully analyze and explore the evidence supporting His existence. It also should be noted that our focus should be on Yeshua, and not on those who are poor representatives of Him.

As will be demonstrated in the next several pages, Yeshua was not merely a fictional character, but was an extraordinary man of history. Though He had no wealth or political power and lived only for a short period of time, He has clearly significantly influenced and impacted the course of history.

THE BEST WITNESS IS AN ADVERSE WITNESS

In the previous chapter, we discovered that the books of the New Covenant are credible documents outlining the historical life of Yeshua and the beginning of His following. The four gospels—Matthew, Mark, Luke, and John—detail the historical ministry of Yeshua. Clearly, some insight can be gained into the life of Yeshua by using these documents. As was already discussed, people often have biases against the New Covenant writings because they are used in religious settings. To appease the skeptical and demonstrate the accumulation of evidence that can be utilized to prove the historical life of Yeshua, non-biblical sources will be used when available. However, because of their historical value, passages from the New Covenant will also be utilized in support of non-biblical evidence.

The primary evidence that will be used in this chapter is referred to in a court of law as testimony from a hostile or "adverse witness." An adverse witness is someone who disagrees with your overall position. In a courtroom, favorable testimony from an adverse witness is considered persuasive, as such a witness is certainly not going to lie or exaggerate to help your case.

For example, if the mother of a man charged with murder testifies that her son left home angry on the day of the murder and almost always carried a handgun, her testimony is extremely beneficial to the prosecution's case. Her testimony is helpful even if she also testifies that her son was headed to his friend's house, which is in the opposite direction of the crime scene (so he could not be responsible). The prosecutor would point out the reliability of the portion of the mother's testimony in which she acknowledges that her son left home angry, and probably had a handgun the night of the murder. As an adverse witness to the prosecution, she would certainly not lie about those facts to help the prosecution.

When I was a young attorney and preparing for one of my first trials, I called my older brother for advice. He is a more experienced attorney, and is now a judge. He shared how he often likes to call an adverse witness as his first witness. This demonstrates how even the opposition agrees with certain key points of his case. I am going to follow my brother's suggestion. Compiled in the following section are three of the many testimonies from individuals who lived around the time of Yeshua, but did not believe Yeshua is the Messiah, thereby making them adverse witnesses to the followers of Yeshua. Nonetheless, they provide statements that Yeshua lived and died at the hands of the Romans, just as the gospels record. We will explore three of the adverse witnesses, although there are others as well.[196]

Adverse Witness 1: Josephus
Adverse Witness 2: The Babylonian Talmud
Adverse Witness 3: Tacitus

Adverse Witness 1: Josephus

The ancient Roman historian Josephus is one of the most well-known and commonly referred to historians of this time in antiquity. As noted in the previous chapter, Josephus was born in Jerusalem in 37 CE and was the son of a highly respected Jewish priest. Josephus would have more than likely heard all about Yeshua while growing up.[197] When Josephus joined the Romans as a historian for the Emperor Vespasian, he recorded that Yeshua was a "doer of startling deeds" and was executed on a cross. Josephus records:

> At that time there appeared Jesus, a wise man. For he was a doer of startling deeds, a teacher of people who receives the truth with pleasure. And he gained a following both among many Jews and among many of Greek origin. And when Pilate [a Roman], because of an accusation made by leading men among us [the Jews], condemned him to the cross, those who had loved him previously did not cease to do so. And up until this very day the tribe of Christians [named after him] has not died out.[198]

As is written by Josephus, the Gospel of Matthew also records that Yeshua lived and was condemned to die at the insistence of the Jewish religious leaders. While on trial with the high priest, Yeshua is asked whether He is the Son of God.[199] Yeshua responds, "You have said so," (Matthew 26:64).[200] After His response:

> The high priest tore his robes and said, "He has uttered blasphemy. What further witnesses do we need? You have heard his blasphemy. What is your judgment?" They answered, "He deserves death," (Matthew 26:65-66).[201]

As this passage from the Gospel of Matthew demonstrates, the Pharisees despised the message that Yeshua preached. What motive does Josephus, a Jewish man writing for the Romans, have to fabricate the existence, "startling deeds," and execution of Yeshua? None!

Adverse Witness 2: The Babylonian Talmud

A second source affirming the life and death of Yeshua comes from the Jewish Babylonian Talmud, a foundational text in Judaism written by rabbinic leaders who did not follow Yeshua. In these writings, the rabbis also provide an account of the crucifixion of Yeshua (whom they call Yeshu, which is a derogatory term often used to describe Yeshua). Their account of the crucifixion of Yeshua is consistent with the narrative in the gospel writings that also place Yeshua's death on the eve of Passover. The Gospel of John records:

> Since it was the day of Preparation (for Passover), and so that the bodies would not remain on the cross on the Sabbath [for that Sabbath was a high day], the Jews asked Pilate that their legs might be broken and that they might be taken away, (parenthetical added), (John 19:31).[202]

The Babylonian Talmud also confirms that Yeshua was crucified on the eve of Passover, just at the gospels record.

> It has been taught: On the Eve of the Passover, they hanged Yeshu. And an announcer went out in front of him, for forty days saying: "He is going to be stoned because he practiced sorcery and enticed and led Israel astray. Anyone who knows anything in his favor, let him come and plead on his behalf." But, not having found anything in his favor, they hanged him on the Eve of Passover.[203]

During this time, "hanged" was synonymous with crucifixion, (when someone is hung on a cross). The same term is used in the New Covenant:

> The Messiah (Yeshua) redeemed us from the curse
> pronounced in the *Torah* by becoming cursed on our
> behalf; for the Tanakh (Old Covenant) says, "Everyone
> who *hangs* from a stake comes under a curse," (paren-
> theticals and emphasis added), (Galatians 3:13).[204]

These rabbis believed that Yeshua was blaspheming against God. As such, they would have desired this movement be dissolved and forgotten as quickly as possible. There is no motive for prominent rabbis to record in the Babylonian Talmud this depiction of the life and death of Yeshua on the eve of Passover, just as the New Covenant notes. Why would they record facts confirming the New Covenant account of the life and death of a man whom they despised, *unless* the facts they wrote were true? They wouldn't. Clearly, Yeshua lived and was crucified on the eve of Passover, as confirmed by the Babylonian Talmud.

Similarly, Maimonides (Rambam) is a very highly regarded 12th century rabbi and scholar. He wrote a 14-volume work called the Mishne Torah in which he made multiple references to Yeshua and his execution. He writes, "Jesus of Nazareth who aspired to be the Messiah and was executed by the court."[205] Maimonides, although not a follower of Yeshua, also acknowledged Yeshua truly lived and was executed.

Adverse Witness 3: Tacitus

The Annals, written by Roman Senator Tacitus in 115 CE, provides a third confirmation from an adverse witness to the life and crucifixion of Yeshua. Tacitus was a Roman senator during the time of active Roman persecution of Christians. *The Annals* reiterates the New Covenant account that Pontius Pilate executed a man named "Christ," and tortured His followers who were known as "Christians:"

Therefore, to squelch the rumor, Nero created scapegoats and subjected to the most refined tortures those
whom the common people called "Christians," [a group]
hated for their abominable crimes. Their name comes
from Christ, who, during the reign of Tiberius, *had been
executed* by the procurator Pontius Pilate. Suppressed for
the moment, the deadly superstition broke out again,
not only in Judea, the land which originated this evil,
but also in the city of Rome, (emphasis added).[206]

Some have argued that because crucifixion was a common practice throughout the Roman Empire, there may have been another
man executed by Pontius Pilate also called "Christ" (which means
Messiah), to whom this quote refers. This argument is without
merit because, as noted in the above excerpt, Tacitus' writings
also describe the "most refined tortures" and execution inflicted
on those who claimed Yeshua was the Messiah ("common people
called 'Christians.'") Thus, Tacitus clearly connects the above passages to Yeshua and His followers. If the existence and execution of
Yeshua were truly a hoax, why would Tacitus record a lie to support
the beliefs of a group of people he probably detested?

LIAR, LUNATIC, OR LORD?

Good documentation, especially from reliable witnesses, will
usually make or break a case. All of the ancient witnesses in this chapter
are extremely reliable because, despite being opposed to Yeshua and
His followers, they confirm the gospel accounts of His life and death.
Individuals who did not have an ulterior motive to perpetuate any
lies about the life of Yeshua penned these three historical documents
relatively close to the time of His life and death. These texts provide
compelling evidence that has led virtually all historians to conclude
Yeshua's life and eventual crucifixion by Pontius Pilate to be true

historical events. Rabbis such as Maimonides (Rabbi Rambam),[207] highly respected modern Jewish scholars such as Dr. Daniel Boyarin (one of the leading Talmudic scholars in the world),[208] and countless others, acknowledge that Yeshua lived and was executed.

However, most who have a problem with Yeshua are not concerned with whether He lived, or even whether He prompted an impressive and long-lasting following. Most who do not believe in the divinity of Yeshua may even claim that He was a wonderful teacher.[209] However, the declarations Yeshua made during His ministry do not allow for such a neutral perspective. Yeshua claimed that He was God in the flesh[210] and had the power to forgive sins.[211] These statements (along with others made by Yeshua) led the Jewish Sanhedrin (the highest council over the Jewish people in Israel at the time) to demand His execution. These statements also led C.S. Lewis to conclude in his highly acclaimed book *Mere Christianity*, that if Yeshua made such claims, He must have either been a liar, a lunatic, or who He said He was, LORD.[212] As we will see in the next chapter, the historical evidence is stacked against Yeshua being either a liar or lunatic. In fact, most rabbis and Jewish leaders today acknowledge that Yeshua was neither a liar nor a lunatic but rather is considered to have been a brilliant rabbi and righteous man.[213]

Can we truly conclude that He is LORD? With the billions of people who have lived over the course of human history, some (albeit, not many) have spurred new religious followings. Most are not bothered by the life of Yeshua, or even His polarizing claims. What truly bothers some is who people claim He is—God in the flesh. It is historically undeniable that Yeshua lived and was executed at the hands of the Romans. His followers believe that He died for the sins of the world, was resurrected from the dead, and is now seated in heaven at the right hand of the Father as the Son of God and prophesied Messiah of Israel. Despite how outlandish these claims may seem, as we will explore in the next chapter, the resurrection of Yeshua is also a remarkably well-documented historical event.

CHAPTER 6

WHAT DO HISTORIANS SAY ABOUT THE RESURRECTION OF YESHUA?

As it appears to be historically indisputable that Yeshua was a man who lived and was crucified, we will now delve into the central aspect of His life—His resurrection. This is an indispensable component of the faith of the followers of Yeshua.[214] If Yeshua did not rise from the dead, His claims and those of His followers are false, and He was simply a charismatic man and false prophet. If He did rise from the dead, then there was clearly a supernatural intervention in His life deserving further exploration.

Let's examine the historical evidence leading billions of people over the course of the last 2,000 years to conclude the seemingly improbable feat—that Yeshua was resurrected from the dead.

HOW CAN HISTORIANS VALIDATE
A MIRACULOUS EVENT?

Despite all of the evidence supporting the resurrection, one question remains: how did this seemingly impossible event occur? We struggle to wrap our minds around this, and justifiably so. We are faced with a daunting paradox: can a historic event be validated despite its miraculous nature?

Some may argue that although miracles were considered a possibility in ancient times, we now understand that they defy the laws of science. However, even in ancient times someone being raised from the dead was astonishing and unexpected. In fact, it is recorded in the Gospel of Matthew that when some of the disciples saw Yeshua resurrected, they doubted.[215] These were the men Yeshua had spent most of the previous three years with, and yet some did not believe He had truly been resurrected from the dead. If resurrections were extremely common and believable in ancient times, why would some of the disciples have initially doubted? It is significant that these same disciples were later willing to be tortured and brutally killed for their belief in the resurrected Yeshua, so obviously their doubts were eliminated.

One of the leading arguments against the historicity of the resurrection is the belief that all events that may seem supernatural actually have natural explanations. As Timothy Keller illuminates in his book *The Reason for God,* this non-acceptance of the supernatural is also rooted in faith. He writes:

It is one thing to say that science is only equipped to test for natural causes and cannot speak to any others. It is quite another to insist that science proves that no other causes could possibly exist.[216]

To *only* believe in science is itself an act of faith. To say that nothing in life can occur without a scientific explanation is no longer a statement of science, but is one with philosophical assumptions behind it.[217]

Similarly, the belief that there are no miracles and the supernatural realm cannot exist is completely extinguished if there is a creator of the universe. As was discovered in Chapter 2, the evidence points to the existence of a creator. It stands to reason that if there is a God, He could easily surpass the laws of nature and physics (that He ultimately created), making miracles a possibility. If you happened to skip over Chapter 2, or need a bit of a refresher on the arguments, I would recommend going back and solidifying whether you believe in God before you continue to read this chapter.[218]

Notably, we should not immediately conclude an event that seems miraculous is in fact a miracle. We should have a critical eye, as many "miraculous events" have been determined to be false. Dr. Francis Collins, one of the core leaders of the Human Genome Project, writes in his book *The Language of God* how important it is to have a "healthy skepticism" with regards to miraculous events. He writes:

> Whatever the personal view, it is crucial that a healthy skepticism be applied when interpreting potentially miraculous events, lest the integrity and rationality of the religious perspective be brought into question.[219]

In other words, claims of a miraculous event should not be taken lightly. However, to completely write off the possibility of a miraculous explanation is to sorely limit our ability to understand what has truly occurred.

Perhaps you do not currently believe in miracles. I would challenge you to continue to read on as we examine the historical evidence for the resurrection of Yeshua. If the evidence is convincing, should we ignore the possibility of a miraculous event?

I believe it will become clear that Yeshua not only lived and was crucified, but also was miraculously resurrected from the dead.

Ancient References to Yeshua's Miracles

Yeshua was not a normal man. As the renowned and highly esteemed Rabbi Maimonides, the respected Roman historian Josephus, the gospel writers, and others describe, Yeshua performed miracles in the presence of many, seemingly everywhere He went. As noted in the previous chapter, Josephus referred to Yeshua as "a doer of startling deeds," which is a similar description he used in referencing the miracles of the Jewish prophet Elisha.[220] [221]

Similarly, the second century Roman author and philosopher Celsus wrote *The True Word,* which was a critique of those following Yeshua.[222] He believed faith in Yeshua was interfering with individuals' allegiance to Rome. Celsus writes this concerning the miracles and life of Yeshua:

> That he (Jesus)… coming to the knowledge of certain *miraculous powers,* returned from thence to his own country, and by means of those powers proclaimed himself a god, (parenthetical and emphasis added).[223]

Celsus was also an adverse witness.[224] He *despised* the followers of Yeshua—he wrote an entire book about why he felt they were crazy! So Celsus clearly had no reason to lie and concede that Yeshua was a miraculous man who had supernatural powers.

The Babylonian Talmud also refers to the supernatural and miraculous nature of the life of Yeshua. It says in *Sanhedrin 43a:*

> On the Eve of the Passover, they hanged Yeshu. And an announcer went out in front of him, for forty days saying: "He is going to be stoned because he *practiced sorcery* and enticed and led Israel astray," (emphasis added).[225]

The writers of these rabbinic commentaries clearly refer to Yeshua practicing "sorcery," which means that He was performing acts that were perceived as being miraculous. Although these writers probably did not regard Yeshua as LORD, they clearly refer to His life as miraculous.

Respected and credentialed biblical theologian Dr. John Meier surmises that in light of the vast amount of documentation of Yeshua's miracles, it would be virtually impossible for them to have been fabricated:

> The miracle traditions about Jesus' public ministry are already so widely attested in various sources and literary forms by the end of the first Christian generation that total fabrication by the early church is, practically speaking, impossible.[226]

The life of Yeshua was clearly perceived as being miraculous. As Yeshua lived a life filled with seemingly supernatural events, it does not seem preposterous to presume another major miraculous event (His resurrection) could have occurred.

THE EVIDENCE FOR THE RESURRECTION

Miracles performed by Yeshua establish a foundation upon which the resurrection can be built; but the ultimate issue is the resurrection itself. As we have seen, historians often draw their conclusions based upon facts that are virtually uncontroverted. In other words, historians determine the explanations for *why* events occurred from the available evidence. Utilizing this method, historians have determined that four compelling facts exist which strongly supports the resurrection. These facts will be referred to as "Exhibits." Each exhibit alone may not convince you of the resurrection of Yeshua. However, any hypothesis denying the resurrection must offer a compelling explanation that addresses *all* four exhibits.

After examining the historical facts for the resurrection of Yeshua, we will then analyze the common alternative theories and explanations offered for the evidence presented—other than the resurrection. For instance, our first "Exhibit" (the empty tomb) is an essentially uncontroverted historical fact. The sealed and guarded tomb in which Yeshua was laid was later found to be empty. However, some have different theories as to *why* His tomb was empty (other than the resurrection of Yeshua). After this examination of the rebuttal theories, I believe you will then be in a position to render a verdict either for, or against, the resurrection of Yeshua. We will start by exploring the evidence of:

> Exhibit A: The Empty Tomb
> Exhibit B: Witnesses to the Resurrected Yeshua
> Exhibit C: The Commitment of the Disciples
>   of Yeshua Amidst Adverse Circumstances
> Exhibit D: Silence from the Opposition

Exhibit A: The Empty Tomb

After Yeshua was crucified, His followers dispersed. They returned to their old jobs and denied their association with Him.[227] That is, until they discovered His empty tomb three days later. As Josephus noted, the following of Yeshua "did not die out" after His death.[228] In fact, it grew rapidly. The momentum of His following would have been abruptly halted if the corpse of Yeshua were discovered, or if there were evidence of foul play. Paul Althaus, a professor of practical and systematic theology at the University of Göttingen, reasons:

> (The resurrection) could have not been maintained in Jerusalem for a single day, for a single hour, if the emptiness of the tomb had not been established as

an undeniable fact for all concerned, (parenthetical added).[229]

Yet, there is no evidence that the corpse of Yeshua has ever been discovered. It seems clear that the tomb in which the body of Yeshua was laid after the crucifixion was empty, which corroborated the testimonies of eyewitnesses claiming that they had seen the resurrected Yeshua.

N.T. Wright, an eminent British New Covenant scholar, concludes, "That is why, as an historian, I cannot explain the rise of early Christianity unless Jesus rose again, leaving an empty tomb behind him."[230]

The Romans despised anything other than allegiance to Rome. The Jewish religious leaders believed Yeshua was blaspheming by claiming that He was the Son of God.[231] They brought Him to Pontius Pilate who ordered the crucifixion of Yeshua.[232] He was a high profile political prisoner who was causing quite a disturbance. The Roman and Jewish leaders would have jumped on any opportunity to demonstrate the illegitimacy of the resurrection of Yeshua, and one foolproof way to accomplish this would have been to simply produce His corpse once word of the resurrection began to spread. Any uprising would have been immediately squelched if the corpse of Yeshua were displayed in a public area. After reviewing the barbaric nature of a Roman Crucifixion, displaying Yeshua's body for all to see seems like a quick and easy solution to the problem presented.[233]

As there is no evidence that either the Jewish or Roman leaders revealed the corpse of Yeshua, it seems plausible that the tomb was, in fact, empty. The Book of Acts, which is a historical documentation of the beginning of the following of Yeshua, mentions the empty tomb. Amazingly, the main debate in Acts is *why* the tomb was empty, not *if* it was empty.[234] No need existed for the disciples to make a major issue of the emptiness of the tomb.

Anyone who was skeptical of the empty tomb could have simply gone to look. If they would have found the body of Yeshua still in the tomb, they could have displayed His corpse for everyone to see. If His tomb were not empty, it would have been an easily verifiable fact that surely would have been documented by either the Jewish or Roman leadership in order to extinguish the uprising.

Some may speculate that the verification could not have been so simple because travel in ancient times was much more difficult. They may presume, perhaps, that people were more akin to believing in things that did not happen because they could not actually go and see it for themselves. Although travel was obviously more difficult in ancient times than it is now, the following of Yeshua began in the *Pax Romana*, a time when the Roman civilization was relatively at peace and there were many accomplishments and advances throughout the empire. Most notably to our discussion, the Romans built an extensive roadway system that would have made travel much easier.[235] Also, Yeshua's tomb was within walking distance in Jerusalem, making it easily accessible for any skeptics who did not believe it was empty.

The story of the resurrected Yeshua would never have circulated so widely without the validation of an empty tomb by eyewitnesses. As the empty tomb seems to be an undisputed fact, this has led to three major theories offered by skeptics to explain why the tomb of Yeshua was empty aside from His resurrection:

Theory 1: The Body of Yeshua Was Stolen
Theory 2: Everyone Looked for Yeshua in the Wrong Tomb
Theory 3: Yeshua Was Never Killed During His Crucifixion

Theory 1: The Body of Yeshua Was Stolen

Response: Yeshua's followers had no access to the tomb, and His enemies had no motive to remove His body.

The most circulated explanation as to why the tomb was empty is that the disciples stole the body of Yeshua. Even the Gospel of Matthew relays that this is a speculation as old as the resurrection.

> While they were going, behold, some of the guard went into the city and told the chief priests that all had taken place. And when they had assembled with the elders and taken counsel, they gave a sufficient sum of money to the soldiers and said, "Tell people, 'His disciples came by night and stole him away while we were asleep.' And if this comes to the governor's ears, we will satisfy him and keep you out of trouble." So they took the money and did as they were directed. And this story has been spread among the Jews to this day, (Matthew 28:11-15).[236]

Just a reminder, if you are rolling your eyes and thinking that the gospels cannot be used as a historical source, please review Chapter 4 explaining their historical value. Although the gospels have not been used exclusively as historical evidence, since they were written within the time frame of 35-70 years after Yeshua's crucifixion, categorically rejecting them seems illogical. As previously noted, any historical evidence written this close to an event during this time in antiquity is deemed extremely reliable.

According to this verse, the Roman guards immediately began the narrative of a con job devised by the disciples. This is significant because it demonstrates that the Jewish leaders did not deny the tomb was empty. Instead, they provided an unsubstantiated theory to *explain* the empty tomb. A major problem with this theory is that those who were motivated to steal the body of Yeshua had no access to the tomb. Again, if there were *any* proof the disciples stole Yeshua's body, the Roman and Jewish leaders would have brought it forth in an attempt to invalidate the narrative being told by Yeshua's close followers, as well as the hundreds of eyewitness who were supporting the claim that Yeshua was resurrected from the dead.

The Roman guards had access to the tomb of Yeshua. Roman soldiers were extremely loyal, if not by choice, then out of self-preservation. Under Roman law, the only people who could be subjected to the torturous execution of a crucifixion were non-Roman criminals and *disobedient Roman soldiers.*

The soldiers guarding Yeshua's tomb would have understood the serious repercussions of abandoning their post, or of allowing someone to steal the corpse of a prisoner. They too could be crucified.[237] George Currie, a scholar of ancient Roman military, describes, "The punishment for abandoning your military post was death, according to the laws."[238] Upholding their post (and guarding the tomb) was quite literally a life or death situation, and these trained guards would not have been careless enough to fall asleep or wander off.

The Roman Empire thrived because of its persistence in ensuring no allegiance was sworn to anyone but Rome. Yeshua came preaching a very different message. He continually referred to the kingdom of God, calling people to "Seek first the kingdom of God and His righteousness," (Matthew 6:33).[239] The Roman leaders undoubtedly despised this message. The motto of the Roman Empire was to seek first the Kingdom of Rome, and maintain allegiance only to Rome. Although the Romans were not yet actively persecuting the followers of Yeshua, they would not have wanted their brutal crucifixion process undermined by the claim that a Jewish peasant carpenter had lived through their most intense form of torture and capital punishment. The Roman Empire chose top-notch guards and not a Barney Fife or Chief Wiggum type.[240]

After the crucifixion of Yeshua, the Pharisees approached Pontius Pilate to remind him that Yeshua claimed that He would defeat death after three days.[241] The Pharisees requested that all precautions be put into place for Yeshua's tomb. Pilate gave them permission to "Make the tomb secure, seal the stone, and set the guard as best they knew how," (Matthew 27:65-66).[242]

Again, non-biblical sources (noted in the previous chapter) thoroughly document that the Jewish religious leaders despised Yeshua and His teachings. They wanted Yeshua to be punished for His blasphemy. Clearly, they would have done everything to make Yeshua's tomb as secure as they could so as not to condone what they believed to be a lie against God. As the Gospel of Mark records, the entrance to the tomb of Yeshua was secured with a large stone:

> When the Sabbath was past, Mary Magdalene, Mary the mother of James, and Salome bought spices so that they might go and anoint him. And very early on the first day of the week, when the sun had risen, they went to the tomb. And they were saying to one another, "Who will roll away the stone for us from the entrance of the tomb?" And looking up, they saw that the stone had been rolled back—it was very large, (Mark 16:1-4).[243]

Although I'm sure these women who lived in an extremely patriarchal society were not exactly body builders, we can imagine that the stone blocking the entrance was extremely large if all three of them thought they could not move it together.

The stone was also "sealed" to prevent individuals from breaking in. The early 20th century New Covenant scholar A.T. Robertson describes the probable process of sealing the tomb. Robertson explains that the Romans likely stretched a cord across the stone covering the entrance to the tomb, and then placed a Roman Seal on either end of the cord.[244] Before placing the seal, the Romans would have ensured the tomb was secured and inescapable. The Roman Seal was held with high regard, and the punishment inflicted upon someone who broke the seal would have been severe.

To summarize, the historical evidence simply does not support the theory that the body of Yeshua was stolen. His followers had no access to His tomb, and His enemies had no reason to steal His body. The Jewish leaders demanded that Yeshua be executed for His blasphemy against God, and because of their influence over the Roman Governor Pontius Pilate, the Romans then executed Yeshua. Although historically Rome was not actively persecuting followers of Yeshua at this time, its leaders still would have not wanted their highest form of torture and death to be undermined; thus, Yeshua's tomb was surrounded by high-level security. Highly loyal and skilled Roman soldiers guarded the tomb, and a large heavy stone was placed in front of the entrance and was then secured by the Roman Seal. Professor D.H. Van Daalen offers up his own sentiments for the reason some adhere to the stolen body theory:

> It is extremely difficult to object to the empty tomb on historical grounds; those who deny it do so on the basis of theological or philosophical assumptions.[245]

Theory 2: Everyone Looked for Yeshua in the Wrong Tomb

Response: It was only a three-day time span between Yeshua's burial and resurrection, so it seems implausible all of His followers and enemies would have forgotten where He was buried.

Some have argued that Yeshua was simply not in the tomb where everyone was looking. They propose that everyone was confused about where Yeshua was buried because all the tombs looked similar. This hypothesis was not even proposed until 1907 by Kirsopp Lake, and it seems to be nothing more than wishful thinking.[246]

It seems unlikely that *everyone* in Jerusalem would have forgotten where this high profile prisoner was placed. Also, it is recorded that the tomb belonged to Joseph of Arimathea who asked Pilate for Yeshua's body so that he could give Him a proper burial.[247] If Joseph were the owner of the tomb, he would have known where it was. If the tomb did not belong to Joseph, he still would have known the location because he had performed Yeshua's burial only three days prior.

Even if Joseph had forgotten which tomb Yeshua was laid in, Mary Magdalene was also a witness to Yeshua's crucifixion and resurrection.[248] It is recorded that she attended the burial of Yeshua, and was one of the women who went to bring spices to anoint His body only to find His tomb empty.[249] She probably would not have forgotten where the man she regarded as her LORD had been buried only three days prior.

If you do not believe the biblical accounts, think about the highly motivated individuals who were trying to stop this new world-changing movement. Once people began to claim that Yeshua was resurrected from the dead, the Jewish or Roman leaders could have easily gone to the correct tomb and presented Yeshua's body. Undoubtedly, the Romans, who would have not wanted their brutal execution process undermined, would have displayed Yeshua's body in a grotesque and public manner. Had this been done, belief in Yeshua would have been immediately extinguished. Instead, the inability of the Jewish and Roman leadership to produce a corpse or a credible explanation for the empty tomb is quite possibly the best evidence that the body of Yeshua was not laying in another tomb. Again, it is clear that the "wrong tomb" theory is unsupported by the historical evidence.

Theory 3: Yeshua Was Never Killed During His Crucifixion

Response: Crucifixions were absolutely brutal. Yeshua would have had to make a miraculous escape after this punishment, and then He would have had to be deemed fully healed by His followers three days later.

Some accept that the tomb was empty, but they do not believe Yeshua was ever truly dead. They believe Yeshua fell unconscious (or swooned), and was never killed during the crucifixion. They believe after He regained consciousness, He simply snuck out of the tomb. While Yeshua was still on the cross, Pilate wanted to confirm that Yeshua was truly dead.[250] Pilate asked his centurion (a Roman military officer) to verify the death of Yeshua. The Romans were well accustomed to death, as crucifixions and executions were common practice throughout the empire, so they would have known what a post-mortem individual looked like.

After Pilate was assured that Yeshua was dead, Joseph of Arimathea prepared His body for burial. Jewish custom required the body be washed, "Then bandaged tightly from the armpits to the ankles in strips of linen about a foot wide."[251] The Gospel of John confirms that this custom was followed.[252] If Yeshua had awoken, He would have had to unwrap his tight whole-body cast, move the large stone that sealed the entrance to the tomb, break the Roman Seal, and sneak out past a heavily guarded entrance.

This would have been a nearly impossible feat for anyone to accomplish, even if someone were in a state of perfect health. Let's remember even skeptics of the resurrection confirm that Yeshua was severely beaten, tortured, and left to die while nailed to a cross by his hands and feet, (refer to Tacitus' quote above).[253] To confirm Yeshua's death, one of the centurions plunged a spear into Yeshua's right side, likely puncturing a lung or one of his vital organs.[254]

Now try to imagine a man who would have been in that kind of condition waking up only to execute a James Bond-esque escape under the noses of the brutal Roman guards. After His miraculous escape, His extensive wounds would have to have been significantly healed in three days in order to persuade hundreds of people who saw Him that He was fully recovered and resurrected from the dead.

Perhaps the most compelling evidence that Yeshua died by crucifixion comes from an in-depth review of the crucifixion of Yeshua published by the esteemed *Journal of the American Medical Association*. This article verifies that Yeshua died on His execution stake. After reviewing the evidence, the article concludes, "Interpretations based on the assumption that Jesus did not die on the cross appear to be at odds with modern medical knowledge."[255] It seems as if the "swoon theory" may take more faith to believe in than the resurrection.

* *

There has yet to be a logical substantiated explanation for the empty tomb of Yeshua, aside from His resurrection. If we choose to deny the resurrection, we are left with the unsolved mystery of why His tomb was empty. If His empty tomb were the only evidence historians could use to validate the resurrection, it would be a fairly convincing case. However, there are still three more historical facts we have yet to explore: the witnesses to the resurrected Yeshua, the commitment of Yeshua's disciples despite severe repercussions, and the lack of evidence from the opposing side.

Exhibit B: Witnesses to the Resurrected Yeshua

Now we are left with this question: if Yeshua was miraculously resurrected from the tomb, where did He go and what did He do? One of the best sources of witnesses of the resurrected Yeshua comes from the first letter to the Corinth Church

("1st Corinthians") written by the Apostle Paul (Rabbi Saul of Tarsus) in approximately 55 CE. Paul was a Pharisee (a very strict, observant Jew) who initially rigorously persecuted those who believed Yeshua was the prophesied Messiah.[256] He stood by and approved as Stephen, a follower of Yeshua, was stoned to death for his beliefs.[257] After a personal supernatural experience on the road to Damascus, Paul immediately became a devoted follower of Yeshua.[258] Paul's transformation from violent persecutor to passionate believer is undeniable. His writings in the New Covenant repeatedly declare his devotion and unwavering commitment to Yeshua.[259]

After his transformation, Paul wrote many letters to the first century churches, some of which are contained in the New Covenant. In 1st Corinthians, Paul writes, "Then he (Yeshua) appeared to more than five hundred brothers at one time, most of whom are still alive, though some have fallen asleep," (parenthetical added), (1 Corinthians 15:6).[260] Paul wrote this passage when most of the 500 witnesses who saw the resurrected Yeshua were still alive![261] If Paul was fibbing or even embellishing, his writings would have been rejected, as there would be no witnesses to support his bold assertions.

Even without Twitter and other social media, the earth-shattering news of a resurrected Messiah would have spread like wildfire. If Paul had lied about the 500 witnesses of the resurrection, there would have been an abundance of people lining up to set the record straight. Remember, travel had become easier during this period in the ancient Roman Empire. Paul even identifies individuals by name who saw the resurrected Yeshua.[262] An opponent to Yeshua could have asked any of the witnesses identified whether Paul's claims were true. *One* denier would have been devastating to Paul's written accounts. However, there is no evidence of such. If either the Roman or Jewish authorities uncovered evidence of false statements by Paul or *any* of the 500 eyewitnesses, the following of Yeshua would have disbanded.

Lastly, in his writings Paul acknowledges that he was a "chief persecutor" of the early followers of Yeshua.[263] This does not appear to be something Paul would fabricate about himself if he were trying to join the group he used to persecute. Such an acknowledgement could cause individuals to be quite suspicious of his newfound allegiance and could have caused him to be heavily scrutinized as a possible spy. Paul's incriminating admission further validates the historical validity of his transforming experience on the road to Damascus.

Since there is little doubt by scholars that individuals believed they had truly seen the risen Yeshua, we will examine one of the more common theories offered to explain why they believed this other than the resurrection of Yeshua.

The Mass Hallucination Theory

Response: Mass hallucinations or visions provoked by feelings of despair are inconsistent with any psychological findings of how hallucinations operate.

Some have argued that over 500 people *believed* they saw Yeshua, but that it was just a mass hallucination or vision caused by their immense grief. This theory claims that hundreds of people all had similar hallucinations. This is significant for several reasons.

First, hundreds of people would have had to make psychological history and experience the same hallucination at the same time. In other words, this would be the first and only time that a mass hallucination has occurred. Clinical psychologist Dr. Gary A. Sibcy points out that even two people experiencing the same hallucination simultaneously has never been known to occur:

> I have surveyed the professional literature [peer-reviewed journal articles and books] written by psychologists, psychiatrists, and other relevant healthcare professionals

during the past two decades and have yet to find a single documented case of a group hallucination, that is, an event for which more than one person purportedly shared in a visual or other sensory perception where there was clearly no external referent.[264]

It is incredulous to believe that over 500 people experienced the same hallucination of a resurrected Yeshua who was walking, talking, and preaching among them again. According to the gospels, Yeshua made several post-resurrection appearances. They were all visual, auditory, and similarly contextual. It seems illogical to conclude that each of these people experienced such similar hallucinations. For instance, if these hundreds of people were so driven to despair by the death of Yeshua that they began hallucinating His resurrection, one would think these personal hallucinations would have varied from individual to individual.

Similarly, this theory does not explain the transformation of Paul. Even if one can overlook the incredible improbability of a mass hallucination, the theory arises from the argument that the hallucination occurred because of immense despair. The transformation of Paul uproots this argument because he was not experiencing despair, yet it is recorded that he saw the risen Yeshua. The belief that hundreds of witnesses hallucinated the same thing at the same time is currently unexplainable and undocumented, making it *extremely* unlikely.

Perhaps even more significant, the mass hallucination theory does not even attempt to address why the tomb of Yeshua was empty.

Exhibit C: The Commitment of the Disciples of Yeshua Amidst Adverse Circumstances

The early followers of Yeshua were making a grand historical claim. They were not simply saying that they believed Yeshua was resurrected in the hearts and minds of those who believed in Him; rather, they were claiming that they had personally interacted with the resurrected Yeshua after He was killed by crucifixion. These early followers were not making these claims based on stories passed down from generation to generation. They were eyewitnesses to the resurrection. Thus, these early followers were either (1) deceived, or (2) attempting to deceive. That is, they all either had the same hallucination of a resurrected Yeshua (and were deceived), or they were deliberately spreading a lie.

As we discussed in the previous section, there were over 500 witnesses to the resurrected Yeshua. Despite what some may propose to be an explanation to account for why there is no refutation of these 500 witnesses, we can agree that they were not simultaneously hallucinating the same thing. This leaves the only other option to be that the early followers were attempting to concoct a grandiose lie. As we will see in the following section, because the early followers of Yeshua were facing extremely challenging circumstances, this does not seem like a plausible explanation either.

Adverse Circumstance 1: Terrible Consequences
Adverse Circumstance 2: Unreliable Witnesses
Adverse Circumstance 3: Hard-to-Believe Facts
Adverse Circumstance 4: Illogical Game Plan

Adverse Circumstance 1: Terrible Consequences

These early followers of Yeshua truly believed in what they were preaching. How do we know this? Because they were willing to be imprisoned, tortured, and killed for their cause. Ten of the original twelve disciples were brutally murdered because of their faith in Yeshua. Although people die for false causes all the time, rarely are they willing to be tortured and killed for causes they know to be false because *they made them up*. New Covenant scholar Dr. Michael Licona in his book *The Resurrection of Jesus* describes the importance of the commitment of the disciples' beliefs:

> Modern martyrs act solely out of their trust in beliefs passed along to them by others. The apostles died for holding to their own testimony that they had *personally seen* the risen Jesus…The disciples of Jesus suffered and were willing to die for what they *knew* to be either true or false, (emphasis added).[265]

If the claims of the followers of Yeshua were false, the disciples (Yeshua's closest followers) would have known because they would have been the ones who made it up![266] Yeshua's followers endured horrific torture, such as being boiled in oil and crucified upside-down.[267] This demonstrates their deep conviction that Yeshua's resurrection truly occurred.

Although false prophets and the branching off of new religious sects are fairly common in the 21st century, this would have been blasphemous to Jewish people in ancient Israel. The initial followers of Yeshua were Jewish. The New Covenant was written entirely by Jews, with the possible exception of the Gospel of Luke and the Book of Acts. These early Jewish believers in Yeshua would have not followed doctrine that they did not truly believe in, as this sort of lie against God could have resulted in harsh consequences.[268]

Even the extremely skeptical German New Covenant scholar Gerd Lüdemann concludes, "It may be taken as *historically certain* that Peter and the disciples had experiences after Jesus' death in which Jesus appeared to them as the risen Christ," (emphasis added).[269]

Now let's turn our attention to the fact that the people telling this story chose poorly constructed ways to do so if they were trying to con individuals into believing something unbelievable. Rather than choosing a believable "fib," they chose a story laced with unreliable witnesses, hard-to-believe facts, and had an illogical game plan to spread their story.

Adverse Circumstance 2: Unreliable Witnesses

What if Yeshua's early followers were trying to sell the most influential and grandiose lie ever told? These early followers were lowly fishermen and tax collectors, not wealthy tycoons or influential people. Even if you do not believe in the deity of Yeshua, the following He inspired has undeniably been one of the most influential movements in the world over the last 2,000 years. The popular historian Will Durant wrote this concerning Yeshua's followers:

> That a few simple men should in one generation have invented so powerful and appealing a personality, so lofty an ethic and so inspiring a vision of human brotherhood, would be a miracle far more incredible than any recorded in the Gospels.[270]

Durant recognizes the unlikelihood of someone choosing the credential-less initial followers of Yeshua if that person were trying to concoct a story. The disciples were not the Bill Gateses, Warren Buffets, or Oprah Winfreys of their day. They were lowly fishermen and tax collectors.[271] Most of these early believers did not have the lofty social status that would be helpful in fabricating a story that would radically change the world.

Adverse Circumstance 3: Hard-to-Believe Facts

Likewise, if the disciples were inventing a story, they were not using very good material. Each gospel writer indicates that Joseph of Arimathea, a prominent man in the Jewish ruling class, performed the burial of Yeshua.[272] A lie about him would have been easy to refute.

The gospels also describe women as the first to discover the empty tomb.[273] At the time, women held no societal power, and any testimony they provided was inadmissible in court.[274] If this truly were a fabricated story, it would have held no credibility. The only way for it to be believable would have been if the women's testimonies were confirmed with physical evidence such as an empty tomb and a multitude of eyewitnesses. If you were going to try to trick people into believing a lie as grandiose as this, it seems you would recruit far better witnesses and develop a far more believable story.

Adverse Circumstance 4: Illogical Game Plan

After the disciples saw the resurrected Yeshua, they did not immediately flee to Athens or Rome to proclaim His resurrection. If they had done so, there would have been no one to refute their testimonies. Although they eventually traveled to spread the news of Yeshua, they initially stayed in Jerusalem where, if they were making everything up, it would have been far easier to discredit their story.[275] Scam artists tend to quickly leave town after they have duped their customers and collected their cash. Yeshua lived, performed many of His miracles, and was crucified in Jerusalem. If the claims of His followers were false and He never lived, performed miraculous acts, and was never resurrected, rebuttal testimonies and evidence would have been readily available. It seems extremely illogical for the disciples to concoct a lie about someone whom many people knew, and then stay in the same place where they were claiming everything took place.[276]

Before Yeshua's resurrection, many of His followers denied that they knew Him. Presumably they did such to avoid punishment. When Yeshua was taken in by the Roman guards to be punished and eventually executed, the disciples "forsook Him and fled," (Mark 14:50).[277] Peter, who was one of Yeshua's closest disciples, denied that he knew Yeshua three times.[278]

Yet, when these same disciples later saw Yeshua alive after His crucifixion, they dramatically changed and professed their allegiance to Him, even though it would mean their own torture and death. Peter, the previous denier, preached the divinity of Yeshua to thousands.[279] Quintus Septimius Florens Tertullianus (try saying that three times fast) was a Christian theologian in the early 2nd century. In his writings entitled *Prescription Against Heretics,* he describes the horrific fate of some of the early disciples and followers (Peter, Paul, and John respectively). He affirms:

> How happy is its church, on which apostles poured forth all their doctrine along with their blood! Where Peter endures a passion like his Lord's! Where Paul wins his crown in a death like John's! Where the Apostle John was first plunged, unhurt, into boiling oil, and thence remitted to his island-exile![280]

The followers of Yeshua were not eagerly waiting by the door for Him to rise from the dead. They believed His death by crucifixion was final. Two of the original twelve disciples—Peter and Thomas—returned to their previous occupation of fishermen, essentially believing that the era of Yeshua was over.[281] Clearly, something drastic and miraculous occurred to give these previously downtrodden men something to believe in. As noted above, just before Yeshua's crucifixion, some disciples did not even acknowledge that they knew Him. After Yeshua's resurrection, His followers stood confidently as they were arrested, tortured, and executed for their allegiance and belief in Him. Author John R. W. Stott, ranked in 2005 by *Time Magazine* as one of the 100 most influential people in the world, confirms this dramatic change in the lives of the disciples of Yeshua. He says, "Perhaps the transformation of the disciples of Jesus is the greatest evidence of all the resurrection."[282] They changed from cowardly deniers into bold proclaimers.

If the only evidence provided were the unexplainable empty tomb, the case for the resurrection would be compelling. The evidence of the empty tomb coupled with hundreds of witnesses to the resurrected Yeshua plus this radical transformation of the disciples amidst severe persecution have yet to find *any* plausible explanations—other than the reality of the resurrection of Yeshua.

Exhibit D: Silence from the Opposition

In a court of law, if the defense were unable to present *any* compelling evidence refuting the position of the prosecutor, it is an open-and-shut case. As has been demonstrated, there is overwhelming evidence supporting the life, healing ministry, death, and resurrection of Yeshua. If the Jewish or Roman leaders were able to present *any* evidence calling into question *any* portion of the narrative circulating about Yeshua's life, death, and resurrection, the evidence would have been provided and the following of Yeshua would have been quickly extinguished. In stark contrast, we find many historic writings *supporting* the resurrection of Yeshua as depicted in the narrative of the gospels.

CONCLUSION

After reviewing the historical evidence, the resurrection stands alone as the only plausible explanation. It is not simply the most likely explanation of the evidence; it is the *only* reasonable explanation.

Dr. Paul L. Maier is a professor of ancient history and author of both scholarly and popular works. He concludes that the evidence for the resurrection supports its historical validity:

> If all the evidence is weighed carefully and fairly, it is indeed justifiable, according to the canons of historical research, to conclude that the sepulcher of Joseph of Arimathea, in which Jesus was buried, was actually empty on the morning of the first Easter. And no shred of evidence has yet been discovered in literary sources, epigraphy, or archaeology that would disprove this statement.[283]

The core of my faith resides in belief in the resurrection of Yeshua, a supernatural event confirming that He is the promised Messiah and the Son of God.[284] Clearly, there are sources offering opposing theories about what occurred after Yeshua's death and burial. As has been discovered, however, the leading rebuttal theories against the resurrection of Yeshua are unsubstantiated. We all must learn to decipher what is truth validated by historical evidence, and what is simply unsupported speculation.

The evidence gathered from adverse ancient witnesses proves Yeshua was a man who lived, was crucified, died, and buried.[285] After Yeshua's crucifixion, His tomb was found empty, hundreds of witnesses claim to have seen Him resurrected, His followers had a drastic change of heart, and His enemies had no verifiable denial. All rebuttal theories have been uprooted and found to be woefully lacking in credibility.

As a former Chief Justice in England Lord Charles Darling affirmed, "No intelligent jury in the world could fail to bring in a verdict that the resurrection story is true."[286]

For most of my life, I thought that believing Yeshua lived and was crucified and resurrected was simply an idea created in the minds of individuals who needed to feel like there was a greater meaning to life. I thought it was illogical and unsupported by evidence to believe the hype about this one man who *possibly* lived centuries ago. Even after becoming a follower of Yeshua, I assumed believing in His resurrection was based on my faith in Him. This faith was based on the vast impact I had felt Yeshua had had on my life. However, after researching the subject for many years, I have discovered there is extremely compelling historical evidence to support His life, crucifixion, and resurrection.

But everything we believe requires some degree of faith. Even seemingly rational, modern-day arguments are often rooted in claims based on faith. As we discussed earlier, one of the most common arguments against the resurrection is the idea that we live in a purely natural world, one in which supernatural intervention is an impossibility. This is ultimately based on the faith that we will never find any evidence to the contrary. Clearly, there is convincing evidence supporting the resurrection of Yeshua, despite its miraculous nature. This evidence should not be ignored or taken lightly despite any preconceived notions about miracles.

If you have been convinced, or your curiosity has been even mildly piqued, I invite you to ask Yeshua if He is the promised Messiah of Israel. One night, over 23 years ago, I was asked if I would like to know Yeshua. I decided that I did want to know Yeshua—*if* He was real. Since that night I have learned that He is very real, and my life has never been the same. Although there was no burning bush or booming voice from the sky, bit by bit He broke down barriers I had previously built up against Him. I believe if you ask God with an open heart to reveal His Son to you, Yeshua will meet you in the most personal way. And once you meet Him, you will understand the true beauty and love of Yeshua, our Messiah, who is far more than just another historical character.

CHAPTER 7

IS YESHUA THE JEWISH MESSIAH?

DOES THE RESURRECTION ALONE PROVE THAT YESHUA IS THE MESSIAH?

As we have seen in Chapters 5 and 6, Yeshua was very clearly a man of history who lived, performed miracles, was crucified by the Romans, and was resurrected from the dead. However, there are some who do not see these miraculous feats as proof that He is the prophesied Messiah of Israel and the Son of God.[287] Instead, they believe that He was merely a man who lived an extraordinary life and was raised from the dead by God. If the resurrection of Yeshua were the *only* piece of evidence for His divinity, this conclusion *might* be valid. There are other individuals in the Old and New Covenant who were also raised from the dead.[288] However, as will be discussed, the claims and ministry of Yeshua make Him very, very different than these other individuals. This chapter will no longer focus on the historical validity of the resurrection of Yeshua, but rather on the astounding proof that He is, in fact, the Messiah.

WHAT IS A MESSIAH?

For some, "Messiah" is a foreign term. For others, it is often misunderstood. As such, it seems pertinent to provide a brief explanation of what Messiah means. The term Messiah (in Hebrew, "Mashiach") appears repeatedly in the Old Covenant.[289] [290] Mashiach translates to "anointed one" or "Christ" (in Greek, "christos"). Since Yeshua is Jesus' Hebrew name, "Jesus Christ" actually translates to "Yeshua the Messiah."

In the writings of the Old Covenant, it is reiterated that we are separated from the glory of God as a result of our wrongdoings (sins).[291] This separation requires some sort of bridge to restore us to a rightful relationship with God. The Old Covenant speaks repeatedly of the sacrificial shedding of blood being that bridge which atones for the sins of the people to restore our relationship with God.[292] Additionally, the rabbis confirm in the Talmud[293] that a blood sacrifice is needed for reconciliation (atonement) with God. The Babylonian Talmud specifically states that, "There is no atonement without blood."[294]

There are over 300 verses in the Old Covenant alluding to a Messiah, or someone who would bridge this separation between God's perfection and the wrongdoings of humanity once and for all.[295] In the Shmoneh Esrey (also known as the Amidah, or Standing Prayer) contained in the Jewish Siddur (prayer book), there are daily prayers related to the Messiah, as well as prayers that deal with salvation, healings, and individuals being raised from the dead.[296] Since the Shmoneh Esrey is a central prayer in Judaism, it follows that the Messiah, salvation, healings, and individuals being raised from the dead are also clearly central tenants of Judaism.

As will be discussed in further depth in this chapter, in the Old Covenant, an animal blood sacrifice was used to atone for sins. Yeshua's brutal crucifixion could certainly be the perfect sacrifice to atone for our sins. Not only does Yeshua fulfill the prophecies of the Messiah recorded in the Old Covenant, but also the timing of His death and resurrection were approximately 40 years before the destruction of the Second Temple in 70 CE.[297] This is significant because after the Temple was destroyed, there was no way for the animal sacrificial system to continue because the sacrifices had to be performed in the Temple. This means that there has been no way to atone for sins for the last 2,000 years.

Some have proclaimed that the Old Covenant describes multiple ways to atone for our wrongdoings against God. Many believe one's sins can be reconciled through the performance of good deeds. However, this conflicts with the previously referenced passages in the Old Covenant and in the Talmud, which states that, "there is no atonement without blood."[298] Further, what I consider good may be completely different than what you consider good, and may be entirely different from what God considers to be good. Lastly, to presume that our idea of what are acceptable good deeds as being able to atone for our sins goes directly against what is written in the Old Covenant—that our good deeds are but "filthy rags" and do not make us righteous before God:

> All of us have become like one who is unclean, and all of our righteous acts are like filthy rags; we all shrivel up like a leaf, and like the wind our sins sweep us away, (Isaiah 64:6).[299]

This point is reiterated in Ecclesiastes.

> Surely there is not a righteous man on earth who does good and never sins, (Ecclesiastes 7:20).[300]

This is undoubtedly why the Jewish prophet Jeremiah writes of God making a "new covenant" with the Jewish people and the world.[301] (This foundational verse contained in the Book of Jeremiah in the Old Covenant will be discussed further below.) As I believe will be made clear, the righteous life of Yeshua: His healings, resurrection, the prophecies He fulfilled, and the miraculous events recorded by the Jewish leaders shortly following His death (discussed below in the section entitled Miracles Proving Yeshua is the Prophesied Messiah) prove that He is the long-awaited Messiah—and that He represents the *new covenant* referred to by Jeremiah. Through the blood sacrifice of Yeshua, we can now find full reconciliation with God.

WHAT WERE THE JEWISH PEOPLE EXPECTING?

The idea of a resurrected Messiah of Israel was not a foreign concept to the Jewish people of the first century, and it still remains a viable part of Judaism today. In *The Thirteen Fundamental Principles of the Jewish Faith* compiled by the prominent 12th century Rabbi Maimonides (Rambam), Maimonides reiterates that it is in accordance with the Old Covenant to believe in a Messiah, and the ability of God to resurrect individuals from the dead.

> Principle 12: I believe with complete faith in the coming of the *Moshiach* (Messiah); and even though he may tarry, nonetheless, I wait daily for his coming, (parenthetical added).

> Principles 13: I believe with complete faith that there will be a revival of the dead at the time when it shall please the Creator.[302]

Also consider this additional Jewish prayer from the Machzor prayer book that speaks of the Messiah having *already* "departed from us" and being wounded for our "transgressions" which shall make us "healed."[303] Excerpts from this common Jewish prayer clearly align with the crucifixion and resurrection of Yeshua.

> Our righteous anointed (Messiah) is departed from us...(He) is wounded because of our transgression...We shall be healed by his wound, (parentheticals added).[304]

Further, the resurrection of Yeshua was clearly an event within the framework of Judaism during the first century. Preeminent Talmudic scholar Dr. Daniel Boyarin affirms that the idea of a Messiah who was divine and would come to Earth was very common at that time. He writes:

> Many Israelites at the time of Jesus were expecting a Messiah who would be divine and come to earth in the form of a human.[305]

This leads one to wonder why the ancient rabbis, who believed a Messiah was coming and believed in a "revival of the dead," would not have recognized Yeshua as that Messiah.

As was discussed in the previous chapter, *some* Jewish religious leaders believed Yeshua was blaspheming, as He did not deny that He was the Messiah and the Son of God. Therefore, they demanded that He be crucified. However, we must realize that many ancient Jews *did* accept Yeshua as the Messiah. All of the early disciples of Yeshua were Jewish. Jewish followers of Yeshua wrote every book in the New Covenant (with the possible exception of the Gospel of Luke and the Book of Acts). Paul wrote a good deal of the New Covenant writings and is often referred to as the "Apostle Paul," but he was then known as the prominent Jewish leader, Rabbi Saul of Tarsus.[306] To state that all Jewish people did not accept Yeshua as the Jewish Messiah is undeniably incorrect.

Some may come at this issue from the opposite side. They may claim that because the Jewish Messiah was expected during this time period, Yeshua was just stepping into the role of "messiah" to gain power. The claims that Yeshua was making were not entirely abnormal during this time period; what made Him different from the other individuals claiming to be the Messiah? For starters, no other individual who claimed to be the Son of God was raised from the dead; it does not seem that God would resurrect a blasphemer.

Further, each of the other "messiahs" would prompt a following that would quickly scatter following the leader's death. The Book of Acts even records that during an exchange among the members of the Jewish Council shortly after Yeshua's death Gamaliel, a highly esteemed Pharisee, describes several recent self-proclaimed messiahs who had prompted short-lived followings. After each of these proclaimed messiahs were killed, their following disbanded. Gamaliel advises the council to leave the followers of Yeshua alone. He reasons that if Yeshua is not the Messiah, His following will quickly dissolve. But conversely he notes that, "If it is of God, you will not be able to overthrow them," (Acts 5:39).[307] Regardless of whether you believe in the historicity of the New Covenant, the logic and rendition of historical events proposed by Gamaliel is sound. If there were other individuals during this time who claimed to be the Messiah and their followings all disbanded, why is the following of Yeshua still widely impactful? There are an estimated *2.2 billion* believers in Yeshua today.[308] It is clear that even from the beginning, there has been something very different about the following of Yeshua.

So what about today? Why does such a large percentage of the Jewish population not believe Yeshua is the prophesied Messiah?[309] Despite the initial following of Yeshua being almost exclusively comprised of Jews, it has morphed into an un-Jewish concept to believe in Yeshua as the Messiah. This is a complex issue. I will try to summarize and critique two of the major objections often raised by Jewish people and others who do not accept Yeshua as the Messiah.[310] Please bear in mind that to categorically reject belief in God or the historical evidence for the resurrection of Yeshua because of these objections seems illogical due to the evidence already presented in the previous chapters. In other words, these objections fail to rebut any of the foundational beliefs already proven regarding the life of Yeshua (i.e., the historical reliability of his life, crucifixion, and resurrection).

Objection 1:   No Peace on Earth
Objection 2:   There is Only One God, and God is Not a Man

Objection 1: No Peace on Earth

The Jewish population has faced horrendous adversities throughout the course of history, and they were not immune to hardship during the time of Yeshua. They were under Roman rule, which eventually led to several Jewish-Roman Wars and the destruction of the Second Temple in 70 CE.[311] The Jewish people not only desired, but also saw a biblical basis for the prophesied Messiah to be one who would conquer and be crowned King in a primarily *political* realm.

This belief has continued to some extent into modern-day Judaism. Some believe that the Messiah will have a dual-role of sorts. He will come as a "suffering servant," *and* as a "conquering king," bringing ultimate and lasting peace. These foundational beliefs come from many passages in the Old Covenant. Two examples are:

Suffering Servant:

When they look on me, on him whom they have pierced, they shall mourn for him, as one mourns for an only child, and weep bitterly over him, as one weeps over a firstborn, (Zechariah 12:10).[312]

Conquering King:

> And in the days of those kings the God of heaven will
> set up a kingdom that shall never be destroyed, nor
> shall the kingdom be left to another people. It shall
> break in pieces all these kingdoms and bring them to
> an end, and it shall stand forever, (Daniel 2:44).[313]

Some feel that because there is not peace on Earth and our world
is still clearly overridden by evil and turmoil, Yeshua cannot be the
Messiah, as He did not fulfill the "conquering king" aspect of the
prophesied Messiah.[314]

The reality is that the "dual-persona" of the Messiah makes
more sense if He comes to Earth two different times, once as a suffering servant as He did 2,000 years ago, and again in the future to
fully restore peace on Earth as a conquering king. Thus, the first
"life" of the Messiah would be one of hardship and trials; the second would be as king. In fact, the Talmud confirms this and states:

> If they (the Jews) are worthy [the Messiah] will come
> 'with the clouds of heaven' (Daniel 7:13); if they are not
> worthy, 'lowly and riding upon a donkey' (Zechariah
> 9:9), (parentheticals added).[315]

The Old Covenant passage of Isaiah 53 is often at the center of the
debate regarding the "suffering Messiah." Some believe this passage
details the suffering that would be inflicted on Israel.[316] Although
somewhat popular now, this belief has not held the majority for
very long.[317] Boyarin writes:

> We now know that many Jewish authorities, maybe
> even most until nearly the modern period, have read
> Isaiah 53 as being about the Messiah; until the last few

centuries, the allegorical (symbolic) reading (that this verse is about Israel) was a minority opinion, (parentheticals added).[318]

Understandably, just because reading Isaiah 53 as being about Israel is a "new" interpretation, does not inherently deem it to be wrong. Reading the text of Isaiah 53 (which can be read in its entirety in Appendix C) however, will demonstrate the inaccuracy in believing this verse is about Israel.

The third verse in Isaiah 53 says that "*He* was despised, and *we* esteemed him not," (emphasis added). Clearly there are two different subjects in this sentence. How can Israel be both the "he" and the "we?" Looking at this verse in the context of the passage, the "we" clearly refers to Israel, so the "he" cannot *also* refer to Israel. The *only* other reasonable subject of this verse that could be referred to as "he" is the Messiah.

Further, the entire passage of Isaiah 53 uses the singular pronoun "he." Although Israel is sometimes referred to in the singular within the texts of the Old Covenant, it is usually as "she." This is not wholly conclusive, but it does add to the probability that this verse is referring to a single person rather than to an entire nation.[319]

If you're not convinced by the above brief analysis, actually reading the text in the context of the entire Old Covenant clearly demonstrates this verse is not about Israel. In his study of Messianic genealogy and prophecy, 20th century Old Covenant and Talmudic scholar Rachmiel Frydland reiterates the inconsistency in believing Isaiah 53 is about Israel and not the Messiah.[320] He writes:

For the servant to be Israel it would mean that Israel was stricken for Israel because of Israel's sin. This would be absolutely contrary to normative biblical principles of atonement. The sacrificial offering for sin, the Sin-Bearer, had to be separate than the sinner.[321]

In other words, for this verse to apply to Israel, it would have to completely contradict the rest of the Old Covenantal texts about sacrificial law. To presume that one passage would be so out of place, so opposed to the rest of the Old Covenant seems to be an ill-suited attempt to compensate for the obvious answer—that Isaiah 53 is about a suffering person rather than the entire nation of Israel.

Perhaps this is why many synagogues do not read Isaiah 53. I vividly recall the first time I read Isaiah 53 as an adult (despite having gone through both Hebrew school and being confirmed after eight years of religious studies), and was certain that it had to be from the New Covenant because it described Yeshua's life, punishment, and crucifixion so accurately.

As the Old Covenant foretold in Isaiah 53 and historians have confirmed, the suffering servant, Yeshua, came to Earth, was crucified, and was resurrected from the dead. His blood sacrifice atoned for the sins of mankind, and now we are able to enter into a relationship with God.[322] He has come as a servant; next, He will come as a King.[323]

Objection 2: There is Only One God, and God is Not a Man

Some presume claiming that Yeshua is both fully-God and fully-man is incompatible with messianic prophecies and Jewish theology. They may view it as blasphemous to declare that anyone other than God in heaven could be divine. These objections will be briefly addressed in this section beginning with the distinction between the phrases "Son of God" and "Son of Man." We will also see that preeminent Jewish scholars confirm that the Old Covenant actually speaks of God in the form of a man and God in the plural.

Does God Have a Son?

Before we delve into the Messianic aspect of the "Son of God" or "Son of Man," one question needs to be answered: does God have a son? The Old Covenant confirms that He does:

> Who has ascended to heaven and come down? Who has gathered the wind in his fists? Who has wrapped up the waters in a garment? Who has established all the ends of the earth? What is his name, and what is his son's name? Surely you know! (Proverbs 30:4).[324]

Clearly, the poetic language of Proverbs is describing God in the first four sentences. This passage closes by asking what is the name of the son of the one "who established all the ends of the earth?" Thus, the Old Covenant confirms that God has a son. (Please also see Psalm 2:7, Isaiah 9:6, and Zechariah 12:10.)

Son of God and Son of Man

However, it gets a bit tricky here. The two terms, "Son of God" and "Son of Man," are used throughout the Bible to allude to two different facets of the Messiah prophesied in the Old Covenant. Contrary to what one may presume, the first title, the "Son of God," refers to the Davidic lineage of the Messiah—or in other words, the "human" aspect of the Messiah. In Ancient Israel when kings were appointed, they were anointed with oil. As you will recall, "Messiah" means "anointed one." The first Book of Samuel describes the process of Saul being anointed as (an earthly) King of Israel.

> Then Samuel took a flask of oil and poured it on his head and kissed him and said, "Has not the Lord

anointed you to be prince over his people Israel... And this shall be the sign to you that the Lord has anointed you to be prince over his heritage," (1 Samuel 10:1).[325]

The prophecies of the future Messiah found in the Old Covenant reiterate that He would be a descendant of David. One of the places where this is recorded is in the first Book of Chronicles. The prophet Nathan speaks to David on behalf of God, and refers to David's descendants as having a throne "forever:"

> Go and tell my servant David, "Thus says the Lord...
> When your days are fulfilled to walk with your fathers,
> I will raise up your offspring after you, one of your
> sons, and I will establish his kingdom. He shall build a
> house for me, and I will establish his throne forever. I
> will be to him a father, and he shall be to me a son," (1
> Chronicles 17:4, 11-13).[326]

Through this promise (and others[327]), scholars have been able to determine that the Jewish Messiah was prophesied to be a descendant of David. Boyarin describes this belief in further detail. He writes:

> The anointed, earthly king of Israel is adopted by God
> as his son; the *son of God* is thus the reigning, living
> king of Israel, (emphasis added).[328]

The first line in the Gospel of Mark reiterates that this is precisely who Yeshua is claiming to be: "The beginning of the Gospel of Jesus Christ, the *Son of God*," (emphasis added).[329]

The second label often given to Yeshua in the gospels is the "Son of Man."[330] After looking at the greater context of the Old Covenant, it is clear that this title refers to a messianic passage in the Book of Daniel with two characters.[331] The first is the Ancient of Days (God in heaven). The second is a younger, *divine being in a human form*, who is given total power and dominion by the Ancient of Days. This second character is believed to be the prophesied Messiah. Boyarin explains that it is "one of the oldest theological ideas in Israel" to believe God is the Father in heaven and also a "second God" as a man on Earth:

> The Messiah-Christ existed as a Jewish idea long before the baby Jesus was born in Nazareth. That is, the idea of a *second God* as viceroy to God the Father is one of the oldest of theological ideas in Israel... these ideas were not new ones at all by the time Jesus appeared on the scene, (emphasis added).[332]

In other words, this idea of a divine Messiah, or "Son of Man" in addition to a heavenly God was not a new concept to the ancient Jewish population. When Yeshua called Himself the Son of Man, the Jewish community knew exactly what He meant.[333] This is apparent when after being asked if He was the Son of God, Yeshua responded by saying, "You have said so. But I tell you, from now on you will see the *Son of Man* seated at the right hand of Power and coming on the clouds of Heaven," (emphasis added), (Matthew 26:64).[334] After this answer, the high priest ripped his robe, and declared this to be reason enough to call for Yeshua's death.[335]

Despite the high priest's misunderstanding, Yeshua fulfilled both the role of Son of God and Son of Man, and is the prophesied Messiah of Israel. Thus, He was fully-God and fully-man, just as Boyarin confirms the Jewish population expected the Messiah to be.

Can God Take the Form of a Man?

Some believe God could never take the form of a man (through Yeshua). However, there are many passages in the Old Covenant that confirm God *has* taken the form of a man.[336] One such passage is found in the Book of Genesis. It is recorded that Jacob wrestled with a *man,* and then says that he saw *God* face to face:

> And Jacob was left alone. And a *man* wrestled with him until the breaking of day... He said to him, "What is your name?" And he said, "Jacob." Then he said, "Your name shall no longer be called Jacob, but Israel, for you have striven with God and with men and have prevailed." So Jacob called the name of the place 'Peniel' saying, "For I have seen *God* face to face, and yet my life has been delivered," (emphasis added), (Genesis 32:24, 27-28, 30).[337]

This passage describes that God came to Earth in the form of a man to wrestle with Jacob.

This is not the only instance recorded in the Old Covenant where God takes the form of a man. In the Book of Genesis, three "men" approach Abraham and one of them is referred to as "Lord:"[338]

> And the Lord appeared to him by the oaks of Mamre, as he sat at the door of his tent in the heat of the day. He lifted up his eyes and looked, and behold, three men were standing in front of him. When he saw them, he ran from the tent door to meet them and bowed himself to the earth and said, "Oh Lord, if I find favor in your sight, do not pass by your servant," (Genesis 18:1-3).[339]

There are many other passages in the Old Covenant depicting God coming to Earth as a man.[340]

The Plurality of God

Some may be a little confused as to how God could still be God *and* come to Earth as Yeshua (or how there could be a plurality of God).[341] It should be initially noted that if there is a God who transcends time and space, we would not be able to fully comprehend His nature and identity. However, we are able to come to a basic understanding of the plurality of God through many Old Covenant verses.[342] One such verse is in the narrative of the beginning of creation recorded in Genesis, the first chapter of the Bible. It is recorded that:

> Then God said, "Let *us* make man in *our* image," (emphasis added), (Genesis 1:26).[343]

Who was with God at the time of creation? To whom was God referring to by saying "us" that would have been in the same *image as God?* Could it not be His Son?

The prophetic Book of Zechariah likewise affirms that God the Father has sent the LORD to live among us on Earth.

> "For I am coming and I will live among you," declares the LORD... "And you will know that the LORD Almighty has sent me to you," (Zechariah 2:10-11).[344]

Since this passage says that the LORD has sent the LORD, it seems as if there are two different forms of God (and one form of God who will "live among" us). The New Covenant notes that Yeshua was sent by God the Father to live among us on Earth, fulfilling this messianic prophecy.[345]

Additionally, when asked what the most important commandment was, Yeshua responded that it was the Shema.[346] The Shema is perhaps the most well-known prayer in Judaism, and refers to multiple forms of God united as one. This famous prayer from Deuteronomy refers to God in the plural in two places:

Shema Yisrael, Adonai eloheynu, Adonai echad.
Hear, oh Israel, the Lord our God, the Lord is one,
(Deuteronomy 6:4).[347]

First, this passage uses the Hebrew word "Adonai" which is the plural word for Lord. It also uses the word "eloheynu" which literally means "our Gods." Judaism makes it clear that there is only one God, so these words cannot be referring to more than one God. Perhaps it is referring to three forms of God united as "one"—God the Father in heaven, the Son of God on Earth (Yeshua), and the Spirit of God.

This passage also includes the word "echad" at the end to describe the oneness of God. The use of the word echad also denotes that this prayer is referring to different forms of God united as one. Echad is translated as one but literally means "complex unity," i.e., God is a "complex unity." Scripture also refers to a husband and wife becoming echad when they wed.[348] That is, they are still two people but they are also united together as one. In this prayer the same is being said about God—He is a complex unity; united as one. Yachid could have been chosen for the word "one" but was not. This seems to be because Yachid means "singular" or "only." So this famous prayer seems to clearly be referring to multiple forms of God united as one.

Finally, in the Old Covenant Book of Isaiah, the triune nature of God is referred to in one sentence—Father, Son, and the Spirit of God (Holy Spirit).

> Draw near to me, hear this: from the beginning I (Yeshua) have not spoken in secret, from the time it came to be I (Yeshua) have been there. And now the Lord God has sent me (Yeshua), and his Spirit, (parentheticals added) (Isaiah 48:16).[349]

The speaker of this passage cannot be God the Father, as the passage states that, "God has sent me." Yet, the speaker was also present "from the beginning," or, during the creation of the world. As was discovered in the Genesis verse above, the "us" at the beginning of creation refers to God and His Son. The speaker in this verse (who we have clarified is Yeshua) describes that His (God's) Spirit has also been sent. Thus, there are *three* dimensions of God described in one verse in the Book of Isaiah in the Old Covenant.

As was already mentioned above, the long-awaited prophesied Messiah who would establish a New Covenant was thought to be divine (from the messianic prophecy in Daniel 7).[350] This belief was also taken from such prophecies as those found in the Book of Isaiah where it is written that a son would be considered a "Mighty God:"

> For to us a *child* is born, to us a *son* is given; and the government shall be upon his shoulder, and his name shall be called Wonderful Counselor, *Mighty God,* Everlasting Father, Prince of Peace, (emphasis added), (Isaiah 9:6).[351]

Clearly the scriptures refer to God in the plural, so there must be more than one form of God. If Yeshua were the prophesied Messiah, then He would have taken on more than one form and been both fully-God and fully-man.

OLD COVENANT PROPHECIES REGARDING THE MESSIAH FULFILLED BY YESHUA

There are over 300 prophecies in the Old Covenant pertaining to the Messiah of Israel. Anyone claiming to be the Messiah would have to fulfill every single one of these prophecies.[352] Some are specific and include such things as: the Messiah would be born in Bethlehem[353] as a descendent from the tribe of Judah;[354] He would enter Jerusalem riding on a donkey;[355] and He would be betrayed for 30 pieces of silver.[356] Of the many individuals who have claimed to be the Messiah, Yeshua is the only man who has ever even come close to fulfilling these prophecies.[357] In fact, many of the potential "messiahs" did not fulfill the most basic and straightforward prophecies.[358]

Some have argued that these fulfilled messianic prophecies are insignificant. They believe Yeshua simply desired to be the Messiah, so He adapted His life to fit the part. Yeshua theoretically could have manipulated some of the prophecies (e.g., remained silent before his accusers[359] and spoke in parables).[360] However, He had no control over many of the prophecies (e.g., lots were cast by His enemies for his garments;[361] a close friend betrayed him;[362] buried in the tomb of a rich man).[363] The statistical likelihood of Yeshua fulfilling just 8 of the over 300 prophecies is a 1 in 100,000,000,000,000,000 chance.[364] No matter how successful Yeshua could have supposedly been in making Himself look like the Messiah, He simply could not have manipulated things in such a way that He was able to fulfill *every* prophecy. Neither

He nor His followers had any control over many of the events that fulfilled the messianic prophecies in the Old Covenant.

It should be acknowledged that the Bible, or any religious text for that matter, could be contorted to perpetuate a particular agenda. The below listed prophecies are often dependent upon understanding the eventual fulfillment by Yeshua. In other words, after witnessing the life, death, and resurrection of Yeshua, His disciples were better able to understand the messianic predictions.[365] These prophecies *alone* may not convince you of the divinity of Yeshua. However, anyone attempting to disprove Yeshua as the Messiah must provide an explanation as to how He was able to fulfill every single prophecy. Cumulatively, these prophecies provide incredible evidence that Yeshua is the Messiah.

In the following section, we will review five of the over 300 prophecies fulfilled by Yeshua. These five prophecies are that the Messiah would:

Prophecy 1:   Heal the Sick
Prophecy 2:   Undergo a Horrific Death
Prophecy 3:   Be Executed Before the Destruction of the Second Temple
Prophecy 4:   Be Raised From the Dead
Prophecy 5:   Atone for the Sins of Humanity

To determine the significance of these prophecies, we will first (1) review the Old Covenant verse in which the prophecy was originally written hundreds of years before it was fulfilled by Yeshua, then (2) document the New Covenant verse in which Yeshua fulfills the Old Covenant prophecy. For those who are still leery of any biblical evidence (despite its proven historical accuracy as was demonstrated in Chapter 4), we will also (3) note where evidence for Yeshua's fulfillment of prophecy is documented outside the Bible.

As I believe will be clear, the mere coincidence of Yeshua fulfilling every single prophecy is simply too unlikely to be the most reasonable explanation.

Prophecy 1: The Messiah Would Heal the Sick.

Old Covenant Reference: Isaiah 35:5-6

> Then the eyes of the blind shall be opened, and the ears of the deaf unstopped; then shall the lame man leap like a deer, and the tongue of the mute sing for joy.[366]

Fulfillment: Yeshua Healed Many People.

New Covenant Reference: Matthew 15:30

> And the great crowds came to him, bringing with them the lame, the blind, the crippled, the mute, and many others, and they put them at his feet, and he healed them.[367]

Non-Biblical Reference: "Antiquities of the Jews" by Josephus

> At that time there appeared Jesus, a wise man. For he was a *doer of startling* deeds, a teacher of people who received truth with pleasure, (emphasis added).[368]

Even individuals such as Josephus (who opposed Yeshua), documented that He was a miraculous man.[369] As is recorded in the four gospels, during the ministry of Yeshua, He often healed the sick.[370]

Prophecy 2: The Messiah Would Undergo a Horrific Death.

Old Covenant Reference: Psalm 22:16-18

> A company of evildoers encircles me; they have pierced my hands and feet- I can count all my bones-they stare and gloat over me; they divide my garments among them, and for my clothing they cast lots.[371]

Old Covenant Reference: Isaiah 52:14

> As many were astonished at you-his appearance was so marred, beyond human semblance, and his form beyond that of the children of mankind.[372]

Fulfillment: Yeshua was Executed by Crucifixion.

New Covenant Reference: Matthew 27:35-37

> And when they *had crucified him*, they divided his garments among them by casting lots. Then they sat down and kept watch over him there. And over his head they put the charge against him, which read, "This is Jesus, the King of the Jews," (emphasis added).[373]

*Non-Biblical Reference: Lucian of Samosata
Letter "The Death of Peregrine"*

> The Christians, you know, worship a man to this day-the distinguished personage who introduced their novel rites, and was crucified on that account.[374] [375]

What makes this prophecy about Yeshua even more remarkable is that the above two referenced Old Covenant verses (Psalm 22 and

Isaiah 52) were written hundreds of years before crucifixion was used by the Roman civilization![376] Although these ancient Jewish writers may not have understood the exact process by which the Messiah would be killed, their descriptions align with and describe the crucifixion process. To presume that these events would just happen to occur in the life of Yeshua seems highly unlikely.

Prophecy 3: The Messiah Would be Executed Before the Destruction of the Second Temple.

Old Covenant Reference: Daniel 9:26

> After the sixty-two weeks, an *anointed one shall be cut off* and shall have nothing. And the people of the prince who is to come *shall destroy the city and the sanctuary* (emphasis added).[377]

Fulfillment: Yeshua was Crucified Around 30 CE, Forty Years Before the Destruction of the Second Temple (which occurred in 70 CE).

New Covenant Reference: Luke 23:46

> Then Jesus, calling out with a loud voice, said, "Father, into your hands I commit my spirit!" And having said this he breathed his last.[378]

Non-Biblical Reference: "Annals" by Tacitus

> Therefore, to squelch the rumor, Nero created scapegoats and subjected to the most refined tortures those whom the common people called "Christians," [a group] hated for their abominable crimes. Their name comes from Christ, who, during the reign of Tiberius,

had been executed by the procurator Pontius Pilate. Suppressed for the moment, the deadly superstition broke out again, not only in Judea, the land which originated this evil, but also in the city of Rome.[379]

Daniel 9:26 predicted that the Messiah would "be cut off" (die) and *then* the "city" (Jerusalem) and "sanctuary" (Second Temple) would be destroyed. As noted by Tacitus in the above writing, Yeshua was crucified during the "reign of Tiberius… by the procurator Pontius Pilate."[380] As you will recall, in Chapter 4 we discussed that a stone has been discovered, verifying Pontius Pilate ruled around 30 CE. Thus, Tacitus has confirmed that Yeshua was crucified in approximately 30 CE as the gospels have recorded. Again, the Romans destroyed Jerusalem and the Second Temple in 70 CE.

Since Yeshua was executed in approximately 30 CE, He died before the destruction of the Second Temple. The above referenced messianic prophecy in Daniel claims that the Messiah would die before the destruction of the Second Temple. Again, the life and death of Yeshua is consistent with Old Covenant prophecies.[381]

Prophecy 4: The Messiah Would Be Raised From the Dead.

Old Covenant Reference: Psalm 16:10

> Because you will not abandon me to the realm of the dead, nor will you let your faithful one see decay.[382]

Fulfillment: Yeshua was Resurrected from the Dead.

New Covenant Reference: 1 Corinthians 15:3-4

> That Christ died for our sins in accordance with the Scriptures, that he was buried, and he was raised on the third day.[383]

Non-Biblical Reference: The empty tomb, over 500 witnesses, the commitment of the disciples amidst intense persecution (imprisonment, torture, and death), and no corpse ever being found (see the previous chapter for more explanation).

Yeshua was resurrected, just as Psalm 22 foretold, and the New Covenant passages and non-biblical sources cited in the previous chapter confirmed. Again, this alone may not convince you that Yeshua was the Messiah. However, the significance of His ministry and the events following it, as well as the hundreds of other fulfilled prophecies and other confirmations I have and will discuss, do strongly support the claim.

Prophecy 5: The Messiah Would Atone for the Sins of Humanity.

Old Covenant Reference: Isaiah 53:5-6

> But he was pierced for our transgressions; he was crushed for our iniquities; upon him was the chastisement that brought us peace, and with his wounds we are healed. All we like sheep have gone astray; we have turned-every one-to his own way; and the LORD has laid on him the iniquity of us all.[384]

Old Covenant Reference: Jeremiah 31:31-34

> "The days are coming," declares the LORD, "when I will make a *new covenant with the people of Israel* and with the people of Judah. It will not be like the covenant I made with their ancestors when I took them by the hand to lead them out of Egypt, because they broke my covenant, though I was a husband to them," declares

the LORD. "This is the covenant I will make with the people of Israel after that time," declares the LORD. "I will put my law in their minds and write it on their hearts. I will be their God, and they will be my people. No longer will they teach their neighbor, or say to one another, 'Know the LORD,' because they will all know me, from the least of them to the greatest," declares the LORD. *"For I will forgive their wickedness and will remember their sins no more,"* (emphasis added).[385]

Fulfillment: Through the Sacrifice of Yeshua, We Have Been Made Righteous in the Eyes of God.

New Covenant Reference: 1 Peter 2:24

He himself bore our sins in his body on the tree, that we might die to sin and live to righteousness. By his wounds you have been healed.[386]

New Covenant Reference: Hebrews 9:12, 22

He (Yeshua) entered once for all into the holy places, not by means of the blood of goats and calves but by means of his own blood, thus securing an eternal redemption… Indeed, under the law almost everything is purified with blood, and without the shedding of blood there is no forgiveness of sins, (parenthetical added).[387]

Non-Biblical Reference: Jewish writings regarding the Yom Kippur miracles (lots from urns, scarlet thread, and Temple Doors) say that they occurred for the first 40 consecutive years following Yeshua's death, indicating that God rejected the Yom Kippur animal sacrifice. Why were the sacrifices rejected? Because a perfect blood sacrifice by Yeshua had already been accomplished (this is explained in the next section).

＊＊

The Old Covenant reiterates that the Messiah would bring restoration between human beings and God.[388] Yeshua, being both the Son of God and the Son of Man, was able to make this atonement. Understandably, this is a grandiose claim to make that, without evidence, would be a matter of mere speculation.

The above listed prophecies and their fulfillment are a statistical anomaly. For some, they alone do not prove that Yeshua is the Messiah. As it was with proving the resurrection, however, if we examine the *compilation* of evidence, it seems far more reasonable to conclude that Yeshua *is* the Messiah. In the following section, we will analyze how the recordings of miraculous acts by the ancient rabbis (these rabbis were adverse witnesses to the resurrection), provide us with powerful evidence further validating that Yeshua is the long-awaited prophesied Messiah.

MIRACLES PROVING THAT YESHUA IS THE PROPHESIED MESSIAH

The Old Covenant is filled with stories of individuals acting immorally. Abraham did not trust God to give him a child and slept with his maidservant.[389] Moses was a murderer.[390] David committed adultery, and then murdered to cover it up.[391] Even reflecting on our own lives, we will see these patterns of immoral behavior (although hopefully, they are not nearly as drastic as these situations). We try to be patient, but when someone cuts us off in traffic, patience is often not our first response. We try to be kind and unselfish, but when it comes down to "us or them," we all too often choose ourselves.

Clearly everyone, including the biblical patriarchs, is not entirely good. In recognizing universal moral inadequacies, the ancient Jewish High Priests would offer sacrifices and perform rituals to atone for their sins. The sacrificial requirements recorded in the Old Covenant were performed in the Temple and were quite extensive.[392] In 70 CE, shortly following the death of Yeshua, the Romans destroyed the Second Temple. Without a place to perform these atoning blood sacrifices, there was no longer a procedure that could be used to take away our sins and restore our relationship with God.[393] That is, unless Yeshua was the perfect sacrifice.[394] God, who is eternal and transcends time, promised throughout the Old Covenant that one day there would be a "new covenant" with the people of Israel (and the world), or a new means by which God would "forgive (our) wickedness" and we would be able to enter into a relationship with Him.[395] The clearest Old Covenant passage where this is promised in Jeremiah 31:31-34, which was quoted in the preceding section.

If Yeshua is the Messiah and our sins are truly are forgiven, we can finally enter into the presence of God without the High Priest having to perform any animal sacrifices in the Temple (which, since the destruction of the Second Temple, can no longer be performed). If Yeshua is the Messiah, then God will have forgiven all "wickedness" and "remembered (our) sins no more."[396] As you will see in the following section, there is extremely powerful evidence that this is exactly what has happened.

The History of Yom Kippur

Yom Kippur, or the Day of Atonement, is considered the most holy day of the year in Judaism. As the name suggests, this is a day set aside to ask for the forgiveness of God (atonement) for our sins. This belief comes from the verse in the Old Covenant, "For on this day shall atonement be made for you to cleanse you. You shall be clean before the LORD from all your sins," (Leviticus 16:30).[397]

To understand the significance of Yom Kippur, we first have to understand ancient Jewish culture. Within the First and Second Temples was the Holy of Holies, which was considered to be the dwelling place of God.[398] The Holy of Holies was separated from the rest of the Temple by a veil. The High Priest was the sole individual permitted to enter the Holy of Holies. The only day he could enter the Holy of Holies was on Yom Kippur.[399]

Before entering the Holy of Holies, the High Priest first sacrificed a young bull as a blood offering to atone for the sins of himself and his family. He would sprinkle some of the blood of the bull on the Mercy Seat within the Holy of Holies.

The High Priest would then choose two goats, and determine which goat was to be killed as an offering to God and which was designated the "scapegoat." The blood of the goat chosen as the sacrifice was sprinkled on the Mercy Seat to atone for the sins of the children of Israel (the Jewish population). The High Priest would then take the second goat (the scapegoat) and declare the sins of the Jewish population on its head, and send it into the wilderness to remove the sins of the people from the camp. (Oy—a lot of rules in the sacrificial system!)

Ancient rabbinic writings offer compelling evidence that Yeshua is the Messiah and that Yeshua's death was the perfect sacrifice that provided redemption and forgiveness for all people. Two such writings that confirm these events are in the Talmud and Zohar. Both of these documents are central authoritative documents in Judaism, and thus, are writings from adverse witnesses.[400] These writings discuss three different miracles lasting for *40 consecutive years* after the death of Yeshua and before the destruction of the Second Temple.

Miracle 1: Same Lot Drawn From Urns
Miracle 2: Scarlet Thread Did Not Turn White
Miracle 3: The Temple Doors Continually Opened

Miracle 1: Same Lot Drawn from Urns

Each year on Yom Kippur, the priest drew lots out of an urn to determine which goat would be the scapegoat, and which would be the sacrificed goat. One lot had inscribed upon it "L'Ha Shem" which means "For the LORD," and the other "L'Azazel" which means "For the scapegoat." It was believed that if the "For the LORD" lot was drawn with the right hand of the priest, God accepted the Yom Kippur sacrifice. If the "For the scapegoat" lot was drawn with the right hand, God did not accept the offering.[401]

According to the *Tractate Yoma 39b* of the Talmud, which was written by the ancient rabbis, the "For the scapegoat" lot was drawn with the priest's right hand each year for 40 consecutive years from approximately 30 CE (the approximate date of the crucifixion of Yeshua) to 70 CE![402] This signified that God had rejected the animal sacrifice. Some may attribute this anomaly to chance, but the statistical likelihood of that happening for 40 consecutive years is greater than 1 to 1 *trillion*! It seems a more reasonable explanation for this incredible anomaly is that an animal sacrifice was no longer needed as Yeshua had made a perfect atoning sacrifice for our sins.

Miracle 2: Scarlet Thread Did Not Turn White

During the same 40 years, Jewish scribes recorded yet another sign signifying God's rejection of the animal sacrifice. Traditionally, part of a scarlet cloth was tied to the horn of the scapegoat, and the other half was tied to the Temple Doors. Some years the thread would turn white, and other years it would remain scarlet. It was believed that if the thread turned white, then the sins of the people were forgiven.[403] This is consistent with the Old Covenant verse, "Though your sins are like scarlet, they shall be as white as snow; though they are red like crimson, they shall become like wool," (Isaiah 1:18).[404]

For the 40 years after the death of Yeshua (in approximately 30 CE) until the destruction of the Second Temple (in 70 CE), the cloth remained scarlet, again indicating that the animal sacrifice had not been acceptable to God and that He did not forgive the sins of the people based on that sacrifice. This rejection is verified in the Babylonian Talmud:

> Forty years before the destruction of the sanctuary, the lot did not come up in the right hand, and the thread of crimson never turned white.[405]

The rejection by God of this long-standing Yom Kippur animal sacrifice seemed to indicate that animal sacrifice was no longer needed to atone for the sins of the people. Why? Once again, the compelling answer is that Yeshua's death had served as the perfect blood sacrifice required.

After the destruction of the Second Temple in 70 CE, Yom Kippur animal sacrifices had to cease as there was no place to perform them. To compensate for this inability to perform animal sacrifices, rabbis decided that purification could be achieved through personal good works. The problem with this approach was addressed earlier in this chapter—no one is completely righteous, and we all have done wrong in the eyes of a perfect God. Further, the same chapter in Leviticus describing the Yom Kippur sacrifices reiterates that this sacrificial practice endures *forever*. It is recorded, "And this shall be a statute forever for you, that atonement may be made for the people of Israel once in the year because of all their sins," (Leviticus 16:34).[406]

So, if God truly rejected all Yom Kippur sacrifices during the years 30-70 CE, one would assume there had been a replacement that was acceptable to God. It seems clear from these miracles surrounding the urns and scarlet thread that God was letting the people know that animal sacrifices were no longer necessary.

There must have been an acceptable sacrifice that atoned for all sins. Clearly, an alternative was needed as the destruction of the Temple has left us with no place to perform blood sacrifices for the last 2,000 years. If Yeshua were truly God in the flesh, He would be completely pure. He could have atoned for the sins of everyone by fulfilling both the role of scapegoat and sacrificial goat. The timing of God's rejection of the animal sacrifices for 40 consecutive years seems like much more than mere coincidence.

Miracle 3: The Temple Doors Continually Opened

Yet another miracle noted in ancient Jewish literature pertains to the Temple Doors. For 40 years beginning in approximately 30 CE, these doors swung open *every* night on their own accord. This miracle is recorded in the Babylonian Talmud:

> Forty years before the destruction of the sanctuary... the doors of the courtyard would open by themselves, until Rabban Yohanan b. Zakkai rebuked them. He said, "Temple, Temple, why will you yourself give the alarm [that you are going to be destroyed? You don't have to, because] I know that in the end you are destined to be destroyed. For Zechariah b. Eido has already prophesied concerning you: 'Open your doors, Lebanon, that fire may devour your cedars,'" (Zechariah 11:1).[407][408]

This passage acknowledges that the Temple Doors continually opened by themselves during this time. Rabbi Johanan b. Zakkai, the leading Jewish authority at the time, understood this significance. He refers to the prophetic words in the Book of Zechariah regarding the destruction of the Temple.[409] He correctly prophesied this as a sign of impending doom, as the Romans destroyed the Second Temple in 70 CE.

The significance of the Temple doors opening every night for the 40 years following Yeshua's crucifixion and resurrection should not be undervalued. The Old Covenant details lengthy and extensive requirements to be met before being able to enter the Temple, and ultimately into the presence of God. However, the doors opening every night for 40 years (14,600 days—if you were wondering), seems to indicate that *all* were now allowed to enter into a close and personal relationship with God. It was no longer just the high priests deemed pure who would be given close access to God. Through the sacrifice of Yeshua, we are all able to enter into a personal relationship with God.

WHAT DO MODERN-DAY RABBIS AND SCHOLARS HAVE TO SAY ABOUT YESHUA?[410]

Ancient scriptures and rabbinical interpretation of Yeshua as the Messiah may not convince some (even though they are written by adverse witnesses to the resurrection). Some may reason that ancient rabbis did not have our modern-day understanding and intellectualism to guide them as they researched Hebrew Scriptures. Even if you have a tendency to reject anything old as being uneducated and primitive thinking, there are still many passionate, intelligent, and esteemed modern-day Rabbis who fervently believe Yeshua is the prophesied Old Covenant Messiah. The powerful testimonies in this section are from the book *Twelve Sons of Israel*.

Orthodox Rabbi Chil Slostowski, a Talmudic scholar and professor at a rabbinical seminary who had previously encouraged his students to despise Yeshua, had his life radically changed after reading the New Covenant. He describes:

While reading (the New Covenant) I felt the creation of a clean heart and of a right spirit within me [Ps. 51:10] and there was new light [Ps. 119:105]. Like a thirsty man drinks greedily when he has found a spring of fresh, cool water, so I drank in page after page of the New Covenant…With every page there grew and deepened the conviction that Yeshua is the Messiah prophesied to us Jews…

I knelt down and prayed… And for the first time prayed in the name of YESHUA. After that prayer there came into my heart such peace and joy as I had never experienced before, not even on Yom Kippur (the Day of Atonement)…

Never before had I felt such certainty of reconciliation with God as I felt then and, thank God, that feeling has remained with me ever since. I knew and had no doubt whatever that the Lord Yeshua is the long-prophesied Messiah of the Jews and the Saviour of the world, and I came to see in Him my personal Redeemer, (parentheticals added).[411]

What a transformation! Someone who had spent his entire academic career studying and teaching the Old Covenant and rabbinic writings saw parallels between the Yeshua described in the New Covenant and the Old Covenant prophesies of the Messiah. He opened his heart, and God met him and filled him with peace and joy like he had never before experienced. Countless people, myself included, have had similar experiences.

Another excerpt from *Twelve Sons of Israel* is a message to the rabbis of Israel delivered by Rabbi Daniel Zion, who was initially credentialed as a chief rabbi of Bulgaria and later as a rabbi in Jaffa, Israel.

Therefore, I tell you, even if I were the only one to believe in Yeshua as the Messiah, I would not consider that to be an imagination; but now I see that millions of men acknowledge Him, among them thousands of highly educated Jews. Some rabbis too, believe in Yeshua as the Messiah. Have they fallen prey to imagination and deception...

Yeshua did nothing but good; He called Israel to repentance and to the Kingdom of God. He did many signs and wonders, as no prophet before Him. He wished to unite people; that they should love each other and also their enemies. Thus He wished to build a bridge between Israel and the nations; there should be peace between them and the prophecies of Isaiah and all the prophets be fulfilled, that the Lord would be King over all the earth.[412]

Rabbi Zion recognizes the miraculous deeds, peace, and love of Yeshua, as well as the "thousands of highly educated Jews" who believe that Yeshua is the Messiah. Rabbi Zion challenges all skeptics to simply open their hearts as he did, so that the light of God will fill them with His abundant love.

Lastly, consider the eloquent words of Rabbi Isaac Lichtenstein, a chief rabbi of Hungary who led Jewish congregations for 40 years before reading the New Covenant for the first time. After reading it, he became a passionate follower of Yeshua. He also notes how mistaken he had been and acknowledges:

I had thought the New Testament to be impure, a source of pride, of hatred, and of the worst kind of violence, but as I opened it, I felt myself peculiarly and wonderfully taken possession of by a sudden glory, a light flashed through my soul. I looked for thorns, and gathered roses, I discovered pearls instead of pebbles;

instead of hatred, love; instead of vengeance, forgiveness; instead of bondage, freedom; instead of pride, humility; instead of enmity, conciliation; instead of death, life, salvation, resurrection, heavenly treasure.[413]

In a letter to his son, Rabbi Lichtenstein also wrote:

From every line in the New Testament, from every word, the Jewish spirit streamed forth light, life, power, endurance, faith, hope, love, charity, limitless and indestructible faith in God.[414]

When Jews become followers of Yeshua they are not "converting to Christianity." They are doing something very Jewish—finding the Messiah of Israel who died for the salvation of Jews and the world. It is not a matter of conversion, but completion—they have found the Messiah who embodies the fulfillment of the Old Covenant prophecies! It is undeniable that the foundational beliefs of Christianity are deeply rooted in Judaism

In fact, Ron Cantor has written an excellent book entitled *Identity Theft*, which details how the "Jewishness" of Yeshua has been lost over the centuries. In his analysis, Cantor notes how three key events celebrated in Christianity coincide with Jewish holidays: Yeshua's crucifixion, His resurrection, and the sending of the Holy Spirit (Ruakh HaKodesh). These world-changing events occurred on Passover, the Feast of Firstfruits, and Shavuot, respectively. It seems the message is clear: it is Jewish to follow Yeshua, as it was the Jewish people who would have been most aware of these three holidays.

As has been previously noted, extra-biblical texts affirm that Yeshua was executed on Passover.[415] The Gospel of John records that Yeshua's crucifixion occurred as the Jews were slaughtering their Passover lambs.[416] Yeshua was the blood sacrifice, whose atoning blood sacrifice on Passover allows us all to be able to enter into a relationship with God.[417] Further, Yeshua's resurrection was on the Jewish celebration of the Feast of the Firstfruits, which was celebrating the blessing of the barley harvest coming forth from the ground.[418] On the day of this festive harvest celebration, Yeshua also rose from the ground.[419] Finally, the Holy Spirit was sent by God on the Festival of Shavuot, which was a celebration commemorating the wheat harvest. Wheat was celebrated as a blessing of nourishment; the Holy Spirit is a daily source of spiritual nourishment. It seems quite likely that these historic world-changing events all coincided with Jewish holidays as an emphatic proclamation by God that it is indeed very "Jewish" to believe in Yeshua as the Messiah.[420]

Contrary to what you may have heard, the belief that Jews cannot, should not, and do not believe in Yeshua as the Messiah is unsubstantiated. Many respected Jewish leaders and scholars see the prophecies about the Jewish Messiah fulfilled through Yeshua.

RELIGION IS NOT THE ANSWER

Although many people believe our sins can be forgiven by the performance of good deeds, this is simply inconsistent with biblical texts.[421] We are told in both the Old and New Covenants that we are in need of a savior. We are utterly lost to our sin, which separates us from a completely good and pure God, and we are in desperate need of a Messiah.[422] Even if you do not wish to take the Bible's word for it—do you truly believe you are 100% good? Do you think you will ever attain a level of perfect morality? Imagine telling the IRS, "I pay my taxes *most* years," or presenting a case in front of the judge claiming that, "I did not kill *most* people." Or, "I do not speed *most* of the time." Could you imagine an outcome in which that would be accepted as a sufficient excuse? If there is a good and pure God, we all fall woefully short of His standards. None of us can even follow the Ten Commandments.[423] As the evidence has shown, Yeshua is the Messiah to bridge the gap between our failures and God's goodness, and allow us all to enter into a relationship with God.

Faith in Yeshua is not about religious activities and customs; it is about your personal relationship with the Messiah. There is no hierarchy of people; we *all* need the sacrifice of Yeshua.[424] If you decide to attend weekly services and act loving and gracious one hour or one day per week—then I have failed in communicating Yeshua's message of forgiveness and love. Similarly, if you go to a synagogue, learn a few Hebrew words, and proudly wear the badge of "Jew" or "Messianic Jew," believing that these things somehow make you more righteous and holy than those who do not—again, I have failed to communicate Yeshua's true love and grace. Although you do not have to convert to Christianity to believe in Yeshua, you have to do something much less challenging, but much more humbling—you have to come to the realization that there is nothing you can do to earn God's forgiveness.

This begins with understanding our desperate need of a savior. This idea is often utterly opposed to what our society perpetuates. Often, we view ourselves as "not as bad as person X." The reality is that if there is a God who is perfectly holy and perfectly good, we all fall short in His sight. Understanding our own fallibility and limitations is perhaps one of the first "steps" to understanding the magnitude of the importance of the sacrifice and resurrection of Yeshua. Religion tells you that you can save yourself by being good. However, this is not about religion. No religious activity or charitable acts (whether they be Christian, Jewish, or any other custom) will bring you any closer to salvation and a relationship with God than turning from your ways and recognizing the depth of the sacrifice of Yeshua.[425]

THE LOVE BEHIND THE SACRIFICE

However, our recognition of the depth of the sacrifice of Yeshua is meaningless if we do not understand the profound love behind this act. Paul Harvey, a popular American radio broadcaster from the 1950s through the 1990s, shared a story entitled "The Man and the Birds." This story truly illustrates the love God exhibited by sending His Son to Earth to show us how to live, both through His rich teachings and by His sacrificial life. I will summarize this story below.

There is a man who was good and kind, but who did not believe in the incarnation (God coming to Earth in the form of a man). One Christmas Eve, the man finally admitted that he could not attend the traditional Christmas church service with his family, reasoning that it would be hypocritical to attend because of his disbelief. So he chose to stay home alone.

While his family was at church, it began to snow heavily. The man heard repetitive tapping on his window and saw some birds attempting to seek shelter in his home amidst the terrible storm. The man had a barn where his children kept their pony that could provide the necessary shelter for these poor birds.

The man quickly prepared himself for the wintery storm, and made the formidable trek to the barn. He knew exactly what they needed for their own protection even though they did not. He flung open the doors and turned around expecting to see the birds immediately fly in. To the man's dismay, the birds remained where they were. He turned the light on in the barn but that did not convince them of what they needed.

He returned to his house to fetch breadcrumbs in an attempt to entice them to enter—again to his disappointment. They ignored and kept flailing around in the cold and snow outside of the protection offered. Their situation was worsening. He tried to shoo them into the barn, but the birds simply scattered in every direction.

The man realized that these birds were afraid of him; he was simply a strange and terrifying creature that they did not understand. He scared them by what he was doing; and because he was so big, they feared him and did not trust him even though he really cared about them.

He thought, "If only I could be a bird and mingle with them and speak their language. Then I could tell them not to be afraid. Then I could show them the way to the safe warm barn, but I would have to be one of them so they could see and hear, and understand."

Just then, the church bells began to ring, and the man had a sudden realization. God tried to show us the way but we didn't get it. So, He became a man, just like us to show us how to save us from life's difficult situations. The truth of what God did for us hit the man, and he sank to his knees in repentance and gratitude with a new, profound grasp of the love of God.[426]

This story depicts the love of our God and His concern for us. As the evidence has clearly shown, Yeshua is the long-awaited prophesied Messiah who came to show us the way because of His profound and incredible love for us. He desires that we would all seek His shelter. Yeshua came to Earth, lived among human beings, and died for us. Despite being wrongfully executed, He cried out to God on the cross saying, "Forgive them, for they know not what they do," (Luke 23:34).[427] Instead of hatred, Yeshua demonstrated love and forgiveness. What a wonderful God we have the opportunity to serve!

CHAPTER 8

CAN A GOOD GOD CO-EXIST IN A WORLD FILLED WITH SUFFERING?

Perhaps you have found the evidence presented for the existence of God, the historical validity of the Bible, and the resurrection of Yeshua to be convincing. But maybe you still have an issue with the *idea* of God. Perhaps you feel that God cannot exist because there is so much evil and suffering in the world. Or, maybe you do not want to think about God (even if He does exist), because of evil and suffering. After learning about devastating acts of terror, witnessing mass destruction in the wake of a tsunami, or hearing of the tragic death of a young child, often an inner conflict ensues. We wonder if there is a good God, then why does He allow so much suffering? The struggle to overcome this conflict and achieve inner consistency (dubbed by scholars as cognitive dissonance) is understandable. We want our beliefs to be harmonious (i.e., God is good and the world is good, or God is bad and the world is bad). After observing the evil and suffering in our world, we experience discomfort (or dissonance), which can lead to an erroneous analysis of God.

Some have proposed that evil and suffering are the biggest obstacles to overcome in order to believe in God. Often these arguments stem from three conclusions drawn from the fact that because evil exists:

Argument 1:   God Does Not Exist
Argument 2:   God is Not Good
Argument 3:   God is Not Powerful

In the following pages, I will attempt to alleviate this dissonance and answer the question: how can a good and powerful God co-exist in a world filled with evil and suffering?

Argument 1: Since Evil Exists, God Does Not Exist

Some believe that because evil and suffering are rampant in our world, the evidence for the existence for God is nullified. In other words, they feel the evidence presented in Chapter 2 is irrelevant because of the existence of evil.[428] However, how can we make a distinction between good and evil unless both of these contrasting realities exist? We all recognize that darkness is nothing more than the absence of light. Similarly, evil is simply the absence of good. If there were no standard of good, then we would have no means of distinguishing something as evil. Renowned author Ravi Zacharias solidifies this point, and notes that evil actually proves the existence of God:

> When you say there's too much evil in this world you assume there's good. When you assume there's good you assume there's such a thing as a moral law on the basis of which to differentiate between good and evil.

But if you assume a moral law, you must posit a moral Law Giver, but that's Who you're trying to disprove and not prove. Because if there's no moral Law Giver, there's no moral law. If there's no moral law, there's no good. If there's no good, there's no evil.[429]

Without some measurability of goodness, we would fail to recognize evil. Reasoning that God does not exist because there is evil in the world is comparable to declaring that you are an orphan because you do not like your parents. To determine the existence of God, we must examine the *evidence* for a creator.[430] All the existence of evil can do is make us not understand or particularly like God. As noted by Zacharias, evil actually provides evidence that there is a contrasting "good" force in the universe.

The Reality of the Alternative

Often those who adamantly reject the existence of God while using suffering as a major reason for their disbelief do so from a naturalistic mindset (or the belief that the natural world is all that exists). These arguments have been at the forefront of a lot of popular atheistic rhetoric (and is particularly evident in the work of Dawkins, Dennett, Harris, and the late Hitchens). They claim that if God existed, He would have to be barbaric and ruthless to allow so much suffering. However, if we are truly only biological beings whose ancestors just happened to have the perfect conditions to eventually lead to our existence billions of years later, then the issue of suffering is irrelevant. Suffering is simply another happenstance, an unfortunate result of the random world in which we live.

In his book *Walking with God Through Pain and Suffering*, author Timothy Keller describes how a naturalistic culture is the first culture that simply does not provide a reason for suffering. As you will see in this chapter, even though a naturalistic mindset does not provide a reason for pain and suffering, they are nevertheless *major* themes throughout the Bible. In other words, a naturalistic culture may not address the reason for suffering, but the Bible does.[431] Other cultures in the past have attributed suffering as being for some higher purpose, thus bringing comfort to those in distress.[432] However, if we are all here by chance, if we are all beings with no greater purpose, then our suffering is irrelevant and meaningless as nothing matters. Everything is irrelevant; life has no higher purpose. If we were never born, if human beings never populated the earth, if the earth had never formed, our suffering would ultimately not matter. Along with our suffering, we would simply be mists in the wind of the cosmos. Keller summarizes the argument often advanced by atheists that there is no greater purpose to our suffering. He specifically addresses Richard Dawkins' views and writes:

> In short, suffering does not mean anything at all. It is an evil hiccup. Dawkins insists that to deny that life is "empty, pointless, futile, a desert of meaninglessness and insignificance" is right, and to look to any spiritual resources to find purpose or meaning in the face of suffering is "infantile."[433]

However, the belief in a higher purpose, which Dawkins describes as being "infantile," is actually much more rational than the alternative. To respond to this, Keller relays the testimony of Andrea Palpant Dilley. Dilley explains how she left the church because she was mad at God about all of the suffering and injustice that she saw in the world. She could not overcome the dissonance between worshipping a good God as the creator, and recognizing abundant evil in the world. But she soon realized that she was being illogical. She writes:

> I came back to church because of that same struggle. I realized that I couldn't even talk about justice without

standing inside of a theistic framework. In a naturalistic worldview, a parentless orphan in the slums of Nairobi can only be explained in terms of survival of the fittest. *We're all just animals slumming it in a godless world, fighting for space and resources. The idea of justice doesn't really mean anything.* To talk about justice, you have to talk about objective morality, and to talk about objective morality, you have to talk about God, (emphasis added).[434]

Or said more simply, without God she realized that there was no point to suffering and no basis for being upset that suffering exists. Taking it a step further, if there is no greater point to life, does it even matter if we try to stop injustice? Why should we care about others if it is simply "survival of the fittest?" If we live in a world in which all we see is a result of the natural, is not injustice simply an unfortunate result of the randomness of life?

I am not proposing that someone who does not believe in God is an immoral or an unjust person. I know many individuals who do not believe in God that are incredibly charitable and are greatly bothered by injustice, even more so than many theists. But from where does that sense of "right and wrong" stem? To declare something to be evil is to propose that there is a contrasting greater good. Nature is neutral, and to look at the world in a naturalistic mindset is to ultimately see suffering as a natural byproduct of this neutrality. Not only is the idea that God cannot exist because of evil not supported by evidence, the argument itself proves that it is implausible. Again, if evil exists, there is some sort of contrasting good that also exists. Rejecting God because of the existence of evil is an irrational reaction, and it fails to address or analyze the overwhelming evidence for the existence of God. Our opinions of God have no bearing on whether He exists.

Argument 2: Since Evil Exists, God is Not Good

Some of you may be asking, "How do we know that God is the 'goodness' that contrasts evil in our world?" Some may believe that the evidence may point to the existence of a creator, but question how any God who created this world riddled with evil can be good, or a God worthy of our worship. Some may reason the characteristics of the creator would be reflected in its creation. By this train of thought, it is assumed the creator of our world is evil because we witness such widespread suffering throughout His creation.

The Issue of Free Will

What if it is not God who is performing acts of evil, but humankind? We probably view ourselves as primarily good and not responsible for the turmoil of the world. We may confess to acting immorally at times: we may fib to a boss, work with another student on an online test, or occasionally lift supplies from the office for our own personal use. However, because we compare ourselves to others with our own biased standards, we often do not believe that we are *evil*.

Free will, or the conscious decisions we make, calls into question our own goodness. Clearly the Holocaust was caused by the choices of Adolf Hitler and the Nazis who supported him. Could an all-powerful God have stopped them? Yes. But had He intervened, He would have been interfering with their free will.[435] Would we want that? Probably—as long as God was putting a halt to the actions of our enemies. But what if God stopped *our* actions? What if God prevented us from pursuing our dream career? What if He intercepted any money we earned above whatever covered our most basic needs because He thought we should donate the balance to the poor?

We may think that God should interfere with the free will of those with whom we disagree, or those who are performing acts of evil, but never with *our* free will because we are not evil. But where would a "good" God draw the line? Should He thwart the desires of the Democrats or the Republicans?

When left to our own interpretation, our standard of "good" versus "evil" will always benefit our own personal agendas and mindsets. Understanding that we are not perfect or particularly "good" may be a hard pill to swallow. If there is an external standard of perfect goodness, we all fall woefully short. If God is the antithesis to evil, His goodness goes beyond anything we can even begin to conceive.

Is Evil Actually Necessary?

However, some may wonder why God did not create beings that possessed free will, but had no desires to act evilly. At first blush, we may think that we have solved the issue of much of the evil in the world! The world would have no political parties or country boundaries; instead, all people would work toward the same noble agenda. What a utopia that would be, right? Notably, if the only choice we have is the choice to do good, then the notion of "good" becomes irrelevant as it is simply doing what we are programmed to do. It is not really *good*; it is just *the only option*.

Acts of kindness like bringing my wife flowers would lose sentimentality, as I would simply be performing an act mandated by my creator. Shoveling the driveway for an elderly widow next door would likewise lose any impact. Humanity would be numb and unable to convey love and thoughtfulness. Our spouses and neighbors would cease to feel any authentic emotions. Well-known 20th century author C.S. Lewis draws a similar conclusion:

> Because free will, though it makes evil possible, is also the only thing that makes possible any love or goodness or joy worth having.[436]

Imagine a scenario in which the government was to completely eliminate all sources of unhealthy food, and then force the entire population to take a serum that would change our taste buds to only desire food that is nutritious. The golden arches of McDonalds would be no more, and people would quickly forget the taste of grandma's homemade apple pie. All citizens would be given their food from the government, and our population would become overwhelmingly healthier. We would have no more childhood obesity; heart disease and cardiac arrest cases would plummet, and the average life expectancy would increase 10 years.

I will admit, this kind of a world may sound ideal to those seeking a healthier human race. In this scenario, however, the choice of eating healthy is eliminated. You are no longer "eating healthy," you are simply "eating" as there is no alternative. Even temporary reprieves where you can overindulge a little would not be possible. Free will, or the ability to make choices, is wholly reliant upon *options*. Without options, any "choices" we would make would be irrelevant—they would simply be the only option.

It is our decision whether we bite into a piece of cheesecake or a carrot. It is our decision to exercise regularly or live a more sedentary life on the couch. It is our decision which political or religious affiliation we align ourselves with. And ultimately, it is our decision if we choose to love and serve our Creator. Although the world may seem as if it would be immeasurably better if we had no free will, taking away our free will would deprive us of our humanity.

If God withheld an individual's choice to act evilly, we would not be *good*; we would be *robots*. The love we would feel from our parents, siblings, spouses, children, and grandchildren would be inauthentic—it would simply be a result of people's programming rendering them essentially mindless. Similarly, we would not be choosing to love and serve God; instead, we would be doing what we were programmed to do. In His infinite wisdom and love, God gave us the ability to make our own decisions. Unfortunately, we do not always make wise choices. But how precious it is when we choose good over evil, and when we choose to love God over our own personal agendas.

I find two analogies noted by others to be illuminating. Blaming God for the problems of the world seems similar to blaming a nearby soap manufacturer for the smelly people in the world who choose not to use the soap that is available to them. Similarly, if we see an artistic masterpiece, we may heap praises on the artist. However, if we later observe that someone defaced and vandalized the masterpiece, we do not blame the artist. We blame the person who defaced and vandalized. There is evil and suffering in this world because of actions inconsistent with God's instructions. We ultimately need to hold ourselves—not God, the artist—accountable for the vandalism that we have done.

Argument 3: Since Evil Exists, God is Not Powerful

Perhaps you agree that God exists and that it is possible for Him to be good even with all of the suffering in our world, but maybe you assume that God cannot do anything about evil. You may believe that He set the world into motion and is now incapable of doing anything about the (at times) horrendous results.

The reasoning behind this argument is particularly difficult for me to understand. Is it plausible to believe that God exists, was the creator of the world, but has somehow *lost* His powers? How did this happen? Although few may make this claim in such obvious terms, it is an argument that is frequently suggested. Some may believe in a supernatural creator, but they do not believe in divine *power*. After creating the world, what was God's "kryptonite" that took away His power?

Further, we attempt to understand these concepts of good versus evil with our own finite capabilities based on our limited years on Earth. But if there were truly an all-powerful, all-knowing, and all-good eternal creator, why would we be able to understand His reasons and categorizations of good and evil?

Relativistic concepts of what is good and what is evil are clear in American politics. Democrats typically believe a higher taxation rate on the wealthy is beneficial for the overall well-being of the population. They believe increasing governmental spending will pump new money into the economy, generate new businesses, and ultimately increase the availability of good jobs. Republicans typically believe lower taxation on businesses and the wealthy will increase entrepreneurial risks taken, which will establish more businesses, and ultimately employ more people.

Depending on your own life experiences, upbringing, current ideals or opinions, you may have very passionate beliefs about which taxation plan will work. These beliefs may evolve and shift over the course of your life. As human beings we all have the ability to choose what to believe (free will), and determine our own opinions on what is good and what is evil. However, we merely have a "worm's eye" view of the world. We are small, finite beings trying to understand a vast, infinite world.

Think of all the times in history when humans have perceived matters incorrectly. We now know that the earth is round, not flat, the heart is the center of the circulatory system, not the liver, and the notorious "mom and dad fantasy" of Freudian psychology has lost the credibility it held less than a century ago. I remember thinking that one day I would have life all figured out—that day has yet to come. If you are over 40, you have probably reflected humorously on the naiveté upon which you based your decisions when you were a teenager. Revisiting the errors of our human intellectual history can help begin to deflate our, at times, immense egos.

Some may claim that if God exists, He is vindictive. They may propose that stories such as Noah's Ark and Abraham potentially sacrificing his son as evidence that God is a bully. However, we have such a finite and miniscule understanding of what is happening in the universe. If there is an all-knowing, all-powerful creator, we will never understand His reasoning during our lifetimes. And just because we cannot conceptualize His reasons does not mean that He is not all-powerful. We may hypothesize reasons for why God may or may not do something, but ultimately, we will never know.[437]

In a comparable way, a fish lives within the realm of an ocean and has no grasp of the world above. Even if the fish gets a glimpse of our world, he will have no comprehension of the complexity of the environment in which we all live. A fish certainly cannot understand life outside the realm of the sea, just as we humans cannot totally relate to the sphere outside of our own realm.

Could you imagine the mind of a being that transcends time? Who was there before time began? Often we naively assume that having the mind of God would be like becoming a more intelligent version of ourselves—when in reality, God is in a realm that we cannot even come close to comprehending.

With all of this in mind, do we truly believe that we can understand with our limited mental capabilities the entire plan for our vast and infinite world? Trying to do so seems akin to a fish trying to relate to our lives and the rest of the world. Do we think so highly of ourselves to reason that if *we* cannot understand the world, then *God* must be powerless?

It requires faith to understand that human rationality cannot grasp the understanding of an infinite being. But everyone must believe in something. Whether you put your faith in Allah, Yeshua, Buddha, or rationality, something is functioning as your standard of truth. And the reality is, God's standard of good and evil may not coincide with our own limited understanding.

OVERCOMING SUFFERING

Joseph is a character in the Old Covenant whose story is riddled with both moral and natural evil.[438] The story of Joseph demonstrates how a seemingly unbearable situation can be used to bring about deliverance and protection. Scholars have noted that the life of Joseph exhibits remarkable parallels and foreshadowing for the life of Yeshua: Joseph was rejected by his brothers; was believed to be dead but was later discovered alive; and was ultimately able to save countless lives.[439]

Joseph's brothers became jealous of him as they thought that he was their father's favorite son. So they threw Joseph into a pit and told their father (Jacob) that Joseph was dead. Joseph was eventually sold into Egyptian slavery. While working, the wife of Joseph's master, Potiphar, continually attempted to seduce Joseph. After he rejected her advances many times, she became enraged and convinced her husband that Joseph had tried to take advantage of her. Joseph was thrown into prison because of the lie of Potiphar's wife. While in prison, Joseph earned a reputation for extraordinarily accurate dream interpretation. This ability led Pharaoh to release Joseph from prison so that he could serve as Pharaoh's own personal dream interpreter.

Pharaoh shared one of his dreams with Joseph. After carefully listening, Joseph interpreted it to mean that there would be seven years of plentiful harvest, followed by seven years of drastic famine. So Joseph suggested that Egypt collect one-fifth of the harvest during the times of plenty to prepare for the times of famine. Following this interpretation, Pharaoh made Joseph his "second-in-command" and gave him immense wealth, authority, and prestige over all of Egypt. Joseph was 30 years old when he was finally given this tremendous authority. Through his interpretation of the Pharaoh's dream, Joseph was able to save countless lives as Egypt was prepared for the famine brought on by the drought.[440] But to get there, Joseph suffered greatly due to the rejection by his brothers, being enslaved in Egypt, and an unjust imprisonment.

Despite all of the evil unjustly inflicted on him, Joseph still proclaims to his brothers who initially enslaved him:

> Do not fear, for am I in the place of God? As for you, you meant evil against me, but God meant it for good, to bring it about that many people should be kept alive, as they are today, (Genesis 50:19-20).[441]

Similarly, some of you may have heard the story of Corrie ten Boom, a Dutch Christian sent to the concentration camps because of her commitment to the Jewish people.[442] Even in those atrocious conditions, she was able to thank God for the lice in the camps because the Nazis no longer kept a close eye on her room for fear of catching the lice. Even after the horrors of enduring the Holocaust, Corrie ten Boom still exclaims, "There is no pit so deep that God's love is not deeper still."[443]

As our faith and trust in God grows despite the circumstances in the world around us, so too does our strength and peace:

> But they that wait for the LORD shall renew their strength; they shall mount up with wings as eagles; they shall run, and not be weary; they shall walk, and not faint, (Isaiah 40:31).[444]

Joseph and Corrie ten Boom can stand as an inspiration to us all. Despite their struggles, they understood that God would work everything for good if they continued to trust Him.

There was a time in my life when I felt like God was letting a bad thing happen to me and I felt like my prayers were going unanswered. In the spring of 2007, I began to experience discomfort in my lower back. It was so uncomfortable that I was forced to virtually eliminate my exercise routine. When my wife and I and two of our children traveled to Yosemite National Park, we were unable to hike on the long trails because I could only walk about 100 yards. I fervently prayed that God would heal my back. No response; no healing.

One month later, I was diagnosed with coronary artery disease. One of my main arteries was 95% blocked, and two of my collateral arteries were 100% blocked. All told, I had 13 blockages. Interestingly, our bodies sometimes create new collateral arteries as alternative routes for blood travel, and fortunately my body did that. Nonetheless, I needed immediate open-heart surgery for six coronary bypasses. Had I been able to hike in Yosemite, as I desired, I may have died right there from a heart attack.

When I felt God was not answering my prayers to heal my back, He had a bigger and better plan—to save my life and strengthen my faith. I was frustrated that I had such extreme back pain and could not enjoy the trails with my family because I could not understand at the time why He would not simply heal my back. In hindsight, I know that He wasn't healing my back because He knew my bad back would save my life!

It is often easy to proclaim the goodness of God when we are comfortable, but when things begin to get uncomfortable, we want explanations. If we only trust God when our lives are easy, we don't trust Him—we are simply trusting comfort, which is obviously easy to do. We like to be in control of our own lives, but unfortunately, we often have no control when a problem or catastrophe presents itself.

When the diagnosis comes back—and it is cancer, or you gaze at where your house once stood before the tornado swept through, it is difficult to accept that God loves you. Choosing to understand our own limited grasp on the world may not be entirely comforting during times of hardship. We want tangible answers for our seemingly pointless suffering. We want to understand why this all-knowing, all-loving, perfectly good God did not take into consideration our happiness.

This is the baseline fallacy in our thought process. God does not promise happiness. There is no scripture reinforcing the notion that the *purpose* of God is to please us. On the contrary, it continually reiterates that the purpose of mankind is to gain a relationship with Him. We are called to "Love the Lord your God with all your heart and with all your soul and with all your might," (Deuteronomy 6:5).[445] Ultimately, we must consider why we ask the question, "Why does God allow suffering?" Are we asking because we believe we understand the grand scheme of humanity better than God? Or are we asking because we believe that the ultimate purpose of God is to perpetuate our personal happiness? Perhaps our frustration lies not in our attempt to rationalize the morality of God, but with our own realization that we are not God.

YESHUA: THE GAME CHANGER

The harsh reality of suffering would leave a bitter sting if it were not for the sacrifice of Yeshua.[446] Thus far in this chapter, we have addressed the logical disconnects that arise between a good God and a world filled with suffering. We can conclude that without an all-good God, we would be unable to distinguish good from evil. Without an all-knowing God, we would have no ability to determine what is "good" using our finite, often self-focused minds. We have learned that because God is all-powerful and all-knowing, He is worthy of our trust. Even in the midst of despair, we can cling to these truths. We can understand that our happiness is not the goal as happiness is based upon current happenings; instead, joy comes from trusting God regardless of what is happening. However, while we are experiencing suffering and unanswered prayers, this rationale and logic can still leave a gaping hole.

Often people wonder whether God cares about our suffering. Although the purpose of God is not to make us happy, the sacrifice of Yeshua tells us that He did not remain distant from our suffering. God did not require us to fend for ourselves. Yeshua came to Earth, both fully-God and fully-man. He came to Earth to bear our sins through His atoning blood sacrifice.[447] God does not ignore our pleas for peace or gaze disdainfully at our problems. The sacrifice of Yeshua says that God cares so deeply about our suffering, that He became a suffering servant for each of us.

The life of Yeshua was filled with suffering.[448] He did not puff up His chest and proclaim that He did not feel pain—He was honest. He wept at the death of a friend.[449] He cried out to God in pain while on His execution stake.[450] We are invited, through the sacrifice of Yeshua, to enter into a similar deep and personal relationship with God, even in the midst of our pain.

It is important to understand the logic behind our faith and to have reasons for why we believe what we do. In some communities where religion is passed down like family heirlooms, this understanding is becoming increasingly important in the face of more vocalized opposing beliefs.

However, rational arguments and logic without the love of Yeshua are often empty, especially in times of suffering. Yeshua has bridged the gap between our imperfection and the perfection of God. He has made the way for us to be able to enter into an enduring relationship with the Creator who can relate to our suffering on a personal level.

Believing in Yeshua will not solve all your problems. It does not guarantee a bigger house, a better credit score, a nicer boss, or the perfect marriage; the challenges of life will continue. However, viewing the world through Yeshua's sacrifice will change the perspective by which you see everything and give you an unparalleled peace amidst the storms of life.

> Who will separate us from the love of the Messiah? Trouble? Hardship? Persecution? Hunger? Poverty? Danger? War? No, in all these things we are superconquerors, through the one who has loved us. For I am convinced that neither death nor life, neither angels nor other powers below, nor any other created thing will be able to separate us from the love of God which comes to us through the Messiah Yeshua, our LORD, (Romans 8:35, 37-39).[451]

EPILOGUE

NOW WHAT?

Hopefully you have found the material compiled in this book to be helpful in further developing your understanding of God, the Bible, and Yeshua. This information is meant to be a basic foundation, and is by no means comprehensive. As such, I encourage you to continue to research the topics that you found interesting. In this life, no one will ever discover even a fraction of all there is to know about God.

> Behold, these are but the outskirts of his ways, and how small a whisper do we hear of him! But the thunder of his power who can understand? *Job 26:14* [452]

Often, our minds can be our biggest obstacle in our quest to understand truth. We have certain biases that can be challenging to dislodge. Open your heart and let God know that you want to know the truth. If you seek God, you will find Him.

You will seek me and find me, when you seek me with
all your heart. *Jeremiah 29:13* [453]

Making a daily habit of reading the Bible will be an invaluable
source of insight and wisdom in your life as you grow in your
relationship with God. The stories and instructions written in the
Bible are not just historically accurate, but are also extremely powerful. They can help to implement change in your life, and the lives
of those around you.

All Scripture is breathed out by God and profitable for
teaching, for reproof, for correction, and for training in
righteousness. *2 Timothy 3:16* [454]

However, individual research and learning, even when reading the
Bible, will only take you so far. Finding a community of people ear-
nestly seeking God is vital. Misleading and incorrect information
about God and Yeshua is everywhere; having other around to help
you discern the truth is crucial.

The early followers of Yeshua did life together.[455] They did
not simply attend a service one day a week for one hour and expect
that they fulfilled their weekly quota of "community time." Even
though many of them had lived with Yeshua for three years and saw
Him after He was resurrected from the dead, they understood the
importance of surrounding themselves with other believers.

Growing up, I always dreaded going to synagogue. However,
when I began attending Messianic congregational services, I felt
tremendous unity and tranquility at the gatherings. I began looking forward to the weekly Shabbat service that was filled with life,
and was far more than simply reading prayers from a prayer book. I
understand that your first attempt to get plugged into a faith community may not be as wonderful as mine was. But please, do not
give up! We cannot do this alone—I strongly encourage anyone who

wants to grow in his or her relationship and understanding of God to get plugged into a community of believers who truly love Yeshua.

> So there are many of us, and in union with the Messiah we comprise one body, with each of us belonging to the others. *Romans 12:5* [456]

Seek God continually, making prayer a part of your daily life. I find that the more I pray, the more vibrant and alive my relationship with God becomes.[457] Just as the glory and magnificence of heaven is unimaginable, so too is a relationship with God in your daily life. I continue to be in awe of the ways God works in my life.

> Don't worry about anything; on the contrary, make your requests known to God by prayer and petition, with thanksgiving. Then God's shalom (peace), passing all understanding, will keep your hearts and minds safe in union with the Messiah Yeshua, (parenthetical added). *Philippians 4:6-7* [458]

All too often, belief in Yeshua is confined to the idea that we want to believe in Him to get to Heaven. Although eternal joy rooted in an enduring relationship with our Creator in Heaven is *extremely important*, it is not the only blessing we can receive. I have experienced far more peace and love through my personal relationship with Yeshua than I ever imagined was possible. Understanding the grace of God, the depth of the sacrifice of Yeshua, and experiencing the comfort and wisdom imparted through the Holy Spirit (Spirit of God)[459] far exceeds anything this world has to offer.[460] Like any relationship, it is an ongoing process. The more diligently we seek and honor Him, the more we learn and receive. As we grow in our relationship with God, our understanding of the fullness of His love likewise grows.

If you have not accepted Yeshua as your LORD, I would encourage you to do so.[461] Truly desiring to know the truth 23 years ago, I asked God if He existed. Since then, God has gradually and radically transformed my life.[462] God wants to meet you right where you are. You do not have to clean up your life before you can come to Him. The Creator of the universe desires a personal relationship with you.

Is there any reason to wait?

APPENDIX A

CAN ALL RELIGIONS BE CORRECT?

Why is it so important to understand and discover spiritual truth? When it comes to religious and spiritual matters, some feel that there is no such thing as absolute truth. While it is obvious that different religions adhere to different beliefs, some feel despite these disparities that all religions can be correct. This is due to the belief that truth is subjective and can vary depending on the circumstances. This belief is loosely defined as relativism. Relativism contends that since we all come with our own unique perspectives, it is narrow-minded to claim that there is such a thing as absolute truth in the spiritual realm. Everything is relative; nothing is absolute. Those are appealing thoughts and it would be nice if they were true. But are they?

As discussed in Chapter 1, it is very clear that there is absolute truth. The physical world is filled with examples. We all need oxygen to live. We cannot claim breathing oxygen may work for some, but breathing helium will work for others if they choose the "helium path." Clearly, oxygen is an absolute truth necessary for our survival.

However, are there also uncompromising truths in the spiritual world? Although individuals have many different beliefs about the specifics of the spiritual realm, it is undeniable there are some *foundational* spiritual truths that surpass subjectivity. For example, either God exists, or does not exist. Either Yeshua is God in the flesh, or He is not. Both sides of these paradoxical realities cannot be true.

As will be shown in the following pages, religions vary drastically in their foundational doctrines regarding spiritual beliefs. These inconsistencies render the "all-spiritual-beliefs-are-correct" philosophy as being illogical. The irony is that everyone believes in absolute truth, even if his or her opinion is that there is no absolute truth. So, even those who advocate for spiritual relativism accept their beliefs as absolute truth. I encourage you to discard the tendency to cling to a theory because it is the "most inclusive" as we all tend to do, and instead let a thoughtful analysis guide your verdict. When the weight of the evidence points in one direction, we must follow the path of reason. Tolerance of those with whom we disagree is admirable, but denying the truth is unwise.

CAN ALL SPIRITUAL BELIEFS BE CORRECT?

There are six major religions, or spiritual belief systems in the world: atheism, Buddhism, Christianity, Hinduism, Islam, and Judaism. You may find that your beliefs do not align perfectly with any of these six spiritual beliefs, as this is not a comprehensive list of all beliefs. As you may notice, I did not create a separate column for "Messianic Judaism" despite identifying as a Messianic Jew. Although I practice Jewish heritage and tradition, my spiritual beliefs more closely align with Christianity than with most *modern-day* Jewish beliefs.[463] As you will recall from Chapter 7, however, I believe the foundation of Christian beliefs are very, very Jewish, as Yeshua is the long-awaited Jewish Messiah.

That being said, the simplification of these beliefs does not undermine the overall analysis. I believe it will become readily apparent that the core tenants adopted by these six belief systems cannot *all* be correct because they maintain opposite stances on foundational spiritual issues. Similarly, it is important to note that the following analyses of these belief systems are based on generalizations about complex ideologies, and there are branches within these groups whose beliefs may drastically vary.[464]

One of the more evident points of distinction among spiritual belief systems is whether they believe in God or a higher power. As you can see from the following chart, there is clear inconsistency. Therefore, it defies logic to contend that they are all correct.

BELIEF IN GOD OR A HIGHER POWER

Spiritual Belief	Belief in God or a Higher Power
Atheism	No
Buddhism	No
Christianity	Yes
Hinduism	Yes
Islam	Yes
Judaism	Yes

If God or a higher power exists, then two of the above spiritual beliefs are mistaken. If God does not exist, then four are off the mark. As was analyzed in Chapter 2, there is persuasive evidence that God *does* exist. Even if you disregarded this evidence, it is still clear that all six spiritual belief systems cannot be correct, unless you believe that the benefits of trusting in God or any higher power are merely psychological. If you assume the benefits of a relationship with God are not real, then the belief in God is essentially a placebo (i.e., any benefit is psychological and comes from our minds rather than a real source ultimately putting you in the "God doesn't exist" category). It seems clear that either:

1. God is a myth and any peace we may think God brings is purely psychological; or
2. God is real but does not bring true peace; or
3. God is real and truly brings peace.

People can obviously believe whatever they want, but it is evident that there are certain ultimate spiritual truths. The *ramifications* of these beliefs are open to interpretation, but the undeniable truth is that with these contradictory beliefs, everyone cannot be right. Gravity still exists regardless of your opinion about its existence. Even if someone does not believe gravity exists, if he or she walks off a 10-story building, they will soon discover the truth. Similar to learning if gravity exists, it seems wise to learn whether God exists, and how His rules impact us for this life and the next.

WHO WAS YESHUA?

As demonstrated in Chapters 5 and 6, there is astounding historical evidence that Yeshua truly lived 2,000 years ago and was crucified by the Romans. There is also proof that a historical event occurred that led many hundreds of witnesses to profess Yeshua's divinity, some of who maintained their beliefs until their own torture and death. We also discovered that the only probable historical event that could have led to this conviction was that Yeshua was resurrected from the dead. The hundreds of fulfilled messianic prophecies and ancient Jewish miracles discussed in Chapter 7 verified that Yeshua was not only raised from the dead, but that His death and resurrection stood as the perfect atoning sacrifice for our sins against God.

Even if you remain unconvinced or disregard the evidence of Chapter 7, it is still apparent that many spiritual belief systems make important and substantial distinctions about Yeshua. As it was with the contrasting beliefs in God, these beliefs are completely contradictory.

Spiritual Belief	Who was Yeshua?
Atheism	A Jewish man who lived 2,000 years ago and was crucified by the Romans.[465]
Buddhism	A Jewish man who exemplified many traits admired in Buddhism.[466]
Christianity	The Son of God and Messiah.[467]
Hinduism	Some sects believe Yeshua was one of many human incarnations of the God Vishnu.[468]
Islam	A prophet sent by Allah.[469]
Judaism	A Jewish man who was a false Messiah and was crucified by the Romans.[470]

If Yeshua was the Messiah, could He also have been a false Messiah? If Yeshua was a prophet sent by Allah, could He have also been an incarnate form of the Hindu God Vishnu? Can Yeshua be just a prophet *and* God? Clearly not.

It is written in the gospels that Yeshua said, "I am the way, and the truth, and the life. No one comes to the Father except through Me," (John 14:6).[471] If He were just a prophet, than Yeshua overstepped His bounds and misspoke. Despite its cultural taboo, we cannot logically advocate for relativism in the spiritual realm. As discussed in Chapter 5, Yeshua has to be either a liar, a lunatic, or LORD. If Yeshua is LORD, then all religions cannot be correct.

Although religious understanding is important, we must refrain from being swept into the allure of a skewed perception of religious tolerance. There are foundationally different beliefs in each spiritual belief system, and those differences cannot always be reconciled. Yes, focusing on what we have in common with those who have different religious backgrounds and preferences than us is important. As believers in Yeshua, we are called to love those who disagree with our beliefs.[472] Often, one of the best means to be able to truly love those with different beliefs than ours is to be willing to enter into kind-hearted, honest conversations about these differences.

Unfortunately, many believers in Yeshua (myself included) often fail in this endeavor to promote open conversations rooted in love. Please do not let our failures cause you to reject the One who offers forgiveness, peace, and everlasting life. I encourage you to resist the societal inclination to adopt spiritual relativism; be willing to seek spiritual truth. I believe this truth resides through faith in Yeshua. God promises that if you open up your heart to Him, He will reveal the reality of this truth to you. Yeshua said:

> Ask, and it will be given to you; seek, and you will find; knock, and it will be opened to you. For everyone who asks receives, he who seeks finds, and to him who knocks it will be opened, (Matthew 7:7-8).[473]

If you search diligently with an open heart, I believe God will meet you right where you are, and reveal His timeless truths and love to you—just as He did for me.

APPENDIX B

CAN THE BIBLE AND SCIENCE BE RECONCILED?

IS THE AGE OF THE UNIVERSE *THE* ISSUE?

"The more I study nature, the more I stand amazed at the work of the Creator. Science brings men nearer to God." [474]

Some may disagree with Louis Pasteur (who many consider to be the father of microbiology) and believe that the time of harmony between science and God is over. They may advocate that we have simply discovered too much about the world to cling to primitive religious beliefs anymore. As was discovered in Chapter 2, this belief is unsupported by evidence. The natural world *needs* a creator in the same way that the jet engine *needed* Frank Whittle. [475] As we continue to discover more specifics about the natural world, one fact remains the same: everything cannot come from nothing; there must be an eternal creator. [476]

In the general population, however, division between science and religion is often not focused on the issue of the origin of the universe. Often, people believe that there is conflict among traditional biblical interpretations and modern-day scientific discoveries, and focus on issues like evolution and the age of the earth. Evolution was discussed in Chapter 2. As you will recall, although evolution as a scientific process can be reconciled with belief in God, it does not make sense as an all-encompassing theory to explain humanity. Our morality and our emotions simply do not align with a "survival of the fittest" mentality.

However, we have yet to address the issue of the age of the universe. As with evolution, I do not believe that the age of the earth is where the issue *truly* lies. Reflecting on all of the evidence for foundational beliefs in following Yeshua (i.e., the existence of a creator and the historical validity for the life, death, and resurrection of Yeshua), the age of the earth is not necessarily a major priority. In other words, although clearly one group is correct and the other is wrong (the world cannot be both 13.8 billion *and* 10,000 years old), it is not a *core tenant* to believing in Yeshua. There are many followers of Yeshua on both sides of this discussion. Regardless, it is still a common issue, so it is one that I want to address.

Often the argument of the age of the earth stems from whether the Hebrew word "day" written in Genesis should be taken literally to mean a 24-hour day, or figuratively to refer to a period of time or an age. Others with far more scientific and linguistic expertise have written ample material on this distinction, and there are biblical scholars on both sides of the debate. As such, I wanted to present an alternative analysis to support the belief that there are far more similarities between science and biblical texts than one may initially believe.

After studying the order of creation generally accepted in the scientific community, it seems clear that the order of the development of our universe, and the order recorded in the first chapter of Genesis are complementary, *not* contradictory. The biblical account of the order of creation aligns with modern scientific views. My hope for anyone reading this is that any barriers one has standing between science and the Bible may begin to deteriorate, allowing you to find the beginning of the universe to be an awe-inspiring topic on both biblical and scientific platforms. If this is a topic that interests you, I strongly suggest reading Dr. Gerald Schroeder's book *The Science of God.* Dr. Schroeder has a PhD in nuclear physics and earth and planetary sciences from MIT.[477] This entire appendix leans heavily on the findings and analysis of his fascinating book.

BIBLICAL AND SCIENTIFIC ORDER OF THE CREATION OF THE UNIVERSE

Day 1

The universe is created, and light is separated from darkness.

Until relatively recently, individuals debated about the beginning of the universe as a philosophical concept. It was all based on theory, as there was no scientific evidence to support any positions. One such position was from Aristotle, who claimed that time was eternal and there was no beginning.[478]

In the mid-20th century, a groundbreaking discovery brought the debate of eternity into the scientific arena. Scientists found radiation emitted during the formation of the beginning of the universe. Today, this discovery is referred to as the "big bang." This has led scientists to conclude that there *was* in fact a beginning. As Dr. Stephen Hawking, the renowned atheist cosmologist, asserts, "All the evidence seems to indicate that the universe has not existed forever, but that it had a beginning about 15 billion years ago."[479]

The discovery of the big bang has validated the accuracy of the first sentence of the Bible.

In the beginning, God created the heavens and the earth, (Genesis 1:1).[480]

Despite what people believed for centuries, there was a beginning of the universe. Physics Nobel Laureate winner Dr. Stephen Weinberg describes the big bang. He explains that the universe would have been so hot that ordinary matter could not have been held together:

At about one-hundredth of a second, the earliest time about which we can speak with any confidence, the temperature of the universe was about a hundred thousands million [10^{11}] degrees Centigrade. This is much hotter than in the center of even the hottest star, so hot, in fact, that none of the components of ordinary matter, molecules, or atoms, or even the nuclei of atoms, could have held together.[481]

Weinberg goes on to describe that because the makeup of the universe was so hot and dense, darkness and light separated. He describes how suddenly the *universe was filled with light*.[482] This pattern aligns perfectly with what is written in the opening passage of the creation account contained in Genesis.

And God said, "Let there be light," and there was light, (Genesis 1:3).[483]

Scientific discoveries validate the first day of the creation story in the biblical text. There was a beginning, and shortly after, the entire universe was filled with light.

Day 2

The heavenly sky (Milky Way Galaxy) is formed, and water is separated as water on the surface, and water in the sky.

Scientists agree that since the big bang, the universe has continued to expand. This continued expansion has resulted in immeasurable stars and galaxies in the "heavenly sky," the nearest being our Milky Way Galaxy. Schroeder explains how this process supports what is written in the creation story in Genesis. He says:

> The Bible tells that on day two the heavenly firmament took shape... from our vantage, the heavens [galaxies] we see are almost totally composed of stars of the Milky Way's main spiral disk.[484]

So, on day two, the heavenly expanse (or our Milky Way Galaxy) is formed.

> And God called the expanse heaven, (Genesis 1:6-7).[485]

Many scientists believe that water was first introduced to the earth after large asteroids and bodies of mass collided with the earth's surface.[486] As the earth continued to cool, this water began to separate and enter into the earth's atmosphere. This resulted in water on the surface of the earth as well as water in the air. So, waters separated into two entities: water in the atmosphere, and water on the planet, confirming what is recorded in Genesis.

> And God made the expanse and separated the waters that were under the expanse from the waters that were above the expanse, (Genesis 1:7).[487]

To recap, there was a beginning, light was separated from darkness, the stars of the Milky Way Galaxy (the heavenly sky) were formed, and waters were separated between the earth and the atmosphere. Day two of the biblical story of creation is also consistent with the chronological order of the origin of the universe accepted by scientists.

Day 3

Oceans and dry land are separated, and vegetation begins to sprout.

The creation story in Genesis begins with a wide-scope of the entire universe, and continually zooms in on the creation of humankind. Day three is the first "day" whose focus lies solely on Earth. Genesis records that next, oceans and dry land separated. Scientists have discovered that this is exactly what happened.

> Let the waters under the heavens be gathered together into one place, and let the dry land appear, (Genesis 1:9).[488]

Next, Genesis records:

> *Let* the earth sprout vegetation, plants yielding seed, and fruit trees bearing fruit in which is their seed, each according to its kind, on the earth, (Genesis 1:11).[489]

This is the first instance where, initially, Genesis *seems* to be out of order with modern-day scientific findings. During this time, scientists believe that life began as simple single-celled bacteria and algae. Initially, this does not seem to align with the "grass, herb-yielding seed, and tree bearing fruit," version of the story recorded in Genesis. Schroeder describes how there actually is no inconsistency. He explains that:

Molecular biology has discovered that some forms of single-celled algae have as much as one hundred times the amount of DNA (genetic information) per cell as do mammals. A genetic library that large could indeed contain the basic information for the forms of plant life that appeared much later.[490]

In other words, on day three the *ability* for grass, herb-yielding seed, and tree bearing fruit is produced. A key word within this verse is *"Let'* the earth sprout vegetation." To propose that this means the earth is *able* to sprout vegetation (not necessarily flourishing in fields of green at the time) seems to perfectly align with the biblical text. The tree may not have actually begun to grow during this time period, but the molecular seed for its eventual growth is planted. Schroeder clarifies that, "The Bible is interested in plants, but the main focus is the flow of animal life leading to humanity."[491] Only mentioning the "seeds" of plant life in their basic form and not following the entire progression does not invalidate the scientific order, nor does it uproot the traditional biblical interpretation of Genesis.

So far in the creation of the universe, we have seen that there was a beginning, light and darkness divided, the stars of the Milky Way Galaxy were formed, waters were separated between the earth and the atmosphere, oceans and dry land separated, and vegetation was able to sprout. The third day in the biblical creation story continues to align with the scientific chronology of our universe.

Day 4

The sun, moon, and stars become visible from Earth.

Earth scientists have discovered that the earth's initial atmosphere contained much lower levels of oxygen than it does now. They have proposed oxygen levels rose because of increased photosynthetic activity (from such organisms as the single-celled algae mentioned previously). Schroder suggests that this change in the atmosphere not only allowed for life, but also changed the atmospheric visibility of the earth. He proposes, "The further cooling of Earth and the rise in atmospheric oxygen, the atmosphere, formerly translucent, became transparent."[492]

Although the sun and moon were not created during this time, after the changes in the atmosphere, they were able to give light and be seen on Earth. Thus, aligning with Genesis:

> God set them (the sun and the moon) in the expanse of
> the heavens to give light on the earth, to rule over the
> day and over the night, and to separate the light from
> the darkness, (parenthetical added), (Genesis 1:17).[493]

To summarize, there was a beginning of the universe, the universe was filled with light as darkness and light separated. The stars of the Milky Way Galaxy were formed, waters were divided into water in the atmosphere and water on the earth, oceans and dry land separated, the seeds for the ability for vegetation were planted. Finally, the atmospheric levels of the earth changed, allowing the sun, moon, and stars to be seen from Earth. Again, science and the account of creation in Genesis can peacefully coexist.

Day 5

The first animal life appears in the water, followed by winged animals.

Discoveries have led scientists to conclude that life on Earth began in the sea, following the order of creation in Genesis.

> Let the waters swarm with swarms of living creatures,
> (Genesis 1:20).[494]

However, most translations of Genesis 1 claim that birds were created next.

> And let birds fly above the earth across the expanse of
> the heavens, (Genesis 1:20).[495]

Scientists have concluded that birds do not come into the picture until after mammals (which may initially seem to create an inconsistency). However, this discrepancy comes from a translation error.

The Hebrew word translated as "birds" is "owph," which can mean flying creatures, fowl, *insects*, or birds. Scientists affirm that insects were next to come onto the scene on Earth. So, as the Bible is probably referring in this instance to *insects* not to *birds*, it still follows the scientific order of creation.

There was a beginning, the universe was filled with light, the stars were formed, waters were separated between the land and the atmosphere, and then separated into oceans and dry land. Next, the ability for vegetation began, the atmospheric levels changed on Earth, life began in the water, and insects appeared. Day five is still consistent between the biblical texts and modern-day scientific discoveries.

Day 6

The creation of land animals, mammals, and finally human beings.

This order precisely follows suit. Scientists propose that life progressed from water to animals on the land, and eventually to human beings.

> Let the earth bring forth living creatures according to
> their kinds—livestock and creeping things and beasts of

the earth according to their kinds… Let us make man in
our image, after our likeness, (Genesis 1:24, 26).[496]

To sum up, there was a beginning, and the universe was filled with
light. Then the Milky Way Galaxy was formed, waters separated
between the atmosphere and the land, and then from oceans to
dry land. Next, vegetation began to sprout, atmospheric levels
changed, life began in the water, followed by insects, land animals,
mammals, and finally human beings. Genesis and modern-day scientific discoveries are completely compatible.

THE VERDICT

Despite what some may propose, science and the order of
creation are not at odds. A book written 4,000 years ago captured
what scientists are still uncovering today.[497] This does not invalidate the significance of scientific discoveries. The Bible describes
the creation of the universe in 31 verses; clearly there are more
intricate processes occurring during these "days" that scientists
have yet to even scratch the surface of.

I implore you to not get swept away into the notion that to
believe in the Bible, we must suspend scientific knowledge and
turn into uneducated beings. Scientific discoveries continue to
point us towards the magnificence of our Creator God.

Day	Biblical Narrative	Scientific Discoveries
Day 1	The universe is created, and light is separated from darkness.[498]	The big bang marks the beginning of the universe. During this time, light and darkness are separated.
Day 2	The heavenly sky (Milky Way Galaxy) is formed, and water is separated between the ground and the sky.[499]	The universe continues to expand, and the stars of the Milky Way Galaxy are formed. After water is introduced to the earth, it begins to separate from the ground into the atmosphere.
Day 3	Oceans and dry land are separated, and vegetation begins to sprout.[500]	Oceans and dry land separate on the earth. Simple single-celled bacteria and algae begin to form.
Day 4	The sun, moon, and stars become visible from Earth.[501]	Earth's atmospheric levels of oxygen increase as a result of photosynthetic activity making the atmosphere translucent (making the sun, moon, and stars visible from Earth).
Day 5	The first animal life appears in the water, followed by winged animals.[502]	Animal life begins in the water, followed by insects.
Day 6	The creation of land animals, mammals, and finally human beings. [503]	Amphibians, reptiles, mammals, birds, and eventually human beings appear on the earth.

APPENDIX C

ISAIAH 53

When I was first given Isaiah 53 to read (before I was a believer in Yeshua), I was sure that it must have come from the New Covenant. It seemed to perfectly describe the crucifixion and atoning death of Yeshua. To my surprise, I learned that Isaiah 53 was penned by the Jewish prophet Isaiah in approximately 700 BCE (over seven centuries *before* the life, crucifixion, death, and resurrection of Yeshua). To me, this is one of the most awe-inspiring prophecies in the Old Covenant. For an in-depth analysis of how this passage has to refer to the Messiah, please see the section "No Peace on Earth" in Chapter 7.

> Who has believed what he has heard from us? And to whom has the arm of the LORD been revealed? For he grew up before him like a young plant, and like a root out of dry ground; he had no form or majesty that

we should look at him, and no beauty that we should desire him.

He was despised and rejected by men; a man of sorrows, and acquainted with grief; and as one from whom men hide their faces he was despised, and *we esteemed him not*. Surely he has borne our griefs and carried our sorrows; yet we esteemed him stricken, smitten by God, and afflicted.

But *he was pierced for our transgressions*; he was crushed for our iniquities; upon him was the chastisement that brought us peace, and *with his wounds we are healed*. All we like sheep have gone astray; we have turned—every one—to his own way; and the LORD has laid on him the iniquity of us all.

He was oppressed, and he was afflicted, yet he opened not his mouth; like a lamb that is led to the slaughter, and like a sheep that before its shearers is silent, so he opened not his mouth. By oppression and judgment he was taken away; and as for his generation, who considered that he was cut off out of the land of the living, stricken for the transgressions of my people? And they made his grave with the wicked and with a rich man in his death, although *he had done no violence,* and there was no deceit in his mouth.

Yet it was the will of the LORD to crush him; he has put him to grief; when his soul makes an offering for guilt, he shall see his offspring; he shall prolong his days; the will of the LORD shall prosper in his hand. Out of the anguish of his soul he shall see and be satisfied; by his knowledge shall the righteous one, my servant, make many to be accounted righteous, and he shall bear their iniquities. Therefore I will divide him a portion with the many, and he shall divide the spoil with the strong, because he poured out his soul to death and was numbered with the transgressors; *yet he bore the sin of many*, and makes intercession for the transgressors, (emphasis added), (Isaiah 53).[504]

After reading about the historical validity of the crucifixion, death, and resurrection of Yeshua (in Chapters 5 and 6), as well as the significance of His death (in Chapter 7), it seems clear that this passage aligns perfectly with Yeshua.

ENDNOTES

Introduction

[1] Karl Marx's full quote is: "Religious suffering is, at one and the same time, the expression of real suffering and a protest against real suffering. Religion is the sigh of the oppressed creature, the heart of a heartless world, and the soul of soulless conditions. It is the opium of the people."

Marx specifically claimed that the purpose of religion was to create a fantasy for the poor. He believed that because the poor were in an economic disparity that they would never be able to overcome, they had to hope for a better life in the afterlife. As you will be able to determine after reading this book, the weight of the evidence clearly shows that spirituality is much more than just a fantasy.

Marx, Karl. "Critique of Hegel's 'Philosophy of Right.'" *Philosophical Books* 12.3 (1971): 20-21. Web.

[2] Obviously, I did not know at the time that the cathedral I was touring (called St. Peter's cathedral) was actually named after a Jewish man who had lived in Jerusalem.

[3] Isaiah 53:5, 7, 12, JPS

[4] Rose's full, powerful testimony can be read in *Appendix B* of my book *A Lawyers Case for God*.

5   Psalm 22:16-18, Isaiah 7:14, 9:6-7, 53, Daniel 9:24-27, and Zechariah 9:9
    are some of the over 300 prophetic verses in the Old Covenant about the
    Messiah that have been fulfilled through Yeshua. For a more in-depth expla-
    nation of these verses, please read Chapter 7.

6   In the Old Covenant, water was often a sign of purity and cleanliness.
    Ceremonial washings were frequently performed (Exodus 19:10; Leviticus
    8:6; Numbers 31:21-24). Similarly, modern-day Jews often perform the
    mikvah ritual, which consists of ceremonial washings and cleansings that
    have been commanded in the Old Covenant writings.

7   For a listing of modern-day prominent Jews who came to believe in Yeshua
    as their Messiah, please go to http://www.messianicassociation.org/profiles.
    htm. This website notes that there are over 200,000 Jewish believers in
    Yeshua *just* in the United States. The list includes:

    • Rabbi Isaac Lichtenstein, Chief Rabbi of Hungary

    • Rabbi Israel Zolli, Chief Rabbi of Rome

    • Rabbi Daniel Zion, Chief Rabbi of Bulgaria during the Holocaust

    • Rabbi Leopold Cohn, Rabbi in Hungary

    • Niels Bohr, Nobel Prize for Physics

    • William Booth, founder of the Salvation Army

    • John Xeres, Talmudic Scholar

    • Daniel Landsmann, Talmudic Scholar

    • Boris Kornfeld, medical doctor and hero of the Gulag

    • Andrew Mark Barron, Aerospace Engineer

    • Mortimer Adler, Professor at the University of Chicago, and chair-
      man of the Board of Editors of Encyclopedia Britannica.

    • Lawrence Kudlow, U.S. Undersecretary of the Office of Management
      and Budget

8   This concept of the "spiritual realm" will be discussed in-depth in the fol-
    lowing chapter.

9   Some books and resources I recommend are contained in Appendix A in my
    first book, *A Lawyer's Case for God,* which can be purchased on Amazon or
    read for free or purchased at JimJacobBooks.com.

Chapter 1

10   A 2011 Gallup and 2012 Pew Research Study confirm this statistic. Newport, Frank. "More Than 9 in 10 Americans Continue to Believe in God." Gallup Headlines. Gallup, Inc., 3 June 2011. Web.; "Religion and the Unaffiliated." Pew Research Centers Religion Public Life. Pew Research Center, 8 Oct. 2012. Web.

11   A more in-depth discussion of some of the polarizing beliefs of different religions can be found in Appendix A.

12   In the Gospel of John, it is recorded that Yeshua says: "I am the way and the truth and the life. No one comes to the Father except through me," (John 14:6).

These words seem to have eternal repercussions. If we witnessed someone who was attempting to constantly breathe helium, we would stop him or her as his or her actions would be fatal. Why would we not have an even greater urgency to share the love and truth of Yeshua if the ramifications *could* be eternal?

13   The Messiah is described in the Old Covenant as being both a Suffering Servant (Son of Joseph) and Conquering King (Son of David). The Messiah is discussed more in Chapter 7.

The Messiah described as a suffering servant: "When they look on me, on him whom they have pierced, they shall mourn for him, as one mourns for an only child, and weep bitterly over him, as one weeps over a firstborn," (Zechariah 12:10). See also Isaiah 53 in Appendix C for another example of the Messiah as a suffering servant.

The Messiah described as a conquering king: "And in the days of those kings the God of heaven will set up a kingdom that shall never be destroyed, nor shall the kingdom be left to another people. It shall break in pieces all these kingdoms and bring them to an end, and it shall stand forever," (Daniel 2:44). See also Zechariah 6:13 for another example of the Messiah as a conquering king.

Chapter 2

14   MacHale, Des. *Wisdom.* London: Mercier Press Ltd., 2002.

15   Another common debate about whether science and the Bible can be reconciled focuses on the age of the earth. Appendix B illustrates the incredible consistencies between the creation story recorded in the Bible and the

discoveries of science. Evidence has been discovered confirming that the order of creation is the *same* in the Bible and science.

16 Keller, Timothy. *The Reason for God: Belief in an Age of Skepticism*, New York: Penguin Group, 2008. 126. Print.

17 Collins, Francis. *The Language of God: A Scientist Presents Evidence for Belief*, New York: Free Press, 2006. 67. Large Print.

18 The renowned founder of the quantum theory, Max Planck, found incredible evidence for God in his discoveries: "All matter originates and exists only by virtue of a force which brings the particle of an atom to vibration and holds this most minute solar system of the atom together. *We must assume behind this force the existence of a conscious and intelligent mind.* This mind is the matrix of all matter," (emphasis added).

Quoted in Braden, Gregg. *The Spontaneous Healing of Belief: Shattering the Paradigm of False Limits.* Carlsbad, CA: Hay House, 2008. 212. Print.

Originally said by Planck, Max. "The Nature of Matter." Florence, Italy. 1944. Lecture.

19 "A Scientist Caught Between Two Faiths: Interview With Robert Jastrow." Interview. *Christianity Today*, 6 August 1982: n.p. Print.

20 Hawking, Stephen. *A Brief History of Time: From the Big Bang to Black Holes*, Toronto: Bantam Books, 1988. Print.

21 Hawking has explained that he believes the multiverse hypothesis accounts for the intricacies of the universe (a theory which will be refuted later in this chapter). For a more in-depth critique of Hawking's beliefs, I suggest reading *God and Stephen Hawking: Whose Design is it Anyway* written by Dr. John Lennox.

22 Collins, *The Language of God*, 67.

23 Craig, William Lane. *Reasonable Faith: Christian Truths and Apologetics.* 3rd ed. Wheaton: Crossway, 1984. 96; 111-126. Print.

24 The whole quote from *The Grand Design*: "Because gravity shapes space and time, it allows space-time to be locally stable but globally unstable. On the scale of the entire universe, the positive energy of the matter can be balanced by the negative gravitational energy, and so there is no restriction on the creation of whole universes. Because there is a law like gravity, the universe can and will create itself from nothing in the manner described in Chapter 6. Spontaneous creation is the reason there is something rather than nothing, why the universe exists, why we exist. It is not necessary to invoke God to light the blue touch paper and set the universe going."

Hawking, Stephen, Leonard Mlodinow. *The Grand Design,* Toronto: Bantam Books, 2010. Print.

[25] Lennox, John. *God and Stephen Hawking: Whose Design is it Anyway?* Oxford: Lion Books, 2011. Print.

[26] Collins, Francis. Interview with Steve Paulson. *The Believer.* *"Francis Collins— Head of the Human Genome Project—Discusses His Conversion to Evangelical Christianity, Why Scientists Do Not Need To Be Atheists, And What C.S. Lewis Has To Do With It."* Salon. 7 Aug. 2006. Web.

[27] Plantinga, Alvin. *Where the Conflict Really Lies: Science, Religion, and Naturalism.* New York: Oxford UP, 2011. 195. Print.

[28] Dyson, Freeman. *Disturbing the Universe.* Basic Books, 1979. Print.

[29] Hawking, Stephen. *Austin American Statesman.* 19 Oct. 1997. Web.

[30] Davis, Paul. *The Cosmic Blueprint: New Discoveries in Nature's Creative Ability to Order the Universe.* Philadelphia: Templeton Foundation Press, 2004. 203. Print.

[31] Hawking, *A Brief History of Time,* Ch. 8.

[32] Two of the many sources in which this example can be found: Collins, *The Language of God,* 77 and Keller, *The Reason for God,* 135-136.

[33] Davies, *The Cosmic Blueprint,* 11, 53. Collins confirms Davies' statement and reasons that, "We have only shifted the problem of cosmic biophilicity up one level. Why? First, because we need to explain where the law of laws comes from," (11).

[34] Dawkins, Richard. *The God Delusion.* Boston: Houghton Mifflin, 2006. 147. Print.

[35] *Expelled: No Intelligence Allowed.* Nathan Frankowski. Ben Stein. Vivendi Entertainment, 2008. Film.

[36] When she was only 15 years old, Malala Yousafzai was shot in the head by the Taliban in Pakistan because of her advocacy for equal education. She survived and has been awarded the Nobel Peace Prize for her relentless efforts to advocate for equal education. She is one name among thousands who are currently fighting for this right around the globe. Her story can be read in her autobiography *I am Malala: The Girl Who Stood Up for Education and was Shot by the Taliban.*

[37] Craig, William Lane. "'Objective' or 'Absolute' Moral Values?" *Reasonable Faith with William Lane Craig.* 8 Dec. 2013. Web.

38   Lewis, C.S. *Mere Christianity.* New York: Macmillan Publishing Company, 1952. 19. Print. Lewis also discusses this topic in the appendix of *The Abolition of Man.*

39   Some may propose that we have a stronger moral compass because of our heightened intelligence. However, after taking one look at some of the behavior of individuals on Wall Street, it is clear that intelligence has nothing to do with one's morality.

40   Dawkins, *The God Delusion,* 101.

41   Keller, *The Reason for God,* 161.

42   Dawkins, *The God Delusion,* 219-220.

43   Ibid., 220.

44   Quoted in Alvin Plantinga, *Where the Conflict Really Lies,* 316.

45   Harris, Sam. *The Moral Landscape: How Science Can Determine Human Values.* New York: Free Press, 2010. Print.

46   Zacharias, Ravi. *Can Man Live Without God?* W. Publishing Group, 1996. 182. Print.

47   Keller, *The Reason for God,* 159.

48   Lennox, John. "As a Scientist I'm Certain Stephen Hawking is Wrong. You Can't Explain the Universe Without God." *Daily Mail.* Associated Newspapers Ltd., 3 Sept. 2010. Web.

Chapter 3

49   This statistic is confirmed by a 2015 Pew Research Center and 2014 Gallup poll. Lipka, Michael. "5 Facts About Abortion." *Pew Research Centers.* Pew Research Center, 11 June. 2015. Web.; Saad, Lydia. "U.S. Still Split on Abortion: 47% Pro-Choice, 46% Pro-Life." *Gallup Headlines.* Gallup, Inc., 22 May 2014. Web.

50   2 Timothy 3:16

51   Professor and Old Covenant scholar K.A. Kitchen has written an in-depth book analyzing the historical validity of the texts of the Old Covenant. Specifically, he addresses the issue of whether the Old Covenant was written during the time period of 2,000-400 BCE. He also seeks to discover if the texts are primarily stories of fiction, or whether they can be looked to for historical truth. Much of the material in this chapter is based on his conclusions. If this is a topic that interests you, I strongly encourage you to read his book as well.

52 This continuing story is made clear through the extensive references in the texts of the New Covenant to Old Covenant passages. Acts 7, Romans 4, and the Book of Hebrews are good places to begin to see the parallels between both the Old and New Covenant.

Similarly, the Book of Acts (which is a historical account of the beginning following of Yeshua) frequently discusses that the disciples of Yeshua used the *Old Covenant texts* to make their case for why Yeshua was the Messiah. Clearly, the beliefs of these early followers were consistent with the texts of the Old Covenant. For more on this topic, please see Chapter 7.

53 The next chapter will detail the evidence supporting the claim that the texts of the New Covenant can be used as historical evidence as well.

54 Old Covenant textual scholar Ernst Wurthwein writes: "No book in the literature of the world has been so often copied, printed, translated, read, and studied as the Bible. It stands uniquely as the object of so much effort devoted to preserving it faithfully, to understanding it, and to making it understandable to others."

Wurthwein, Ernst. "The Theological Significance of Textual Criticism and the History of the Text." *The Text of the Old Testament: An Introduction to the Biblia Hebraica.* Grand Rapids: Eerdmans, 1979. 121. Print.

55 Quoted in Randall Price, *The Stones Cry Out.* Eugene: Harvest House Publishers, 1997. Print.

Original quote by Nelson Glueck. *Rivers in the Desert: A History of the Negev.* New York: Farrar, Strauss & Cudahy, 31. 1959.

56 Ibid., 324-325.

Original quote by W.F. Albright. *The Archaeology of Palestine.* London: Penguin Books, 128. 1954.

57 Agard, Margaret. *Historical Proofs of the Bible.*

58 Abraham is considered to be the "founding father" of Judaism, as well as Islam and Christianity.

59 Genesis 49:31-32

60 David officially began ruling Israel in 1003 BCE, but was the leader of a fairly large number of Israelites beginning in 1010 BCE. The reason for this delay came from a conflict between David and his predecessor Saul, and can be read about in the first Book of Samuel in the Old Covenant.

Kitchen, K.A. *On the Reliability of the Old Testament.* Grand Rapids: W.B. Eerdmans, 2003. 83. Print.

61 Prior to 853 **BCE**, the Israelites did not have contact with any "super-powers" of the day (e.g., Assyria). There is no mention of the Israelites in the Egyptian records during this time, because there is no evidence that the Egyptians led any imperial campaigns against Israel after their exodus during the reign of Ramesses III in 1175 **BCE**.

Understanding the limits and context of the eras for which we attempt to discover evidence will help lead to a better understanding of the evidence discovered. In other words, finding *anything* specifically referring to King David in a non-biblical context during this time in history is quite significant.

Kitchen, *On the Reliability of the Old Testament*, 88-91.

62 Ibid., 92.

63 Ibid., 93.

64 1 Chronicles 18:14

65 The significance of the destruction of the Second Temple will be discussed in Chapter 7.

66 Please refer to the section "Fulfilled Prophecies of the Old Covenant" in this chapter for a fulfilled prophecy about King Cyrus.

67 Ezra 6:3

68 2 Chronicles 32:30; also see 2 Kings 20:20

The pool of Siloam is also mentioned in the Gospel of John in the New Covenant when Yeshua restores a blind man's vision, (John 9:1-12). The historical reliability of the texts of the New Covenant and the life of Yeshua will be discussed in Chapters 4 and 5.

69 Price, *The Stones Cry Out*, 323.

70 Jeremiah 36:32

71 Kitchen, *On the Reliability of the Old Testament*, 23. Pages 30-32 also detail the approximate years that each King of Israel reigned.

72 Schoville, Keith N. "Top Ten Archaeological Discoveries of the Twentieth Century Relating to the Biblical World." *Stone Campbell Journal* 4:1 (2002): n.p. Web.

Some skeptics have suggested that because of the consistency between the Dead Sea Scroll texts and our modern-day texts of the Old Covenant, the modern-day Old Covenant texts were not written very long before the Dead Sea Scrolls were recorded. Because of the archeological discoveries discussed in the text, this assumption seems highly unlikely and ill suited.

Kitchen wrote an in-depth analysis in his book *On the Reliability of the Old Testament* addressing this very objection.

73 Licona, Michael. *The Resurrection of Jesus: A New Historiographical Approach.* Downers Grove: InterVarsity Press, 2010. 68-69. Print.

74 For a list of more archaeological discoveries supporting the historicity of the Old Covenant, please refer to my first book, *A Lawyer's Case for God.*

75 Throughout this book, when referring to God as "**LORD**," all the letters will be capitalized. As is clear from this verse, while reading the Bible, you may notice that sometimes this is the case when "**LORD**" is used there as well.

In Exodus, God reveals His name. His name is translated into English as YHVH (the tetragrammaton), (Exodus 3:13-15). The ancient Israelites sought to preserve the sanctity of God's holy name so strictly, that they would not utter it aloud. Instead, they would pronounce God's name as "Adonai" which is a Hebrew word meaning Lord or Master.

So, anytime "**LORD**" is in all capital letters in the Bible or ancient Hebrew texts, it is a reference to YHVH or God. Anytime it is not in all capitals, it can also be referring to God, or to a lord or master (the context of the verse is important for this distinction).

76 Jeremiah 9:16

77 Isaiah 11:12

78 God's supernatural fulfillment of His promises was apparent over Israel during the War of Independence in 1948, and during the Six-Day War in 1967 when Israel defended itself against attacks by much larger and more powerful armies.

On the first day that Israel existed as a nation in 1948, five Arab nations defied the United Nations and simultaneously attacked Israel from all sides. Israel barely had an army, had drastically less weaponry, and was tremendously outnumbered. Yet Israel won this war!

Israel being victorious is comparable to New Jersey prevailing against an attack by a country that is the size of the United States. The only logical explanation for this victory is that God was protecting His people's return to their land, just as He said He would: "For I will take you from among the nations, gather you out of all countries, and bring you into your own land," (Ezekiel 36:24).

David Ben Gurion, the first Prime Minister of Israel, concluded, "In Israel, in order to be a realist, you must believe in miracles," (CBS interview, October 5, 1956).

79   "Book of Isaiah." *Got Questions.* Got Questions Ministries, n.d. Web.

80   Wood, Bryant G. "The Discovery of the Sin Cities of Sodom and Gomorrah." Associates for Biblical Research. 16 April, 2008. Web.

81   Konig, George. Ray, Konig. "10 Prophecies Fulfilled by Nineveh and Babylon." *100 Prophecies,* 116.

82   Isaiah 13:19

83   "Babylonian Exile, Jewish History." *Encyclopedia Britannica Online.* Encyclopedia Britannica, 25 Nov. 2014. Web.

84   Jeremiah 25:12, NKJV

85   Isaiah 35:1, JPS

86   Isaiah 27:6

87   Boyd Farrow. CNBC *European Business News,* Nov. 2007. Web.

88   Fedler, John. *Focus on Israel: Israel's Agriculture in the 21st Century.* Israel Ministry of Foreign Affairs, December 24, 2002.

89   Konig, George, Ray, Konig. "Biblical Prophecy Fulfilled by Nations Around Israel." *100prophecies.org.* N.p., n.d. Web.

90   Deuteronomy 28:49-52

91   "The Cyrus Cylinder." *British Museum.* N.p., n.d. Web.

92   Isaiah 44:24-28

93   Ezra 1:2; Please also refer to and 2 Chronicles 36:23 for additional fulfilled prophecies about King Cyrus.

94   The fulfillment of the below listed prophecies further demonstrates that God's Word is true:

    1.   *The re-establishment of the nation of Israel in literally one day.* This occurred when the United Nations approved of the establishment of Israel. (Independence was officially declared on May 14, 1948.) This was foretold 2,700 years ago in Isaiah 66:8: "Shall the earth be made to give birth in one day? Or shall a nation be born at once?"

    2.   *The resurrection of Hebrew as an everyday language in the 20th Century after being a dead language for almost 2,000 years.* No other extinct language has ever been revived! The return of Hebrew as an everyday language in 1948 was foretold in Zephaniah 3:9 in approximately 641 BCE: "For then I will restore to the peoples a pure language." Notably, in his commentary on Zephaniah 3:9, Rabbi and esteemed commentator Ibn Ezra said that Zephaniah 3:9 says: "They will speak Hebrew, the pure and holy tongue." Hebrew, as an everyday language was *dead*

at this time, and yet, Rabbi Ezra was confirming that Zephaniah was speaking of its restoration. (Stone Edition Tanakh edited by Rabbi Nosson Scherman, p.1398 [1996, 2001].)

3. *The Land of Israel prospering under Jewish control.* In 1867 Mark Twain described Israel as a physically undesirable place, "a desolate country...a mournful expanse...a desolation." Satellite pictures of the Middle East today show the entire region to be a barren wasteland except Israel, which contains many rich, lush, and varied vegetation areas. This prospering was foretold in approximately 500 BCE by Ezekiel 36:10–35: "[T]he cities shall be inhabited and the ruins rebuilt... I will...do better for you [Jewish people] than at your beginnings. Then you shall know that I am the Lord.... I will give you a new heart and put a new spirit within you; I will take the heart of stone out of your flesh and give you a heart of flesh.... And I will multiply the fruit of your trees and increase of your fields, so that you need never again bear the reproach of famine among the nations.... So they will say, 'This land that was desolate has become like the garden of Eden.'" Also, see Amos 9:11, 14, 15.

[95] 2 Samuel 22:31

[96] Jeremiah 31:35-36

[97] The existence and thriving of the Jewish people today is a testimony of God's faithfulness and is evidence that He keeps His promises. God does so for the sake of His name.

"I will establish my covenant between me and you and your offspring after you throughout their generations for an everlasting covenant, to be God to you and to your offspring after you," (Genesis 17:7).

"Thus says the LORD: 'If the heavens above can be measured, and the foundations of the earth below can be explored, then I will cast off all the offspring of Israel for all they have done,' declares the LORD," (Jeremiah 31:37).

Also see Genesis 12, Leviticus 26:43-44, Deuteronomy 4:26-27, 7:9, 28:63-64, 31:8, 2 Kings 8:19, 2 Samuel 7:22-26 and many other passages in the Old Covenant.

[98] Pascal, Blaise. Thomas M'Crie, W.F. Trotter, and Richard Scofield. *Blaise Pascal: The Provincial Letters: and, Pensees, and Scientific Treatises.* Chicago. Encyclopedia Britannica, 1990. Print.

[99] Mark Twain, "Concerning the Jews," Harper's Magazine, 1899.

100 "The Book of Job, Old Testament." *Encyclopedia Britannica Online.* Encyclopedia Britannica, n.d. Web.

101 Job 28:25-27

102 "Discovering Air." *Nova Online Adventure.* PBS Online, Nov. 2000. Web.

103 "Probable Occasion When Each Psalm Was Composed." *Blue Letter Bible.* Sowing Circle, 2015. Web.

104 Psalm 8:6-8

105 Thomas, Brian. "NASA's Ocean Currents Study Confirms Providential Care." Institute For Creation Research, n.d. Web.

106 Smith, Jay. "Zechariah Summary." *BibleHub.* Biblos.com, n.d. Web.

107 Zechariah 14:4

108 More Old Testament prophecies and examples of scientific foreknowledge can be found in *A Lawyer's Case for God.* Some of the examples discussed are:

 1. The medical benefits of circumcision on the 8th day (Genesis 17:12)

 2. Blood circulation is critical for sustaining life (Leviticus 17:11)

 3. Pork and shellfish transmit disease (Leviticus 11:7)

109 Dawkins, *The God Delusion.*

110 One of my favorite books, and the material that is most heavily used in this section, is Paul Copan's book *Is God a Moral Monster?* If you are intrigued by this topic, I strongly suggest reading Copan's well-researched and thought-provoking book.

111 Leviticus 25:39-40, 43

112 Refer to Genesis 3

113 Exodus 21:20-21

114 Copan, *Is God a Moral Monster?* 135-136.

115 Exodus 21:24

116 Exodus 21:26-27

117 Copan, *Is God a Moral Monster?* 130.

118 Deuteronomy 15:12-14

119 Notably, many abolitionists made the case that the Bible was actually very *against* slavery. For a deeper look into this issue and its implications on our culture today, I suggest reading *The Civil War as a Theological Crisis* by historian Mark Noll.

120 The life, death, and resurrection of Yeshua will be discussed in further depth in Chapters 5-7.

121 Deuteronomy 20:16-17

122 Kitchen, *On the Reliability of the Old Testament*, 173-174.

123 Deuteronomy 7:2-3. Another example can be found in Joshua 23:12-13

124 Copan, *Is God a Moral Monster?* 176.

125 Ibid., 175.

126 Joshua 6:21

127 Copan, *Is God a Moral Monster?* 182-183.

128 Psalm 68:5

129 David Lamb writes this in his book *God Behaving Badly*: "Compared to other ancient Near Eastern literature, the Old Testament is shockingly progressive in its portrayals of divine love, acceptance of foreigners and affirmation of women. The Old Testament was not only divinely inspired, it was also culturally engaged."

Lamb, David T. *God Behaving Badly: Is the God of the Old Testament Angry, Sexist and Racist?* Downers Grove, IL: InterVarsity Press, 2011. 23. Print.

130 Psalm 36:5

131 Psalm 86:15

Chapter 4

132 Old Testament/Hebrew Scriptures/Tanakh

133 New Testament/Messianic Scriptures/Brit Chadasha

134 The 27 books of the New Covenant were chosen using four major criteria:

1. An apostle or a colleague of an apostle wrote the text

2. The text was orthodox (aligned with the teachings of Yeshua)

3. The material was relevant to the body of believers

4. There was a widespread and long-lasting usage of the text by the followers of Yeshua.

Licona, Michael. "How Did The Bible Become Compiled Into One Volume?" Houston University. n.d. Lecture.

135 The New Covenant makes a grand *historical* claim. The writers declare that Yeshua was a man who lived and was resurrected from the dead. The texts do

not claim that this merely happened within the heart of His followers, or in the spirit of those who believe. The New Covenant texts affirm that Yeshua was a real human being who spoke, walked, and ate with individuals following His death and resurrection (Luke 24:39-43; John 21:1-25).

As such, if the claims of the followers of Yeshua are proven to be overwhelmingly historically incorrect, their spiritual validity is nullified as well. However, as we will discover in the next two chapters, the historical evidence for the life, crucifixion, death, and resurrection of Yeshua is outstanding.

136   One of the most important historical non-gospel New Covenant texts to provide evidence for the resurrection is found in Paul's first letter to the church at Corinth (specifically, the passage is 1ˢᵗ Corinthians 15:3-8). There is a brief analysis of this verse in Chapter 6. For a more in-depth discussion, I suggest reading Michael Licona's book, *The Resurrection of Jesus*, pages 223-235.

137   In 2005, distinguished professor Dr. Gary Habermas conducted a study of scholarly publications regarding the historical Jesus over a 30-year time span (1975-2005). His research of over 1,400 publications found that 75% of these publications supported the argument for the historical validity of the empty tomb. He recognizes, "Thus, while far from being unanimously held by critical scholars, it may surprise some that those who embrace the empty tomb as a historical fact still comprise a fairly strong majority."

Habermas, Gary R. "Resurrection Research from 1975 to the Present: What are Critical Scholars Saying?" *Journal for the Study of the Historical Jesus,* 2005. 135-153. Web.

138   Notably, there are only 193 remaining fragments of manuscripts of the play *Oedipus the King* (compared to the 5,838 discovered fragments of manuscripts of the New Covenant).

Battezzato, Luigi. *History of Scholarship: A Selection of Papers from the Seminar on the History of Scholarship Held Annually at the Warburg Institute.* New York: Oxford, 2006. 92. Print.

139   Licona, Michael. "The Basis of our Biblical Text Manuscripts." Houston Baptist University. n.d. Lecture.

140   Brumbaugh, Robert S. "Plato Manuscripts: Toward a Completed Inventory." *Manuscripta,* July 1990. Web.

141   Licona, "The Basis of our Biblical Text Manuscripts."

142   Quoted in Lee Strobel's *The Case for Christ:* "The New Testament, then, has not only survived in more manuscripts than any other book from antiquity,

but it has survived in a purer form than any other great book—a form that is *99.5 percent pure*," (emphasis added).

Original quote by Norman L. Geisler, and William E. Nix. *A General Introduction to the Bible.* Chicago: Moody Press, 1980. 361. Print.

This point was also discussed during Michael Licona's lecture *The Basis of our Biblical Text Manuscripts.*

[143] Licona, "The Basis of our Biblical Text Manuscripts."

[144] 1 John 1:4, CJB

[145] 1 John 1:4, NKJV

[146] Quoted in Josh McDowell, *The New Evidence that Demands a Verdict,* 34.

Original quote by John W. Montgomery. *History and Christianity.* Downers Grove: InterVarsity Press, 1971.

[147] There is some speculation regarding the authorship of the four gospels. However, after analyzing the evidence, many historians have no qualms with assigning each gospel to its traditionally named author.

Papias wrote in approximately 125 CE that the Gospel of Mark "made no mistakes" in accurately recording Peter's eyewitness. Papias also records that Matthew had preserved the teachings of Yeshua correctly. This suggests two of the four gospels were independently verified to be historically accurate within the first century of the following of Yeshua.

Further, in 180 CE, Irenaeus, who was an early leader in the following of Yeshua, affirms the accurate recording and traditional authorship of *all four* gospels.

Strobel, Lee. *The Case for Christ.* Grand Rapids: Zondervan, 1998. 28-29. Print.

[148] Bruce, F.F. *The New Testament Documents: Are They Reliable?* Grove: InterVarsity, 1960. Print.

Lee Strobel also verified these dates in *The Case for Christ.* During an interview with Craig Blomberg, Strobel recognizes Blomberg is "One of the country's foremost authorities on the biographies of Jesus, which are called the four gospels," (40).

Blomberg says, "The standard scholarly dating, even in very liberal circles, is Mark in the 70's, Matthew and Luke in the 80's, and John in the 90's," (40). Although the dates are slightly different than those proposed by Bruce and recorded in the text, the timeframe is still the same (35-70 years following the death of Yeshua), thus further affirming the historical credibility of the gospels.

Strobel, *The Case for Christ*, 40.

[149] Strobel also recognizes just how expansive the post-resurrection testimonies would have been in a court of law. He writes: "To put it in perspective, if you were to call each one of the witnesses to a court of law to be cross-examined for just fifteen minutes each, and you went around the clock without a break, it would take you from breakfast on Monday until dinner on Friday to hear them all. After listening to 129 straight hours of eyewitness testimony, who could possibly walk away unconvinced?"

Strobel, *The Case for Christ*, 320.

The Apostle Paul confirms that over 500 people (at once) saw the resurrected Yeshua: "And that He appeared to Cephas, then to the twelve. Then he appeared to more than *five hundred brothers at one time*, most of whom are still alive, though some have fallen asleep. Then He appeared to James, then to all the apostles. Last of all, as to one untimely born, he appeared also to me," (emphasis added), (1 Corinthians 15:5-8).

For additional non-biblical evidence supporting the resurrection, please see Chapter 6.

[150] Some may question how such seemingly innocuous details like the number of loaves and fish Yeshua broke to feed 5,000 could be remembered and correctly recorded 30 years later, (Matthew 14:13-21). However, if you are over the age of 30, I am sure that you can recall details of many events from a number of years prior (i.e., your graduation, meeting your spouse for the first time, your wedding day). Days of significance often lead to significant memory retention.

[151] Louis "Louie" Zamperini, a one-time U.S.A. Olympian, was captured and held as a POW in a Japanese prison camp during WWII. Along with two of his crewmembers, Louie was stranded on a raft for 47 days before being captured. Louie was held in various prison camps for over two years before the end of WWII and his release. When he came home, he eventually found peace, joy, and hope in the love of Yeshua. His testimony of survival and forgiveness is truly incredible.

The details of his triumphant story can be read in *Unbroken: A World War II Story of Survival, Resilience, and Redemption* by Laura Hillenbrand.

[152] Matthew 14:22-33

[153] Luke 9:16

[154] Licona, *The Resurrection of Jesus*, 223.

[155] 1 Corinthians 15:3-9

156 Tacitus, who will be discussed in-depth in the next chapter, records: "Suppressed for the moment, the deadly superstition broke out again, *not only in Judea*, the land which originated this evil, but also in the city of Rome."

Quoted in Michael Licona, *The Resurrection of Jesus*, 243.

Original quote in Tacitus *Ann.* 15.44. English translation by Meier (1991), 89-90.

157 1 Timothy 4:13; This tradition is also recorded in Justin Martyr's *First Apology* written in 125 CE.

158 There only needed to be one person who revealed the corpse of Yeshua, and any claims of the early followers of Yeshua would have been immediately dismantled.

159 Stanford, Miles J. *Fox's Book of Martyrs: A History of the Lives, Sufferings, and Deaths of the Early Christian and Protestant Martyrs.* Grand Rapids: Zondervan, 2003. Print.

160 Romans 1:1-6

161 *Livius: Articles on Ancient History.* 2004. Web.

162 Quoted in Lee Strobel, *The Case for Christ*, 82.

163 Matthew 28:2-7

164 John 20:12

165 Matthew 27:32

166 Mark 15:21

167 Luke 23:26

168 The Gospel of John (Chapter 19) details John's account of the crucifixion and burial process.

169 Mark 15:21

170 Dr. William Lane Craig summarizes this point nicely in his Q&A titled *Inerrancy and the Resurrection*. He writes, "The problem with focusing on discrepancies is that we tend to lose the forest for the trees. The overriding fact is that the Gospels are remarkably harmonious in what they relate. The discrepancies between them are in the secondary details."

Craig, William Lane. "Inerrancy and the Resurrection." *Reasonable Faith with William Lane Craig.* 30 July 2007. Web.

171 As will be described in Chapter 5, this is evidence from an "adverse witness," and will be the primary external evidence utilized to prove the historicity of the life, death, and resurrection of Yeshua.

172   Licona, *The Resurrection of Jesus*, 72-73.

173   The debate primarily arose from the question of whether full salvation could be received through belief in Yeshua, or if one had to remain obedient to Mosaic Law as well. Paul addresses this issue directly in his letter to the Galatians. He writes, "For in Christ Jesus neither circumcision nor uncircumcision counts for anything, but only faith working through love," (Galatians 5:6).

      Paul also writes about circumcision in his letter to the Romans. "For circumcision indeed is of value if you obey the law, but if you break the law, your circumcision becomes uncircumcision. So if a man who is uncircumcised keeps the precepts of the law, will not his uncircumcision be regarded as circumcision? Then he who is physically uncircumcised but keeps the law will condemn you who have the written code and circumcision but break the law. For no one is a Jew who is merely one outwardly, nor is circumcision outward and physical. But a Jew is one inwardly, and circumcision is a matter of the heart, by the Spirit, not by the letter. His praise is not from man but from God," (Romans 2:25-29). See also Acts 15:5-11.

174   This "tradition" was instituted by God as a covenant with the Jewish people in the Book of Genesis. "And God said to Abraham, 'As for you, you shall keep my covenant, you and your offspring after you throughout their generations. This is my covenant, which you shall keep, between me and you and your offspring after you: Every male among you shall be circumcised,'" (Genesis 17:9-10).

175   This point is discussed in further depth in Chapter 6 during the "Swoon Theory" section.

176   Matthew 8:23-27

177   Mark 9:33-37

178   John 18:15-18, 25-27

179   Luke 1:1-4

180   William Mitchell Ramsay was an early 20th century archaeologist and New Covenant scholar who was the leading authority on the history of Asia Minor. He writes this about Luke: "Luke is a historian of the first rank…This author should be placed along with the very greatest of historians."

      Ramsay, William Mitchell. *The Bearing of Recent Discovery on the Trustworthiness of the New Testament*. Grand Rapids: Baker Book House, 1953. Print.

181   Hemer, Colin J., and Conrad H. Gempf. *The Book of Acts in the Setting of Hellenistic History*. Tubingen: J.C.B. Mohr, 1989. Print.

182   Matthew 27:2

183   "Therefore, to squelch the rumor, Nero created scapegoats and subjected to the most refined tortures those whom the common people called 'Christians,' [a group] hated for their abominable crimes. Their name comes from Christ, who, during the reign of Tiberius, had been executed by the procurator Pontius Pilate. Suppressed for the moment, the deadly superstition broke out again, not only in Judea, the land which originated this evil, but also in the city of Rome."

Quoted in Michael Licona, *The Resurrection of Jesus*, 243.

Original quote by Tacitus, Ann. 15.44., 89-90.

184   "And when Pilate, because of an accusation made by the leading men among us, condemned him to the cross, those who had loved him previously did not cease to do so. And up until this very day the tribe of Christians [named after him] has not died out."

Quoted in Michael Licona, *The Resurrection of Jesus*, 239.

Original quote translated by Meier (1991), 61.

185   There are also references to Pilate in the writings of first century philosopher Philo of Alexandria.

186   Archeologists have discovered the inscription discovered on the stone "not only confirms the historicity of Pilate, it clarifies the title that he bore as governor." This evidence coupled with the other writings of antiquity validate that Pontius Pilate is one of the best historically attested individuals in the crucifixion narrative.

Schoville, Keith N. "Top Ten Archaeological Discoveries of the Twentieth Century Relating to the Biblical World." *Stone Campbell Journal* 4:1 (2002): n.pag. Web.

187   John McCay writes, "The burial cave is located in the Peace Forest, south of the Gehenna Valley, near the Government House," (225). These details have led archeologists to identify the site as the burial cave for the family of Caiaphas, the Jewish High Priest who Yeshua was brought before in the crucifixion process, (Matthew 26:57).

McCay, John. "The Empty Tomb of Jesus." *Evidence for God: 50 Arguments for Faith from the Bible, History, Philosophy, and Science*. Ed. William A. Dembski, Michael R. Licona. Grand Rapids: Baker Books, 2010. 224. Print.

This discovery was also verified in the article by Keith Schoville, "Top Ten Archaeological Discoveries of the Twentieth Century Relating to the Biblical World."

[188] Ibid., 235.

[189] Quoted in G.J. Goldberg's *John the Baptist and Josephus*. Web. Original quote by Josephus *Antiquities* 18.5.2.116.

[190] Mark 6:27

[191] Quoted in Michael Licona, *The Resurrection of Jesus*, 236. Original quote translated by Meier (1994), 281.

[192] Mark 6:2-3

[193] The remains of a crucified man were discovered by Vassilios Tzaferis in 1968. In his Biblical Archaeology Review, Tzaferis writes, "He (the discovered crucified victim) was a Jew, of a good family, who may have been convicted of a political crime. He lived in Jerusalem shortly after the turn of the era and sometime before the Roman destruction of Jerusalem in 70 A.D," (parenthetical added). This discovery confirms the gospel accounts that Yeshua could have been buried in a tomb after His crucifixion.

Tzaferis, Vassilios. "Crucifixion—The Archaeological Evidence." *Biblical Archaeology Review*, Jan/Feb 1985, 44-53.

[194] Bruce, *The New Testament Documents: Are They Reliable?* Notably, F.F. Bruce is the author of over 40 books—not exactly a slouch.

Chapter 5

[195] Skiena Steven, and Charles B. Ward. "The 100 Most Significant Figures in History." *Time*. 10 Dec. 2013. Web.

[196] Dr. Michael Licona has a fairly comprehensive list and analysis of the ancient adverse witnesses to the life and early following of Yeshua in his book *The Resurrection of Jesus*, 235-248. His analysis (aside from the three witnesses described in the text: Josephus, the Babylonian Talmud, and Tacitus) includes the following sources:

1. The Roman Senator (and friend of Tacitus) Pliny the Younger wrote a letter to the Emperor Trajan (written around 111 CE).

2. The Roman historian Suetonius wrote a biography in which he mentioned early followers of Yeshua (written between 117-122 CE).

3. The Syrian Stoic Mara bar Serapion wrote a letter to his son from a Roman prison (written around 73 CE).

4. The historian Thallus affirmed information recorded in the New Covenant in his history of the eastern Mediterranean world (written around 55 CE).

5. In *The Passing of Peregrinus*, Lucian (who was a Syrian) referred to Yeshua (written around 165 CE).

6. The author Origen wrote an attack on Christianity (which will be discussed in further depth in Chapter 6). (This work was written sometime between 177-180 CE.)

Although Josephus, the Babylonian Talmud, and Tacitus are not the only sources that affirm the life, death, and crucifixion of Yeshua, for our analysis, they have been deemed the most useful. If you are interested in this subject, I suggest further researching the above listed ancient sources.

Licona, *The Resurrection of Jesus*, 235.

[197] Ibid.

[198] Quoted in Michael Licona, *The Resurrection of Jesus*, 239.

Original quote translated by Meier (1991), 61.

It should be noted that there is often a dispute regarding the authenticity of portions of this passage. Some scholars have noted that in some versions, it appears as if the original message may have been changed. However, the portion I have quoted in the text does not contain any of these disputed passages. Further, Josephus' *Antiquities* were translated into Arabic, which few followers of Yeshua spoke. (In other words, the Church would not have had as much influence over being able to alter Josephus' original writings.) Thus, having duplicative fabrications of Josephus' writings would have been highly unlikely.

[199] The significance of the title "Son of God" will be explained in Chapter 7.

[200] Matthew 26:64

[201] Matthew 26:65-66

[202] John 19:31

As Lee Strobel confirms in *The Case for Christ*, breaking the legs of crucified victims would have sped up their death. Without the ability to push up and hold their weight with their legs, they would have died from asphyxiation within minutes, (268).

However, the soldiers discovered that Yeshua was already dead, so they did not break His legs. This fulfilled the messianic prophecy written hundreds of years in advance, "He keeps all of his bones, not one of them is broken," (Psalm 34:20).

203 Quoted by Mark Eastman. *Blue Letter Bible.* Sowing Circle, n.d.. Web. Original quote in b. Sanhedrin 43a. Also quoted in Michael Licona, *The Resurrection of Jesus*, 247, with slightly different wording.

204 Galatians 3:13, CJB

205 Eastman, *Blue Letter Bible.*

206 Quoted in Michael Licona, *The Resurrection of Jesus*, 243

Original quote in Tacitus *Ann.* 15.44., 89-90.

207 As noted in the text, Maimonides writes, "Jesus of Nazareth who aspired to be the Messiah and was executed by the court," validating the life of Yeshua, as well as His "execution" by the order of the Jewish Sanhedrin.

Eastman, *Blue Letter Bible.*

208 Dr. Boyarin is widely accepted as one of the greatest rabbinic scholars in the world. In his book entitled *The Jewish Gospels: The Story of the Jewish Christ*, Dr. Boyarin affirms the following of Yeshua is deeply rooted in Jewish traditions. Dr. Boyarin's analysis will be discussed further in Chapter 7.

209 The Gospel of John offers excellent insight into the wisdom, love, and forgiveness of Yeshua. John records that Torah scholars and Pharisees (religious leaders) were ready to stone a woman caught in the act of committing adultery. In their minds, this was a necessary act in order to comply with their understanding of Torah. Yeshua quieted this uprising with these simple words: "Let him who is without sin among you be the first to throw a stone at her," (John 8:7). The crowd laid down their stones and departed, one by one. Yeshua then exhorted the woman and said, "Neither do I condemn you; go, and from now on sin no more," (John 8:11). The gospels records this mercy and compassion demonstrated by Yeshua time and time again.

210 John 5:17-18, 10:30-33, 14:1-9; 1 Timothy 3:16

211 Mark 2:5-7

212 Lewis, *Mere Christianity.*

213 Just two examples of Jewish leaders who have acknowledged that Yeshua was a brilliant rabbi and a righteous man are Rabbi Shmuley Boteach and Professor Alan Dershowitz.

Rabbi Boteach is a media personality who has authored the popular book *Kosher Jesus.* He writes, "There are many reasons for accepting Jesus as a man of great wisdom, beautiful ethical teachings, and profound Jewish patriotism."

Boteach, Shmuley. *Kosher Jesus.* Jerusalem: Gefen, 2012. Print.

Alan Dershowitz is a renowned Harvard Law Professor. In a CNN interview on April 7, 2000, Professor Dershowitz echoed the sentiments of Rabbi Boteach. He said, "I think of Jesus as the first reform rabbi, a wonderful teacher, who tried to make Judaism less formalistic and more ethical."

Chapter 6

[214] 1 Corinthians 15:17

[215] Matthew 28:17

[216] Keller, *The Reason for God*, 88.

[217] Perhaps one day medical science will be able to verify that resurrections are a scientific possibility.

[218] Notably, if you have already made up your mind that history cannot prove a miraculous event, then there will most likely be no evidence that will be convincing to you. I would challenge you, however, to find a more plausible explanation than the resurrection of Yeshua after an analysis of the evidence presented in the chapter.

[219] Collins, *The Language of God*, 75.

[220] Below are some of the miracles of Elisha recorded in the Old Covenant: 2 Kings:

2:14- The Jordan river divided

4:35- After praying to God, Elisha raised a child from dead

4:43- Bread multiplied

6:17- Sight to the blind

13:21- Man comes to life by touching Elisha's bones

[221] Keener, Craig S. *Miracles: The Credibility of the New Testament Accounts.* Grand Rapids: Baker Academic, 2011. Print.

[222] Although *The True Word* manuscript has yet to be discovered (and may never be), it is quoted at length in the rebuttal *Contra Celsum,* written by Origen of Alexandria in the third century.

[223] Quoted by Peter Kirby. "Historical Jesus Theories." *Early Christian Writings.* 2015.

Originally quoted in *Contra Celsum, Ch. XXXVIII.*

[224] Just a reminder, an adverse witness is someone who disagrees with your overall position. In a courtroom, favorable testimony from an adverse

witness is considered persuasive, as such a witness is certainly not going to lie or exaggerate to help your case.

225 Quoted by Mark Eastman. *Blue Letter Bible.* Sowing Circle, n.d.. Web. Original quote in b. Sanhedrin 43a.

Also quoted in Michael Licona, *The Resurrection of Jesus,* 247, with slightly different wording.

226 Licona, *The Resurrection of Jesus,* 283.

227 They "forsook Him and fled," (Mark 14:50), and returned to their old profession as fishermen (John 21:2-3).

228 "And when Pilate, because of an accusation made by the leading men among us, condemned him to the cross, those who had loved him previously did not cease to do so. And up until this very day the tribe of Christians [named after him] has not died out."

Quoted in Michael Licona, *The Resurrection of Jesus,* 239

Original quote translated by Meier (1991), 61.

229 Quoted in Josh McDowell. *Evidence that Demands a Verdict: Historical Evidences for the Christian Faith.* San Bernardino: Here's Life Publishers, 1981. 244. Print.

Originally quoted in Pannenberg, Wolfhart. *Jesus—God and Man.* Trans. by L.L. Wilkins and D.A. Priebe. Philadelphia: Westminster Press, 1968.

230 Wright, N.T. "The New Unimproved Jesus." *Christianity Today.* 13 Sept. 1993.

231 "'I adjure you by the living God to tell us if you are the Christ, the Son of God.' Jesus said to him, 'you have said so. But I tell you, from now on you will see the Son of Man seated at the right hand of Power and coming on the clouds of heaven.' Then the high priest tore his robes and said, 'He has uttered blasphemy,'" (Matthew 26:63-65). The significance of this claim will be discussed in further depth in the next chapter.

232 Matthew 27:11-26

233 Undoubtedly, this would probably not have included the Romans holding the hands of any doubters and politely showing them that they were incorrect. It would have been more akin to putting the brutalized corpse of Yeshua out in the public square for everyone to see.

234 It seems as if Yeshua's body were still lying in His tomb, thousands would not have been convinced of His resurrection. Acts 2 describes Peter's first sermon in which Peter unabashedly proclaims Yeshua lived, was crucified,

died, and buried, and was resurrected by God. It is recorded that about 3,000 people came to believe in the resurrection of Yeshua that day, (Acts 2:41). Please also refer to Matthew 28:11-15 quoted in the text.

235 "Ancient Rome—The Pax Romana." *U.S. History.* Ancient Civilizations. Independence Hall Association. n.d. Web.

236 Matthew 28:11-15

237 Some may wonder what happened to the Roman soldiers during the resurrection of Yeshua. The Gospel of Matthew records that after an angel appeared at the tomb to tell the women that Yeshua had been resurrected, the guards were terrified. "And for fear of him (the angel) the guards trembled and became like dead men," (parenthetical added), (Matthew 28:4).

238 McDowell, *The New Evidence that Demands a Verdict*, 237.

239 Matthew 6:33

240 Barney Fife was a bumbling deputy on the Andy Griffith TV Series in the 1960s. Chief Wiggum is an incompetent police officer on The Simpsons.

241 Matthew 12:40, 16:21

242 Matthew 27:65-66

243 Mark 16:1-4

244 Quoted in Josh McDowell, *The New Evidence that Demands a Verdict*, 237.

Originally quoted in Robertson, Archibald Thomas. *Word Pictures in the New Testament.* Vols. I-V. Nashville: Broadman Press, 1930. Reprint, New York: R.R. Smith, Inc., 1931.

245 Van Daalen D.H. *The Real Resurrection.* London: Collins, 1972. 41. Print.

246 Craig, William Lane. "Accounting for the Empty Tomb: The Quest for the Risen, Historical Jesus." *American*, n.p., 1 Apr. 2013. Web.

247 Luke 23:50-53; John 19:38-40

248 Despite the *recent* controversy surrounding the life of Mary Magdalene (from such books as *The Da Vinci Code),* she is an important figure in the resurrection story.

If you find *The Da Vinci Code* controversy interesting, I would suggest either listening to or reading through the transcript of the "DaVinci Code Forum" hosted by the Johnson Ferry Baptist Church in Marietta, Georgia. The two scholars in this forum are Dr. William Lane Craig and Dr. Michael Licona. They debunk the conspiracies regarding Mary Magdalene in a succinct and comprehensive manner. This forum can be found on Dr. Craig's website, *Reasonable Faith with William Lane Craig.*

249 Mark 15:47, 16:1-3

250 Mark 15:44-45

251 McDowell, *The New Evidence that Demands a Verdict*, 281.

252 John 19:39-40

253 "Therefore, to squelch the rumor, Nero created scapegoats and subjected to the most refined tortures those whom the common people called 'Christians,' [a group] hated for their abominable crimes. Their name comes from Christ, who, during the reign of Tiberius, had been executed by the procurator Pontius Pilate. Suppressed for the moment, the deadly superstition broke out again, not only in Judea, the land which originated this evil, but also in the city of Rome."

     Quoted in Michael Licona, *The Resurrection of Jesus*, 243.

     Original quote by Tacitus, Ann. 15.44., 89-90.

254 John 19:34

255 Edwards, William D., Wesley J. Gabel, and Floyd E. Hosmer. "On the Physical Death of Jesus Christ." *The Journal of the American Medical Association.* 255.20, 1986. Web.

256 In Acts, Paul says that he studied under Gamaliel, one of the chief rabbis of the day, (Acts 22:3).

257 Acts 22:20

258 Acts 9:1-22

259 There is some debate among some scholars as to whether all of the following letters were authored by Paul. Notably, there is virtually no debate over Paul's authorship of 7 letters (*). However, the full list of the traditional 13 Pauline Epistles (writings/letters) are: Romans*, 1 Corinthians*, 2 Corinthians*, Galatians*, Ephesians, Philippians*, Colossians, 1 Thessalonians*, 2 Thessalonians, 1 Timothy, 2 Timothy, Titus, Philemon*

260 1 Corinthians 15:6

261 In *The Resurrection of Jesus*, Dr. Licona writes: "It is believed that Paul wrote the letter we now refer to as 1 Corinthians in A.D. 54 or 55. If Jesus died in A.D. 30, we are reading a letter that was written within twenty-five years of Jesus' death by a major church leader who knew a number of those who had walked with Jesus," (223).

262 Acts 15:3-8

263 Galatians 1:13-14

264 Strobel, *The Case for Christ*, 322.

265 Licona, *The Resurrection of Jesus*, 370.

266 Time and time again it is written in the texts of the New Covenant that these are accounts from *eyewitnesses*. This means that the writers would have known if what they were writing was historically true or false. "For we did not follow cleverly devised myths when we made known to you the power and coming of our Lord Jesus Christ, but we were eyewitnesses of his majesty," (2 Peter 1:16).

267 "How happy is its church, on which apostles poured forth all their doctrine along with their blood! Where Peter endures a passion like his Lord's! Where Paul wins his crown in a death like John's! Where the Apostle John was first plunged, unhurt, into boiling oil, and thence remitted to his island-exile!"

"Ante-Nicene Fathers, Vol. III: The Prescription Against Heretics." *Christian Classics Electronic Library.* Chap XXXVI. 1998. Web.

268 The Jewish population would have taken the claim that Yeshua was the Son of God very seriously. The first of the 10 Commandments given to Moses on Mount Sinai is to worship "no other Gods," (Exodus 20:3; Deuteronomy 5:7).

Some Jews to this day do not accept Yeshua as the Son of God because of their interpretation of this commandment. As will be discussed in further depth in Chapter 7, the evidence that Yeshua is the Jewish Messiah and the Son of God is overwhelming. This means that the followers of Yeshua understand that they are worshipping God, not an idol or a man.

269 Ludemann, Gerd. *What Really Happened to Jesus: A Historical Approach to the Resurrection.* trans. John Bowden. Louisville: Westminster John Knox Press, 1996. 8. Print.

270 Durant, Will. *Caesar and Christ.* Vol. 3. New York: Simon & Schuster, 1994. Print.

271 Mark 3:13-19 lists the names of the 12 disciples before the crucifixion of Yeshua.

272 Matthew 27:57-60; Mark 15:42-46; Luke 23:50-53; John 19:38

273 Matthew 28:1-10; Mark 16:1-8; Luke 23:55; 24:1-12; John 20:1-2

274 Habermas, "The Empty Tomb of Jesus." *Evidence for God*, 169.

275 Dr. William Lane Craig reiterates that "one of the most remarkable facts about the early Christian belief in Jesus' resurrection was that it flourished in the very city where Jesus had been publicly crucified."

Craig, *Reasonable Faith*, 361.

276 It is recorded that Paul preached in Jerusalem (Acts 26:20).

²⁷⁷ Mark 14:50

²⁷⁸ Mark 14:66-72

²⁷⁹ Acts 2

²⁸⁰ "Ante-Nicene Fathers, Vol. III: The Prescription Against Heretics." *Christian Classics Electronic Library.*

²⁸¹ John 21:2-3

²⁸² McDowell, *The Evidence that Demands a New Verdict*, 252.

²⁸³ Maier, Paul L. *In the Fullness of Time: A Historian Looks at Christmas, Easter, and the Early Church.* Grand Rapids: Kregel Publications, 1997. 203. Print.

²⁸⁴ "And if the Messiah has not been raised, your trust is useless, and you are still in your sins," (1 Corinthians 15:17, CJB). The next chapter will dive further into examining the validity of the claim that Yeshua is the Son of God.

²⁸⁵ As was discussed in Chapter 5.

²⁸⁶ Green, Michael. *Man Alive.* Chicago: InterVarsity Christian Fellowship, 1969. 54. Print.

Chapter 7

²⁸⁷ The Old Covenant affirms that God has a son: "Who has established all the ends of the earth? What is his name, and what is his son's name? Surely you know!" (Proverbs 30:4). This point will be discussed in further depth throughout this chapter.

²⁸⁸ The following is a list of other instances in the Bible when individuals were raised from the dead. Notably, these people were all raised from the dead by the power of God, *or* by the power of God *through Yeshua.*

Old Covenant:

1 Kings 17:17-24 (Elijah raised the son of Zarephath's widow from the dead)

2 Kings 4:35 (Elisha raised the son of a Shunammite woman from the dead)

2 Kings 13:21 (A man touched the bones of Elisha, and was raised from the dead)

New Covenant:

Matthew 9:18-26 (Yeshua raised Jairus' daughter from the dead)

Matthew 27:52-53 (Saints were raised from the dead after the crucifixion of Yeshua)

Luke 7:13-15 (Yeshua raised the widow's son at Nain from the dead)

John 11:43-44 (Yeshua raised Lazarus from the dead)

Acts 9:36-42 (Peter raised Tabitha from the dead by the name of Yeshua)

Acts 20:9-12 (Paul raised Eutychus from the dead by the name of Yeshua)

[289]   There are many other expectations of the Messiah, including that he would be well versed in Jewish law, and observant of its commandments (Isaiah 11:2-5). He also would be a charismatic leader, inspiring others to follow in his example.

Rich, Tracey R. "Judaism 101: Mashiach: The Messiah." *Judaism 101: Mashiach: The Messiah.* N.p., n.d. Web.

[290]   The prophet Isaiah foretells the coming of a child who will be the Messiah. He also prophesies that this child will be a "Mighty God... Prince of Peace:"

"For to us a *child* is born, to us a *son* is given; and the government shall be upon his shoulder, and his name shall be called Wonderful Counselor, *Mighty God*, Everlasting Father, Prince of Peace. Of the increase of his government and of peace there will be no end, on the throne of David and over his kingdom, to establish it and to uphold it with justice and with righteousness from this time forth and forevermore. The zeal of the **LORD** of hosts will do this," (emphasis added), (Isaiah 9:6-7).

The prophet Daniel also describes that the Messiah will establish a kingdom that will never be conquered:

"I saw in the night visions, and behold, with the clouds of heaven there came one like a son of man, and he came to the Ancient of Days and was presented before him. And to him was given dominion and glory and a kingdom, that all peoples, nations, and languages should serve him; his dominion is an everlasting dominion, which shall not pass away, and his kingdom is one that shall not be destroyed," (Daniel 7:13-14).

[291]   "But your iniquities have made a separation between you and your God, and your sins have hidden his face from you so that he does not hear," (Isaiah 59:2).

[292]   "He shall kill the goat of the sin offering that is for the people and bring its blood inside the veil and do with its blood as he did with the blood of the bull, sprinkling it over the mercy seat and in front of the mercy seat. Thus he shall make atonement for the Holy Place, because of the uncleanness of the people of Israel and because of their transgressions, all their sins," (Leviticus 16:15-16).

"For the life of the flesh is in the blood, and I have given it for you on the alter to make atonement for your souls, for it is the blood that makes atonement by the life," (Leviticus 17:11).

293   The word "Talmud" is a Hebrew word meaning "learning" and "instruction," and consists of what are known as the *Gemara* and the *Mishnah*. The Talmud is a central text of mainstream Judaism and contains rabbinical discussions and commentary on Jewish history, law, customs, and culture.

294   Babylonian Talmud (Yoma 5a) citing Leviticus 17:11

295   These verses will be discussed in further depth in the section "Old Covenant Prophecies Regarding the Messiah Fulfilled by Yeshua."

296   The Shmoneh Esrey in the Jewish Siddur prayer book includes these three daily prayers:

Prayer #2: Individuals Raised from the Dead: "You, O L-rd, are mighty forever, you revive the dead. You are mighty to save."

Prayer #8: Healing: "Heal us, O L-rd, and we shall be healed; save us and we shall be saved."

Prayer #15: The Messianic King (notably, the subtitle was assigned to this prayer by Maimonides who has been discussed in previous chapters): "Speedily cause the offspring of David, Your servant, to flourish, and lift up his glory by Your divine help because we wait for Your salvation all the day. Blessed art thou, O L-rd, who causes the strength of salvation to flourish."

297   The significance of this timing will be discussed in further depth in the text during the analysis of Daniel 9.

298   Babylonian Talmud (Yoma 5a) citing Leviticus 17:11

299   Isaiah 64:6, NIV

300   Ecclesiastes 7:20

301   Jeremiah 31:31-34

302   Rich, Tracey R. "Mashiach: The Messiah." *Judaism 101.* N.p., 2011. Web.

303   The Machzor is the Jewish prayer book used on the High Holidays of Rosh HaShanah and Yom Kippur.

304   The Machzor prayer in its entirety: "Our righteous anointed is *departed* from us: horror hath seized us, and we have none to justify us. He hath borne the yoke of our iniquities, and our transgression, and is *wounded* because of our transgression. He beareth our sins on his shoulder, that he may find pardon for our iniquities. We shall be healed by his wound, at the time that the Eternal will create him (the Messiah) as a new creature. O *bring him up* from the circle of the earth. Raise him up from Seir, to assemble us the *second time* on Mount Lebanon, by the hand of Yinnon," (parenthetical and emphasis added).

Machzor, Prayers for the Day of Atonement. Revised edition (New York: Rosenbaum & Werbelowsky, 1890), pp. 282, 284.

[305] Boyarin, Daniel. *The Jewish Gospels: The Story of the Jewish Christ.* New York: Perseus Distribution, 2012. 6. Print.

[306] Paul writes in his letter to the Romans: "I ask then, has God rejected his people? By no means! For I myself am an Israelite, a descendant of Abraham, a member of the tribe of Benjamin. God has not rejected his people whom he foreknew," (Romans 11:1-2).

Clearly, Paul was a Jew.

[307] This entire exchange can be read in Acts 5:17-42.

[308] Chappell, Bill. "World's Muslim Population Will Surpass Christians This Century, Pew Says." *NPR.* NPR, 2 Apr. 2015. Web.

[309] Notably, the number of Jewish people who believe that Yeshua is the prophesied Messiah has grown significantly over the last several decades. As footnoted in the Introduction, it is estimated that there are over 200,000 Jewish followers of Yeshua, many of who are quite prominent, (Messianicassociation.org/profiles.htm). Further, the 2012 International Religious Freedom Report claimed that there was a "community of approximately 20,000 Messianic Jews," living in Israel alone.

"International Religious Freedom Report for 2012." *U.S. Department of State.* U.S. Department of State, n.d. Web.

[310] One book I recommend that addresses this subject is Dr. Daniel Boyarin's *The Jewish Gospels.* Dr. Boyarin is an Orthodox Jew and is one of the most respected Talmudic scholars in the world. Much of the information in the following section is based on the evidence and conclusions he communicates in his book *The Jewish Gospels.*

[311] The ancient work *The War of the Jews* by the Roman historian Josephus details his account of this historic event.

[312] Zechariah 12:10

[313] Daniel 2:44

[314] Another verse regarding the Messiah being a conquering king is in the Book of Amos: "'Behold, the days are coming,' declares the **LORD**... 'I will restore the fortunes of my people Israel... I will plant them on their land, and they shall never again be uprooted,'" (Amos 9:13-15).

[315] b. Sanhedrin 98a

[316] Others believe it is quite possibly some of the best biblical evidence that Yeshua is the Messiah.

317 There are several ancient rabbinical sources that refer to Isaiah 53 as being about the Messiah, *not* about the nation of Israel. The Targum Jonathan, a 2nd century rabbinic commentary about Isaiah 53, affirms that the Old Covenantal text is about the Messiah.

"Behold my servant *Messiah* shall prosper; he shall be high, and increase, and be exceedingly strong: as the house of Israel looked to him through many days, because their countenance was darkened among the peoples, and their complexion beyond the sons of men," (emphasis added).

The same interpretation of Isaiah 53 being about the Messiah is found in the Babylonian Sanhedrin (98b): "The Messiah—what is his name?... The Rabbis say, the leprous one; those of the house of Rabbi say, the sick one, as it is said, 'Surely he hath borne our sickness.'"

Frydland, Rachmiel. "The Rabbis' Dilemma: A Look at Isaiah 53." Jews for Jesus, 1997. Web.

318 Boyarin, *The Jewish Gospels*, 132.

319 Another reason why Isaiah 53 cannot be about Israel is because the subject of the passage will do no violence: "He has done no violence and there was no deceit in his mouth," (Isaiah 53:9). However, we know that Israel *has* been involved in many violent conflicts. In light of this, along with the analysis in the text, it does not seem this passage can be referring to Israel.

Some also claim that Isaiah 53 cannot be about the Messiah because the subject of the passage has "offspring:" "He shall see his offspring," (Isaiah 53:10). We know that Yeshua did not have any children. However, the Hebrew word translated as "offspring" is also translated as "seed." The Bible often uses words in a poetic form, so the word could be used to refer to a spiritual, rather than a literal seed. When coupled with the analysis offered in the book, this passage seems to clearly be about the Messiah, Yeshua.

320 For additional ancient Rabbinic sources validating that Isaiah 53 refers to the Messiah and not the nation of Israel, please see Babylonian Talmud Sanhedrin 98b, Soncino Talmud edition: Ruth Rabbah 5:6, *Answering Jewish Objections to Jesus* by Michael L. Brown, and *The Fifty-Third Chapter of Isaiah According to the Jewish Interpreters* by AD. Neubauer and S.R. Driver.

321 Frydland, Rachmiel. *What the Rabbis Know About the Messiah*. 3rd ed. Cincinnati: Messianic Publication, 1993. 86. Print.

322 Although Yeshua did not come as a conquering king, He still left peace on Earth. The Gospel of John records that Yeshua has left us with His peace. "Peace I leave with you; my peace I give to you. Not as the world gives do I give to you. Let not your hearts be troubled, neither let them be afraid," (John 14:27).

Yeshua further reminds those who believe in Him that He has overcome the world, and has brought peace to each of us. "I have said these things to you, that in me you may have peace. In the world you will have tribulation. But take heart; I have overcome the world," (John 16:33).

323   Prophecy: Daniel 7:14

"And to him was given dominion and glory and a kingdom, that all peoples, nations, and languages should serve him; his dominion is an everlasting dominion, which shall not pass away, and his kingdom one that shall not be destroyed."

Future fulfillment: Revelation 17:14

"They will make war on the Lamb (Yeshua), and the Lamb will conquer them, for he is Lord of lords and King of kings," (parenthetical added).

324   Proverbs 30:4

325   1 Samuel 10:1

326   1 Chronicles 17:4, 11-13

327   Two passages along with others are: Psalm 11:3, 72, 89:2-4.

328   Boyarin, *The Jewish Gospels*, 28.

329   Mark 1:1

330   More often than not, Yeshua is the one who calls Himself the "Son of Man." One such example is in the Gospel of Mark. "Which is easier, to say to the paralytic, 'Your sins are forgiven,' or to say, 'Rise take up your bed and walk'? But that you may know that the *Son of Man* has authority on earth to forgive sins," (emphasis added), (Mark 2:9-10).

331   Daniel 7

332   Boyarin, *The Jewish Gospels*, 44.

333   Examples of Yeshua referring to himself as the Son of Man can be found in: Mark 2:10, 2:28; Matthew 9:6, 26:64; Luke 5:24, 9:22, 22:69

334   Matthew 26:64

335   Matthew 26:65-68

336   I have a more in-depth analysis of the validity of God taking the form of a man in my book *A Lawyer's Case for God*.

337   Genesis 32:24, 27-28, 30

338   The first reference to God in this passage is with the tetragrammaton, (yod, hay vov, hay) which is how the Sacred Name of God is written in Hebrew. When Abraham is addressing God, he refers to Him as Adonai (and not the

tetragrammaton) as the name of God is so sacred that the Jewish people did not pronounce it. Further, the word Adonai is used in these passages to refer to God: Ezekiel 16:3, 38:3; Psalm 68:12, 130:2.

339 Genesis 18:1-3

340 Asher Intrater, a highly esteemed Messianic author, leader, and speaker, has noted that the following passages refer to God in the Old Covenant in the form of a man:

1. In Genesis 18 a heavenly man visits Abraham and is referred to on the one hand as an angel from God, and on the other hand as YHVH Himself.

2. In Genesis 32 the angel who wrestles all night with Jacob is referred to as both man and God (El Shaddai).

3. In Exodus 3 the figure inside the burning bush who talks to Moses is called an angel but also YHVH God Himself.

4. In Exodus 14 the same God/Angel appears inside the pillar of fire and cloud, and leads the children of Israel through the Red Sea and through their wanderings in the desert.

5. In Exodus 24 Moses and Aaron, along with seventy elders of Israel, see the God of Israel in the form of a man on the mountain and eat with him.

6. In Joshua 5, the same figure who is in the burning bush meets Joshua before the battle of Jericho. He is called the captain of the angelic armies of God, yet Joshua bows down and worships him, taking off his shoes as Moses did at the burning bush.

7. In the Ezekiel 1 vision, at the top of the glory fire is a throne with a "Man" sitting on it. Again, this is a revelation of God appearing to mankind in the form of a man.

8. In Zechariah 2-3 this angel of the Lord appears standing before Joshua the high priest. In chapter 2 verse 10 he says that he is YHVH, and in verse 11 he says that YHVH has sent him.

9. In Daniel 7 this divine Messiah is brought before the throne of the Ancient of Days. He is given eternal authority over all the nations, and those nations worship Him.

10. In Daniel 10 the divine angel of the Lord appears in lightening and fire and tells Daniel what will happen in the end times.

For a detailed analysis of these passages, I recommend the book *Who Ate Lunch with Abraham* by Asher Intrater.

[341] As you research more about the beliefs of the followers of Yeshua, you will run across this idea of a "triune nature of God." This belief is based on biblical references to God in three distinct forms: God the Father, God the Son, and God the Holy Spirit. These three forms are separate, yet one in character, nature, and purpose. The Son of God, which has been analyzed in the text, refers to Yeshua who proclaims that, "I and the Father are one," (John 10:30).

However, some may be surprised that the Spirit of God (or the Holy Spirit) is also extensively referenced in both the New *and* the Old Covenants. In fact, the Spirit of God is mentioned in the Old Covenant over 100 times. It is referenced within the first two verses of the Old Covenant texts.

"In the beginning, God created the heavens and the earth. The earth was without form and void, and darkness was over the face of the deep. And the *Spirit of God* was hovering over the face of the waters," (emphasis added), (Genesis 1:1-2).

The Spirit of God is likewise mentioned in the Book of Isaiah. "And now the **LORD** God has sent me, and his *Spirit*," (emphasis added), (Isaiah 48:16).

The Holy Spirit (or Spirit of God) is also discussed extensively in the New Covenant as our Comforter and Guide. "But you will receive power when the Holy Spirit has come upon you, and you will be my witnesses in Jerusalem and in all Judea and Samaria, and to the end of the earth," (Acts 1:8).

Although we may hear of three parts of God and presume this is an avocation that God is a polytheistic being, He is three-parts, yet still wholly one God. Think of water. Water can come in three distinct forms: liquid, solid, and gas. These three forms are not any more or less water. In their alternate forms, they are still purely and wholly water. In a similar manner, God is still completely one being, while taking three different forms.

[342] The Zohar, which is the ancient foundational book on Jewish mysticism (Kabbalah), likewise refers to the mystery of the three forms of one Holy God: "The Ancient Holy One is revealed with three heads, which are united into one, and that head is three exalted. The Ancient One is described as being three: because the other lights emanating from him are included in the three. But how can three names be one? Are they really one because we call them one? How three can be one, can only be known through the revelation of the Holy Spirit."

Zohar, Vol. 111, 288; Vol. 11, 43, Hebrew editions

[343] Genesis 1:26

344 Zechariah 2:10-11, NIV

345 While on Earth, Yeshua spoke of Psalm 110:1 in the Old Covenant, which is a reference to His divinity and records God speaking to God. Thus, there are two forms of God in this passage.

"David himself, in the Holy Spirit, declared, 'The **LORD** said to my Lord, 'Sit at my right hand, until I put your enemies under your feet,' (Psalm 110:1), David himself calls him the Lord," (Mark 12:36-37).

346 Matthew 22:37-39

347 Deuteronomy 6:4

348 Genesis 2:24

349 Isaiah 48:16

350 "I saw in the night visions, and behold, with the clouds of heaven there came one like a son of man, and he came to the Ancient of Days and was presented before him. And to him was given dominion and glory and a kingdom, that all peoples, nations, and languages should serve him; his dominion is an everlasting dominion, which shall not pass away, and his kingdom one that shall not be destroyed," (Daniel 7:13-14).

351 Isaiah 9:6

352 Before our analysis, it should be noted that the first coming of Yeshua to Earth (in the first century) did not fulfill every Messianic prophecy. His followers believe that the unfulfilled prophecies will be fulfilled the second time He comes to Earth. However, the prophecies He has fulfilled has led believers to anticipate that He will eventually fulfill every single prophecy. For ease in the duration of this chapter, we will claim that Yeshua has fulfilled every single prophecy.

353 Prophecy: Micah 5:2

"But you, O Bethlehem Ephrathah, who are too little to be among the clans of Judah, from you shall come forth for me one who is to be ruler in Israel, whose coming forth is from of old, from ancient days."

Fulfillment: Matthew 2:1

"Now after Jesus was born in Bethlehem of Judea, in the days of Herod the king, behold, wise men from the east came to Jerusalem."

354 Prophecy: Genesis 49:10

"And the scepter shall not depart from Judah, nor the ruler's staff from between his feet, until tribute comes to him; and to him shall be the obedience of the peoples."

Fulfillment: Luke 3:23-38

The genealogy of Yeshua

355 Prophecy: Zechariah 9:9

"Rejoice greatly, O daughter of Zion! Shout aloud, O daughter of Jerusalem! Behold, your king is coming to you; righteous and having salvation is he, humble and mounted on a donkey, on a colt, the foal of a donkey."

Fulfillment: Matthew 21:6-9

"The disciples went and did as Jesus had directed them. They brought the donkey and the colt and put on them their cloaks, and he sat on them. Most of the crowd spread their cloaks on the road, and others cut branches from the trees and spread them on the road."

356 Prophecy: Zechariah 11:12-13

"Then I said to them, 'If it seems good to you, give me my wages; but if not, keep them.' And they weighed out as my wages thirty pieces of silver. Then the Lord said to me, 'Throw it to the potter—the lordly price at which I was priced by them.' So I took the thirty pieces of silver and threw them into the house of the Lord, to the potter."

Fulfillment: Matthew 26:14-15

"Then one of the twelve, whose name was Judas Iscariot, went to the chief priests and said, 'What will you give me if I deliver him over to you?' And they paid him thirty pieces of silver."

357 Some of the individuals who have claimed to be the Messiah but failed to fulfill some of the most basic prophecies were:

Judas Maccabeus (167-160 BCE)

Rabbi Akiva (135 CE)

Simon bar Kokhba (2nd century CE)

Shabbetai Zevi (17th century)

Menachem Mendel Schneerson (20th century)

In his Defenders 2 podcast, Dr. William Lane Craig recounts something that historian N.T. Wright had said.

"In no case across the first century before Jesus or the first century after Jesus do we have any of the followers of these failed Messianic movements claiming that their would-be king really was the Messiah after all or that he had been raised from the dead. He says when your favorite Messiah got himself killed, you basically had two choices: either you went home or you got yourself a new Messiah! But what happened in the case of Jesus is unique – it is extraordinary. And that calls out for some explanation."

Craig, William Lane. "Doctrine of Christ (part 21)." *Reasonable Faith with William Lane Craig*. Reasonable Faith, n.d. Web.

[358] One of the most recent "messiahs," Menachem Mendel Schneerson, was born in the Ukraine, died of old age, and has never been resurrected from the dead. Admittedly, he never declared to be the Messiah, but he had quite a following that believed that he was.

[359] Prophecy: Isaiah 53:7

"He was oppressed, and he was afflicted, yet he opened not his mouth; like a lamb that is led to the slaughter, and like a sheep that before its shearers is silent, so he opened not his mouth."

Fulfilled: Matthew 27:12-14

"But when he was accused by the chief priests and elders, he gave no answer. Then Pilate said to him, 'Do you not hear how many things they testify against you?' But he gave him no answer, not even to a single charge, so that the governor was greatly amazed."

[360] Prophecy: Psalm 78:1-2

"Give my ear, O my people, to my teaching; incline your ears to the words of my mouth! I will open my mouth in a parable; I will utter dark sayings from of old."

Fulfilled: Matthew 13:34

"All these things Jesus said to the crowds in parables; indeed, he said nothing to them without a parable."

[361] Prophecy: Psalm 22:18

"They divide my garments among them, and for my clothing they cast lots."

Fulfilled: John 19:23-24

"When the soldiers had crucified Jesus, they took his garments and divided them into four parts, one part for each soldier; also his tunic. But the tunic was seamless woven in one piece from top to bottom, so they said to one another, 'Let us not tear it, but cast lots for it to see whose it shall be.'"

[362] Prophecy: Psalm 41:9

"Even my close friend in whom I trusted, who ate my bread, has lifted his heel against me."

Fulfilled: Luke 22:4-6

"He went away and conferred with the chief priests and officers how he might betray him to them. And they were glad, and agreed to give him money. So he consented and sought an opportunity to betray him to them in the absence of a crowd."

363 Prophecy: Isaiah 53:9

"And they made his grave with the wicked and with a rich man in his death, although he had done no violence and there was no deceit in his mouth."

Fulfilled: Matthew 27:57-60

"When it was evening, there came a rich man from Arimathea, named Joseph, who also was a disciple of Jesus. He went to Pilate and asked for the body of Jesus. Then Pilate ordered it to be given to him. And Joseph took the body and wrapped it in a clean linen shroud and laid it in his own new tomb, which he had cut in the rock. And he rolled a great stone to the entrance of the tomb and went away."

364 Stoner, Peter Winebrenner, and Robert C. Newman. Science Speaks; Scientific Proof of the Accuracy of Prophecy and the Bible. Chicago: Moody, 1969. Print.

365 For example, before the resurrection of Yeshua, the story of Jonah would not have been looked to for any sort of Messianic foreshadowing. However, after Yeshua spoke, "For just as Jonah was three day and three nights in the belly of the great fish, so will the Son of Man be three days and three nights in the heart of the earth," His followers were better able to understand the greater significance of the story of Jonah, (Matthew 12:40).

Dr. William Lane Craig has an excellent analysis regarding this same topic on his website *Reasonable Faith with William Lane Craig* in the article titled "Old Testament Prophecies of Jesus' Resurrection."

366 Isaiah 35:5-6

367 Matthew 15:30

368 Quoted in Michael Licona, *The Resurrection of Jesus*, 239.

Original quote translated by Meier (1991), 61.

369 As was discussed in the previous chapter.

370 Some of the references in the gospels to the healings performed by Yeshua: Matthew 8:5-17, 8:28-34, 9:1-8, 18-33, 12:10-13, 22, 15:29-31, 17:14-19; Mark: 1:23-34, 40-45, 2:1-12; Luke 5:1-11, 7:11-17, 8:37-43, 13:10-13, 22:51; John 2:1-11, 4:46-52, 5:1-9

371 Psalm 22:16-18

372   Isaiah 52:14

373   Matthew 27:35-37

374   Fowler, H.W., and F. G. Fowler. "Works of Lucian, Vol. IV: The Death of Peregrine." *The Works of Lucian of Samosata.* N.p., n.d. Web.

375   For a succinct analysis proving the historical validity of the life and crucifixion of Yeshua, please see Chapter 5.

376   Historians do not know precisely when the Romans first used crucifixion. However, at the time Psalm 22 and Isaiah 52 were written, it clearly was not a *common* form of execution.

377   Daniel 9:26

378   Luke 23:46

379   Quoted in Michael Licona, *The Resurrection of Jesus*, 243.

      Original quote by Tacitus, Ann. 15.44., 89-90.

380   Ibid.

381   Notably, Daniel 9:25-26 predicts the *exact time* when the Messiah would come to Earth.

      "Know therefore and understand that for the going out of the word to restore and build Jerusalem to the coming of an *anointed one* (Messiah), a prince, there shall be seven weeks. Then for sixty-two weeks it shall be built again with squares and moat, but in a troubled time," (parenthetical and emphasis added), (Daniel 9:25).

      Recall from the text that the very next passage says that after this time, the sanctuary (Temple) would be destroyed. The Temple was destroyed by the Romans in 70 CE. So, this passage accurately predicts that the Messiah would come before the destruction of the Temple. All of this information was already stated in the text, but if you will bear with me through some math, this prophecy becomes even more impressive.

      Daniel 9 states the Messiah would be "cut off" at a certain time (after 69 [62+7] "weeks"). Since there are 7 days in a week, we can multiply 69 weeks by 7 to get 483. It seems as if this passage was meant to prophecy that the Messiah would come 483 years after the prophecy was written.

      Nehemiah 2:1 records that the order to build the Temple was enacted in 444 BCE. So, Daniel 9 accurately predicts the death of the Messiah in approximately 39 CE.

      These numbers may seem slightly off (although, still admittedly impressive). However, if the 483 years are converted from the Hebrew calendar (360 days per year), to the Daniel solar calendar (365 days per year) which would have been used at the time the prophecy was made, then the passage in Daniel has actually predicted that the Messiah's death would occur in 32 CE. This is the approximate year many historians place Yeshua's historical resurrection.

Can we claim with absolute certainty that this is an accurate analysis of this passage in Daniel? No. But it certainly is cause to make us stop and think about the probability of this prophecy being so intricately accurate.

382 Psalm 16:10, NIV

383 1 Corinthians 15:3-4

384 Isaiah 53:5-6; Please refer to Appendix C for the entire powerful Messianic passage of Isaiah 53.

385 Jeremiah 31:31-34, NIV

386 1 Peter 2:24

387 Hebrews 9:12, 22; As you will recall from earlier in the chapter the ancient Rabbis attest that "There is no atonement without blood," (Talmud–Yoma 5a).

388 "He shall pray to God, and He will delight in him, he shall see His face with joy, for He restores to man His righteousness," (Job 33:26).

"'Come now, and let us reason together,' says the Lord, 'Though your sins are like scarlet, they shall be as white as snow; though they are red like crimson, they shall be as wool,'" (Isaiah 1:18).

389 Genesis 16:1-4

390 Exodus 2:11-15

391 2 Samuel 11

392 Leviticus 4, 17

393 Leviticus 4:35, 5:10

394 "He entered once for all into the holy places, not by means of the blood of goats and calves but by means of his own blood, thus securing an eternal redemption," (Hebrews 9:12).

395 Quoted from Jeremiah 31:31-34.

396 Ibid.

397 Leviticus 16:30

398 1 Kings 5-6 details the process of building the First Temple, and Ezra 3-6 describes building the Second Temple. Before either temple was built, sacrifices to God were offered in the Tabernacle (a portable dwelling place for God

described in Exodus 25-27). For ease, we will just refer to the "Temples" in the text, but the same processes were also utilized in the Tabernacle.

399   Leviticus 16, 23:27

400   The importance and persuasiveness of utilizing evidence from an adverse witness was discussed in Chapter 5.

401   "Talmud—Mas. Yoma 2a." *English Babylonian Talmud.* Halakhah, n.d. Web.

402   Ibid.

403   Ibid.

404   Isaiah 1:18

405   Talmud—Mas. Yoma 2a.

406   Leviticus 16:34

407   Zechariah 11:1

408   Talmud—Mas. Yoma 2a.

409   Zechariah 11:1

410   The quotes used in this section are from *Twelve Sons of Israel*, a book I *highly* recommend. *Twelve Sons of Israel* contains the testimonies of 12 prominent rabbis (10 of whom were Orthodox) who lived in the 19th and 20th century, and who joyfully proclaimed Yeshua was their Messiah. You can download this book at twelvesonsofisrael.com. You can also order a hard copy of this book by email at info@cityofdavid.com, or by phone at (905) 761-8118.

411   "Rabbi Chil Slowtowski." *Twelve Sons of Israel: Dramatic Accounts of Twelve Rabbis Who Sought for the Messiah—and Found Him.* Fourways, ZA: Messianic Good News, 2013. 81. Print.

412   "Rabbi Daniel Zion," *Twelve Sons of Israel*, 97.

413   "Rabbi Isaac Lichtenstein," *Twelve Sons of Israel*, 50.

414   Ibid., 49

415   "It has been taught: On the Eve of the Passover, they hanged Yeshu." A more complete quote from this excerpt of the Babylonian Talmud can be read in Chapter 5.

     Quoted by Mark Eastman. *Blue Letter Bible.* Sowing Circle, n.d.. Web.

     Original quote in b. Sanhedrin 43a.

416   "Now it was the day of Preparation of the Passover. It was about the sixth hour. He said to the Jews, 'Behold your King!'" (John 19:14).

417 In the Passover story recorded in Exodus, the Hebrews were protected from the "angel of death" by covering their doorposts with the blood of the sacrificed Passover lamb, (Exodus 12:29-30). In a similar way, Yeshua, who was the Passover lamb, has protected us from spiritual death. "Through death he might destroy the one who has the power of death," (Hebrews 2:14-15).

Further, just as the afikomen (the middle matzah) is broken on Passover, wrapped in a cloth, and hidden, only to be discovered later on (for which the discoverer receives a reward), Yeshua was broken, wrapped in a burial cloth, and sealed in a tomb. Whoever finds Him receives an eternal reward.

Additionally, the afikomen is eaten at the end of the meal as dessert. Orthodox Judaism teaches that the Passover lamb used to be eaten at the end of the meal and that nothing could be eaten after it. Recall that the Passover lamb was the lamb that was slain so that its shed blood could save the Jewish people. That is precisely what Yeshua was and did. He is the Passover lamb who was slain so that His blood could save His people. In today's Seder, the afikomen has replaced the Passover lamb as the last thing to be eaten. Thus, the afikomen is now the Passover lamb. So we have more evidence that the afikomen is Yeshua—the middle matzah that is wrapped in a cloth, hidden, and later found. And a reward is even given to the one who finds it. Amazing!

418 Leviticus 23:9; John 20:1; 1 Corinthians 15:23

419 The apostle Paul emphasizes the parallel between the atoning death of Yeshua and the Festival of the Firstfruits in his first letter to the Corinthians. "But the fact is that the Messiah has been raised from the dead, the firstfruits of those who have died. For since death came through a man, also the resurrection of the dead has come through a man. For just as in connection with Adam all die, so in connection with the Messiah all will be made alive," (1 Corinthians 15:20-22, CJB).

420 Cantor, Ron. *Identity Theft*. Shippensburg, PA: Destiny Image Pub., 2013. Print.

421 Recall the Talmudic passage referenced above that states "there is no atonement without the blood." As noted previously, this is also discussed in the Old Covenant: "For the life of the flesh is in the blood, and I have given it for you on the altar to make atonement for your souls, for it is the blood that makes atonement by the life," (Leviticus 17:11).

422 Isaiah 64:6-7; Romans 3:23

423 Have you ever used God's name as a curse word and violated the 3rd Commandment? Have you ever failed to honor the Sabbath and violated the 4th Commandment? Or have you ever stolen even a small item and

violated the 8th Commandment? When was the last time you longed for the possessions of another, breaking the 10th Commandment? If you're anything like me, it was probably very recently.

424   Isaiah 53:6; Psalm 37:38

425   "For to this day, when they read the old covenant, that same veil remains unlifted, because only through Christ is it taken away. Yes, to this day whenever Moses is read a veil lies over their hearts. But when one turns to the Lord, the veil is removed," (2 Corinthians 3:14-16).

426   Harvey, Paul. "The Man and the Birds." N.p., n.d. Web.

427   Luke 23:34

Chapter 8

428   Just a refresher of the major arguments made in Chapter 2:

1.   Cosmological Argument (something has always had to exist)

2.   Fine-Tuning Argument (the world is too delicately created to have been simply created by chance)

3.   Morality (our distinction of "right" and "wrong" shows that there is something more than just neutral nature)

One cannot propose that the "immorality of God" is a reason to not believe in His existence (in the same way that someone cannot propose Old Covenant atrocities are a reason to not believe in the historical validity of the Bible). Even if we do not *like* God, this feeling of dislike does not mean that He does not exist.

429   Zacharias, *Can Man Live Without God?* 182.

430   As you will recall from Chapter 2, the evidence for the existence of God is very good.

431   Arguably the entire theme of the Book of Job and many of the Psalms is about how to deal with suffering. I believe one of the most powerful verses from the story of Job is when Job, after losing everything, still glorifies God. He says, "Naked I came from my mother's womb, and naked shall I return. The Lord gave, and the Lord has taken away; blessed be the name of the Lord," (Job 1:21).

432   Keller, Timothy. *Walking with God Through Pain and Suffering.* New York: Penguin Group, 2013. 17-20. Print.

433   Ibid., 21.

[434] Ibid., 106.

[435] Some may argue that God does intervene with the free will of some. One example cited for such beliefs can be found in a well-known narrative in the Old Covenant, the story of Moses freeing the Israelites from Egyptian slavery.

After Moses was instructed by God to free the Israelites, God warned him that it would not be an easy task as God said that, "I will harden his (Pharaoh's) heart so that he will not let my people go," (parenthetical added), (Exodus 4:21).

But let's examine the passage more closely. According to Adam Clarke's commentary, the Hebrew word translated as harden "literally signifies to strengthen, confirm, make bold or courageous." An illustration commonly utilized is that of a sponge squeezed (made hard) in the hand. Anything that comes from the squeezed sponge was already there. So, when God "hardened" Pharaoh's heart, He simply forced out what was already there, strengthening Pharaoh's own convictions.

Now let's examine the passage in context. Moses returned to Israel and pleaded with Pharaoh to let the Israelites go into the wilderness and offer sacrifices to God. Pharaoh refused. A pattern began: Moses would go to Pharaoh to ask him to let the Israelites go into the wilderness, Pharaoh would say no, God would send a plague, Pharaoh would often repent and tell Moses that they could leave, the plague would stop, and because "Pharaoh's heart remained hardened," he would not allow the Israelites to leave. This pattern continued for ten devastating plagues over the land of Egypt. Following the final plague, Pharaoh finally let the Israelites leave.

Can we truly believe that God is good if He hardened the heart of Pharaoh leading to such devastation in Egypt? Further, can there even be an argument of free will if God arguably intercedes in the instances of some and not of others? These questions have been at the forefront of many scholarly discussions, and there are many different perspectives and answers to these questions. One such response was by the renowned analytical philosopher Dr. William Lane Craig. Craig describes how the ultimate issue is not with whether God actually intervened and hardened the heart of Pharaoh, but the perspective from which God can view the heart of Pharaoh. He describes how:

"What God knows is not only what a person will do—that is simple foreknowledge—but more than that he knows what they would do under any circumstances they might be in which is even more radical and something that is completely beyond us."

In other words, God did not harden the heart of Pharaoh; He already knew how Pharaoh, in his free will, would act in response to the situation. We must recall that Pharaoh had already hardened his own heart. Had God intervened, He would have been interfering with the free will of Pharaoh.

God simply allows us to continue on the path that we have chosen. Again, if any of this is problematic to you, please recall that it has no bearing on whether God exists. It simply means that you do not like what He does and does not do.

[436]   Lewis, *Mere Christianity*.

[437]   An argument sometimes used against the morality of God is with His plan for salvation. We do not understand the mind of God, and that includes questions of eternity. Thankfully, we are not the ultimate judge. Although we may have difficulty wrapping our finite minds around God's ultimate plan for the restoration of the world, our trust in His plan is not misplaced. We will never understand who God has revealed Himself to in the darkest jungles or in their final breaths, (Romans 1:19-20).

[438]   To read the entire story of Joseph, please see Genesis 37-50.

[439]   The story of Joseph is believed by many to be foreshadowing of the deliverance provided by Yeshua. Here are a few of the parallels:

1. Joseph was rejected by his brothers; Yeshua was rejected by many of his Jewish brethren.

2. Joseph was believed to be dead but was later found alive. The same happened with Yeshua after His crucifixion.

3. Joseph's brothers initially did not recognize him in his foreign Egyptian garb, and he had to remove his Egyptian covering to reveal himself to them. Yeshua has not been recognized by much of His Jewish brethren and has been revealing Himself to them in large numbers over the last few decades.

4. Joseph stored up grain to feed people who would have otherwise starved and died during the drought and famine. Yeshua feeds us spiritually and offers eternal life.

[440]   Drought is an example of natural evil (as opposed to moral evil).

[441]   Genesis 50:19-20

[442]   Her story can be read in *The Hiding Place* which was written by Elizabeth and John Sherrill, as well as Corrie ten Boom herself.

[443]   Boom, Corrie ten, Elizabeth Sherrill, John Sherrill. *The Hiding Place*. Jacksonville: Perma-Bound. 1990.

[444]   Isaiah 40:31, JPS

445 Deuteronomy 6:5

446 Ultimately, suffering is the result of our fallen world, (Genesis 3). No human beings have the ability to be perfect, and our sins separate us from God, (Isaiah 59:2). Yeshua, as the perfect sacrifice, reconciles us, and we are able to enter into a relationship with God, (Romans 5:12-18). This relationship enables us to enter Heaven where there will be no tears, sorrow, and pain, (Revelation 21:4). God is not the problem; our *separation* from God is the problem.

447 The evidence of these claims were discussed in Chapter 7.

448 As has been undeniably verified by historians, Yeshua was brutally killed by a Roman Crucifixion. The evidence and implication of Yeshua's crucifixion can be read in Chapters 5, 6, and 7.

449 The shortest verse in the Bible "Jesus wept," is also incredibly powerful, (John 11:35). After seeing his friend Lazarus lying dead, Yeshua was moved to tears. Through these acts of emotionality, Yeshua ultimately gave us permission to feel despair when people die (although we know that we will see them again in Heaven). He invited us to cry out to God in the midst of true despair (while still glorifying Him). Our all-knowing, all-powerful God already knows the emotions that we are feeling; why should we try to hide these feelings in an attempt to appear perfect?

450 Matthew 27:46; Psalm 22 is considered by many to be a messianic prophecy. Thus, by crying out with the first line of this verse (which the Jewish population of the day would have been familiar with), Yeshua seems to be declaring that He is indeed the prophesied Messiah. (Psalm 22 was discussed in Chapter 7.)

451 Romans 8:35, 37-39, CJB

Epilogue

452 Job 26:14

453 Jeremiah 29:13

454 2 Timothy 3:16

Even if you do not believe the Bible is the inspired Word of God, it is still an invaluable tool with tremendous insights for life.

455 Acts 2:44-47

456 Romans 12:5, CJB

457   During prayer time, God often speaks silently to our hearts and minds. The Old Covenant refers to this as God's "still small voice," (1 Kings 19:12).

458   Philippians 4:6-7, CJB

459   Ruakh HaKodesh is Hebrew for the Holy Spirit.

The Holy Spirit is the Spirit of God that we can invite to reside in us to be our Comforter and Guide.

"But you will receive power when the Holy Spirit has come upon you, and you will be my witnesses in Jerusalem and in all Judea and Samaria, and to the end of the earth," (Acts 1:8).

"And who has also put his seal on us and given us his Spirit in our hearts as a guarantee," (2 Corinthians 1:22).

460   1 Timothy 6:7 Wealth, power, and prestige are fleeting, but the love of God is enduring forever.

461   Here is a suggestion of a short prayer, similar to the prayer I prayed over 23 years ago:

God, I want to know if you are real. Please give me a better understanding of you. Help the Bible come alive to me so that I better see your plan of salvation through your Son, Yeshua. In Yeshua's name I pray, Amen.

This prayer is modeled after Paul's letter to the Ephesians in which Paul prayed this for others.

"For this reason, ever since I heard about your trust in the Lord Yeshua and your love for all God's people, I have not stopped giving thanks for you. In my prayers I keep asking the God of our Lord Yeshua the Messiah, the glorious Father, to give you a spirit of wisdom and revelation, so that you will have full knowledge of him. I pray that he will give light to the eyes of your hearts, so that you will understand the hope to which he has called you, what rich glories there are in the inheritance he has promised his people, and how surpassingly great is his power working in us who trust him. It works with the same mighty strength he used when he worked in the Messiah to raise him from the dead and seat him at his right hand in heaven, far above every ruler, authority, power, dominion or any other name that can be named either in the 'olam hazeh or in the 'olam haba. Also, he has put all things under his feet and made him head over everything for the Messianic Community, which is his body, the full expression of him who fills all creation," (Ephesians 1:15-23, CJB)

462   More of my testimony can be found in the Introduction of this book, and is also in the last chapter of *A Lawyer's Case for God*. If you are interested

in additional materials and resources that I recommended, they can also be found in Appendix A in *A Lawyer's Case for God*.

Appendix A

[463]   More precisely, Messianic Judaism is a Judeo-Christian belief system whose foundations are established in the Old Covenant and continue in the New Covenant.

[464]   Especially with Hinduism and Buddhism whose beliefs are less concrete and defined.

[465]   Will Durant, a famous historian in the 20th century, became an atheist. Even as an atheist, Durant solidified the historical validity of the beliefs of the followers of Yeshua.

"The denial of that existence seems never to have occurred even to the bitterest gentile or Jewish opponents of nascent Christianity. That a few simple men should in one generation have invented so powerful and appealing a personality, so lofty an ethic and so inspiring a vision of human brotherhood, would be a miracle far more incredible than any recorded in the Gospels."

Durant, Will. Caesar and Christ. Vol. 3. New York: Simon & Schuster, 1994. Print.

[466]   Sister Ajahn Candasiri is a senior nun at the Amaravati Buddhist Monastery in Hertfordshire. Upon reflection, she saw many Buddhist ideals and practices evident in the life of Yeshua, as were recorded in the gospels. She specifically discusses the inner-peace and "fulfilled perfection" by Yeshua during the crucifixion narrative. She writes:

"When we hear of his last hours: the trial, the taunting, the agony and humiliation of being stripped naked and nailed to a cross to die—is an extraordinary account of patient endurance, of willingness to bear the unbearable without any sense or blame or ill will. It reminds me of a simile used by the Buddha to demonstrate the quality of metta, or kindliness, he expected of his disciples: 'Even if robbers were to attack you and saw off your limbs one by one, should you give way to anger, you would not be following my advice.' A tall order, but one that clearly Jesus fulfills to perfection: 'Father, forgive them for they know not what they do.'"

Candasiri, Ajahn. "Jesus Through Buddhist Eyes." BBC News. BBC, 17 Nov. 2009. Web.

[467]   "If you confess with your mouth that Jesus is Lord and believe in your heart that God raised him from the dead, you will be saved," (Romans 9:10).

468   In an article on the comparison between Christianity and Hinduism, it is recognized that some believe Yeshua may have been an incarnate form of the God Vishnu:

"There are no hard and fast rules as to how God reveals His knowledge and chooses His messengers... In His aspect as Lord Vishnu, He incarnates upon earth in human form several times to restore order and destroy evil."

V, Jayarum. "Hinduism and Christianity, Jesus in India." Hinduwebsite. com, n.d. Web.

469   It is written in the Qur'an, which is regarded as a holy and sacred scripture in Islam, that:

"We believe in Allah, and the revelation given to us, and to Abraham, Isma'il, Isaac, Jacob, and the Tribes, and that given to Moses and Jesus, and that given to (all) prophets from their Lord: We make no difference between one and another of them."

"Surah Al-Baqarah (The Cow) 2:136." The Noble Qur'an. Sunnah.com, 2015. Web.

470   The renowned 12th century Rabbi Maimonides writes, "Jesus of Nazareth who aspired to be the Messiah and was executed by the court." Thus, Maimonides verifies the life and crucifixion (execution) of Yeshua.

Eastman, *Blue Letter Bible.*

471   John 14:6

472   Matthew 5:43

473   Matthew 7:7-8

Appendix B

474   Louis Pasteur revolutionized the medical field with vaccines for rabies, anthrax, and chicken cholera. He also developed the process for the pasteurization of milk, and laid the foundation for the control (and eventual development of vaccines) for tuberculosis, diphtheria, tetanus, and many other diseases.

Quoted in Michael Patrick Leahy. *Letter to an Atheist.* Nashville, TN: Harpeth River, 2007. 61. Print.

475   As you will recall from Chapter 2, Sir Frank Whittle discovered the laws of physics to explain the jet engine. Dr. John Lennox uses this example as a helpful analogy regarding the distinction between defining the origin (or agent) of a cause, and further understanding the process of a cause.

Lennox, "As a Scientist I'm Certain Stephen Hawking is Wrong. You Can't Explain the Universe without God."

476 Dr. Francis Collins, one of the leaders in the Human Genome Project, explains that: "The big bang cries for a divine explanation. It forces the conclusion that nature had a defined beginning. I cannot see how nature could have created itself. Only a supernatural force that is outside of space and time could have done that."

Collins, *The Language of God*, 67.

477 Schroeder, Gerald L. *The Science of God: The Convergence of Scientific and Biblical Wisdom.* New York: Free, 1997. Print.

478 Aristotle. "Physics." *The Internet Classics Archive.* N.p., n.d. Web.

479 Hawking, Stephen. "The Beginning of Time." *Stephen Hawking: The Official Website.* N.p., n.d. Web.

480 Genesis 1:1 (Day 1)

481 Weinberg, Steven. "Introduction: The Giant and the Cow." *The First Three Minutes: A Modern View of the Origin of the Universe.* New York: Basic, 1977. 14. Print.

482 Ibid., 15.

483 Genesis 1:3 (Day 1)

484 Schroeder, *The Science of God*, 71.

485 Genesis 1:6-7 (Day 2)

486 Cain, Fraser. "Where Did the Earth's Water Come From?" *Universe Today.* N.p., 14 Oct. 2013. Web.

487 Genesis 1:7 (Day 2)

488 Genesis 1:9 (Day 3)

489 Genesis 1:11 (Day 4)

490 Schroeder, *The Science of God*, 212.

491 Ibid., 213.

492 Ibid., 72.

493 Genesis 1:17 (Day 4)

494 Genesis 1:20 (Day 5)

495 Genesis 1:20 (Day 5)

496 Genesis 1:24, 26 (Day 6)

[497] More examples of scientific foreknowledge can be found in Chapter 3, and in Chapter 2 of my book *A Lawyer's Case for God*. Also, please refer to K.A. Kitchen's book *On the Reliability of the Old Testament* for evidence that the Bible was written within the last 4,000 years.

[498] Genesis 1:1-5

[499] Genesis 1:6-8

[500] Genesis 1:9-13

[501] Genesis 1:14-19

[502] Genesis 1:20-23

[503] Genesis 1:24-31

Appendix C

[504] Isaiah 53

ACKNOWLEDGMENTS

I would like to thank my amazing wife, Cathy, for her patience, prayers, and love throughout our 35 years of marriage. Her modeling of God's unconditional love has drawn me to want to know Him more. Knowing her has been one of the greatest gifts I have ever received. Her help (and patience) with this book has been absolutely invaluable. Researching and writing this book has truly been a labor of love.

I also want to thank my children who have inspired me greatly over the years. They are a tremendous blessing! They all had very helpful suggestions to make this book more impactful. I am also grateful to Rabbi Don Goldstein, Rabbi Shmuel Wolkenfeld, Amy Adler, and others who assisted with the research and writing of this book. A special shout-out to Cara Strike who worked tirelessly on this for a year and a half.

I am also thankful to God for His protection, patience, and unconditional, everlasting love. How comforting is it to know that as I sojourn through life, He is with me 24/7. He has graciously forgiven me and allowed me to experience the depths of His love, which I never knew existed until I was 39 years old.

In closing, I want to thank my mother, brother, sister, and stepfather for the impact they have had on my life. My father passed away from lung cancer when I was 10, and my mother was suddenly faced with the daunting challenge of raising three young children alone. She masterfully accomplished this task while working full-time. She made innumerable sacrifices that have continued to be a blessing in my life. She eventually married my stepfather who helped to raise my siblings and me. My stepfather treated me like his own son. Without his constant support, I do not believe I would be a lawyer today.

Growing up, I was very close to my older sister and brother. I moved from St. Louis to Kansas City, and during my visits to my hometown, my sister was *always* a gracious hostess, and has played a big role in creating many family memories. My brother, who is also a lawyer, has imparted many words of "fatherly" advice and wisdom that have significantly influenced the direction of my life. My family has been, and will always be, a huge blessing in my life. I love them all dearly.

ABOUT THE AUTHOR

Jim Jacob has been a senior partner at his law firm since 1979. He has been privileged to represent prominent civic leaders, large U.S. companies, and countless individuals. For many years, Jim has held the highest rating from Martindale-Hubbell, a prominent company that evaluates lawyers nationwide. Jim has been admitted to practice law before the United States Supreme Court, and was selected for membership to Outstanding Lawyers of America. Jim has written articles on legal topics for both the *Kansas City Star* and *Missouri Lawyers Weekly*.

Jim's first book, *A Lawyer's Case for God*, has received international acclaim and has been translated into three languages.

Jim and his wife, Cathy, have been married for 35 years and have four children. Jim and Cathy have served for many years in varying leadership roles at their congregation. Jim also serves two international not-for-profit organizations—one as a legal advisor, and one as a board member and officer.